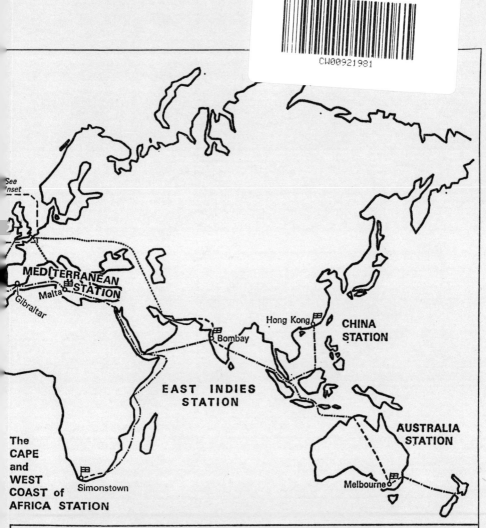

See
Inset

MEDITERRANEAN
STATION
Malta
Gibraltar

Bombay

Hong Kong

CHINA
STATION

EAST INDIES
STATION

AUSTRALIA
STATION

The
CAPE
and
WEST
COAST of
AFRICA STATION

Simonstown

Melbourne

1. Strategic Communications of the Royal Navy circa 1878.

—·—·—· British owned Deep Sea Cables
— — — — Landline links in British Territory
·············· Landline links through Foreign Territory

Note: This map does not show all cables by any means. There were, for instance,
a number of transatlantic cables at this time. Telegrams could be sent from
most ports in the United Kingdom and Europe. Landlines also crossed the
United States from coast to coast and across Russia and Siberia to the
Far East.

The Electron and Sea Power

By the same author

THE SUBMARINE AND SEA POWER
AIRCRAFT AND SEA POWER

THE ELECTRON
AND SEA POWER

Vice-Admiral Sir Arthur Hezlet
K.B.E., C.B., D.S.O., D.S.C.

PETER DAVIES : LONDON

Peter Davies Limited
15 Queen Street, Mayfair, London W1X 8BE
LONDON   MELBOURNE   TORONTO
JOHANNESBURG   AUCKLAND

432 06732 9

First published 1975

Printed in Great Britain by
Cox & Wyman Ltd
London, Fakenham and Reading

Contents

Contents

Illustrations

PHOTOGRAPHS

MAPS AND DIAGRAMS

Preface

WHEN I WAS in the Royal Navy, I was never an electrical, communication or radar specialist, although of course as a submarine officer I was a user of this sort of equipment. In some ways for this book this has been an advantage, since as a writer on sea power in its broader forms I can see the subject without bias.

I have always been intrigued by these aspects of naval warfare. My interest dates from the early thirties when I was a Midshipman in H.M.S. *Royal Oak* in the Mediterranean. It was first awakened by an extremely interesting and lucid lecture on wireless communications given by Commander Lord Louis Mountbatten, who was then the Fleet Wireless Officer. The idea for this book, however, emanates from the discussion period of a lecture at the Joint Services Staff College at Latimer early in 1950. The lecture was given by Sir Henry Tizard, then the Chairman of the Defence Research Policy Committee. He indicated that he believed the three great influences on naval warfare of the twentieth century to be the invention of aircraft and the submarine and also the discovery of electromagnetic waves. I have covered the effect of the first two influences in my books *The Submarine and Sea Power* and *Aircraft and Sea Power* and this work is a companion volume which attempts to complete the picture. I have slightly enlarged the subject from the use of electromagnetic waves to the introduction of all electrical and electronic devices; hence the title which seems to me to embrace the whole subject and which I hope purists will accept.

A great deal of the material for this book is taken from published sources, but most of the information about the early days of wireless and asdics in the Royal Navy is from Admiralty papers now in the Public Record Office. I have of course been somewhat inhibited in the last chapter by security and have been confined to published sources which are fortunately fairly detailed and I hope accurate. The subject is, as in my first two books, treated internationally and covers much the same period although it goes back rather more into the nineteenth century. Inevitably with a theme such as this, there must be a certain amount of technical discussion. I have done my best to make the text intelligible to the general reader without removing much that is of real interest to the naval officer or the expert in electrics or electronics. I have made no attempt to standardize terms and I use for instance asdics or sonar, radio or wireless, as seems most appropriate to the period and the country with which I am dealing.

My thanks are, as ever, due to the publishers who commissioned the book and who permitted me to put it aside for over a year while I got a book on a very different subject off my chest. They were also very patient when I ran badly over their deadline. My thanks are also due to Rear-Admiral Buckley and the staffs of the Admiralty Library and the Naval Historical Division of the Ministry of Defence, who have always been very ready to assist. The staffs of the Library of the Royal United Services Institution, the Photographic Section of the Imperial War Museum and the Rolls Room of the Public Record Office have also been most courteous and helpful. Finally my gratitude goes to Mrs Gocher for her astonishing skill at deciphering my untidy drafts and typing them so accurately.

Bovagh House,
Aghadowey,
Co. Londonderry,
Northern Ireland.

I

Warships and Electricity in the Nineteenth Century

A FEW YEARS before the Battle of Trafalgar, a major advance was made in the science of electricity. Volta invented his 'Voltaic pile', or what we now know as a primary battery, which was capable of producing electricity in a steady flow by chemical means.

Electricity itself was no new discovery. It had been known as early as 600 BC, when the Greeks had found that if they rubbed amber it had the property of attracting or repelling light bodies. They had also found that some fish could impart electric shocks. The systematic study of these phenomena did not begin however until the sixteenth century and only made real progress during the eighteenth century. Development was limited, although with the invention of the Leyden jar in 1745, electricity could be accumulated and stored. Many leading scientists applied themselves to the subject, and by the end of the eighteenth century had not only made a systematic study of many materials with the same electrical properties as amber, but had found that sparks were emitted from strong charges and had realized that electricity was connected with lightning.

They had discovered too that electricity could be conducted, and that some substances conducted better than others. They had found that there were two kinds of electricity, positive and negative, and that like kinds repelled and opposite kinds of electricity attracted each other. Many important facts had therefore been established but electricity was as yet of interest only to the scientist and had not left the laboratory. A number of proposals were indeed made for various kinds of telegraph but none of them was practical, and the study of electricity was continued mainly as a contribution to knowledge in general.

It is only possible to identify two useful outcomes of all this work. The first was the invention of the lightning conductor by Franklin in 1752 and the second was the exploding of gunpowder by electricity by Sir William Watson, who had actually fired a musket by electricity in 1747. The method used made it hopelessly impractical and less efficient than conventional methods, and it was over a century before this discovery was put to effective use. By 1805, although the existence of electricity was known and had been subjected to much study, it had occurred to no one that it would have the slightest effect upon sea power.

During the next thirty years immense progress was made in the laboratory, especially in the theory of electricity and its measurement. Many improved types of primary battery were produced, the phenomenon of induction was discovered as well as the power of electricity to magnetize steel. The main practical application was still seen to be some form of telegraph and a vast number of proposals were made. Few of these proved commercial propositions and many, such as one with a separate wire for each letter of the alphabet, were altogether too unwieldy. Nevertheless the essential ingredients were there, and in 1828 a telegraph was worked over a distance of eight miles on Long Island in the U.S.A. It used a single wire with earth return and a coded system of signalling which was recorded on litmus paper. A few years later the telegraph became cheaper when it was found that a line conductor need not be insulated over its whole length but only had to be supported by insulators at intervals. In the late eighteen-thirties and early forties Morse perfected his code, short lines were laid in both England and the U.S.A. (Note 1) and telegraph companies were formed. The 'Electric Telegraph' as a reliable method of communication now began to spread throughout the civilized countries of the world.

In these days, when rapid communication is taken for granted, it is difficult to imagine how long news took to travel before the invention of the telegraph. For letters from Great Britain to the Mediterranean, steam despatch vessels had replaced sailing ships in 1830 and they could complete a round voyage from Falmouth to Corfu and back via Cadiz, Gibraltar and Malta in about six weeks (Note 2). In the thirties it like-wise took a very long time to get to the Far East, all traffic being by sailing ship round the Cape. A reply to a letter could not be expected in under nine months. In 1839, by arrange-ment with the French Government, the mails for India were sent overland to Marseilles and then by Admiralty steam packet to Malta and Alexandria, whence they were carried overland to Suez and onwards by a steamer of the East India Company.

During the First China War, the new Commander-in-Chief East Indies, Sir William Parker, made an exceptionally fast passage to take up his appointment by this route. The last part of his journey was by the East India Company's steam frigate *Sesostris* in which he arrived at Macao on 9 August 1841, sixty-eight days after leaving England. On the other side of the world, the United States Navy's Pacific Squadron had to communicate with the Navy Department in Washington by despatch vessel sailing round Cape Horn (Note 3). Conse-quently in 1846 they did not know of an outbreak of war with Mexico until an officer travelling overland managed to get a message through privately.

In 1842 the Admiralty still maintained their telegraph system by semaphore from hill to hill all the way from London to Portsmouth. In this year they began to receive suggestions about the electric telegraph. A line from London to the railway terminus at Gosport was offered to them for a rent of £2,500 per year: two gentlemen, Messrs Wright and Bains, sent a description of their 'electro-magnetic printing telegraph' and a Mr Elwin proposed a plan for 'transmitting secret corres-pondence instantaneously by electric current'. Their lordships were interested as the semaphore was expensive and subject to serious delays in foggy or hazy weather. In 1843 they requested Michael Faraday to 'give his attention to this mode of com-munication on the Portsmouth railway' as they were anxious to have his opinion. In 1845 they made up their minds and came to an agreement for the hire of a telegraph line from London to Gosport where they set aside a room for it in the Victualling Yard. Two years later, they were sufficiently happy with the new system to close down the old semaphore although they kept it in reserve (Note 4). By this time the inland tele-graph system in the U.S.A. was sufficiently developed for communication between the Navy Department in Washington and ships and squadrons in ports on the east coast to be established using a code (Note 5).

By 1849 the telegraph was continuous from the Admiralty to Admiralty House at Portsmouth: the old semaphore was now finally discontinued and the property disposed of.

In 1850 the first submarine cable was laid between England and France. It failed almost at once but another was laid from Dover to Calais with complete success the following year, thus connecting the telegraph systems of Great Britain and the Continent. This meant that in theory telegraphic communication could be established between the Admiralty and the British Mediterranean fleet. Although there is no record that the Admiralty used it before the Crimean War in 1854 they showed interest and assisted in the laying of the Channel cable by lending the paddle steamers *Fearless, Blazer* and *Monkey*.

In 1851 the Admiralty were informed that the electric telegraph was open throughout the whole of British North America. At the time their own interests were more parochial. The inland telegraph to Portsmouth was by now in fairly general use and in 1852 it was extended to Plymouth.

During the next few years a number of submarine cables were laid with varying success. The Admiralty co-operated as before enthusiastically with the telegraph companies in this work. H.M.S. *Adder* and *Fearless* helped with the cable from Orfordness to Scheveningen; H.M.S. *Lizard, Cuckoo, Vivid* and *Princess Alice* assisted with the cable from the South Foreland to Belgium and H.M.S. *Porcupine* and *Asp* with the cable from Portpatrick to Donaghadee. The spread of the telegraph was therefore slow but steady and by the Crimean War, the Admiralty was in touch with most of the other dockyards in the United Kingdom. The Governments in London and Paris were also communicating by telegraph before the outbreak of the war in March 1854.

At this time the inland telegraph in Europe reached Kiel, Copenhagen, Danzig, Marseilles and as far east as Belgrade. The normal communication with the British fleet that entered the Baltic under Sir Charles Napier was by courier overland to Danzig and thence by despatch vessel to the fleet. Despatches sent this way, roughly once a week, took from seven to fourteen days according to where the fleet lay but on one occasion took as long as twenty-one days. The first recorded naval use of the telegraph was to report the capture of Bomarsund on August 16, the message being sent from Danzig on the arrival of H.M.S. *Basilisk* there with the news three days later. By this time the Press was also using the telegraph from Danzig to report the progress of the war, but the Admiralty continued to rely on letters. In December, Sir Charles Napier, then at Kiel in his flagship, had no hesitation in using the telegraph to request leave of absence for urgent private reasons. The Admiralty replied by the same means and this seems to have been the first time that they sent a message by telegraph in the Crimean War. In the Baltic campaign of the following year, despatches were still sent through Danzig. On the arrival of Admiral Dundas in May, he wished to stop a notice of blockade being published with which he did not agree and sent H.M.S. *Conflict* to Copenhagen to telegraph to the British Minister at Stockholm to cancel it. In August the successful bombardment of Sveaborg was reported by this means, arriving at about the same time as the Press reports. In the Baltic, therefore, the telegraph was only used in emergency, to compete with the Press or to make up for some lack of foresight, and its use never became general.

Normal communication with the British fleet in the Black Sea under Vice-Admiral Dundas (Note 6) was also by letter. In this case despatches were sent by courier overland to Marseilles and thence by mail steamer to Constantinople. Here they were collected by a naval despatch vessel for delivery to the fleet. Letters sent this way took from sixteen to twenty days and the courier left rather more often than once a week. The first use of the telegraph in this campaign was from London: to overtake the courier and intercept him at Marseilles so as to correct an important despatch which he was carrying. This telegram was in cipher addressed to the Consul at Marseilles.

On 24 January 1855 a telegram was sent from the Crimea to the Foreign Office in an attempt to institute a faster service via Bucharest, to which place the inland telegraph had now been extended. It was sent by despatch vessel to Varna and thence by road to Bucharest where it arrived on January 29 and was at once telegraphed to London arriving the same night. It was not until March 5 that the Admiralty sent a telegram to the Commander-in-Chief by this route. Towards the end of 1854 the Admiralty decided to extend the electric telegraph all the way to the Crimea. A specially fitted vessel arrived at the end of January 1855 and laid a cable from Varna to Balaklava. By the time this was completed the inland telegraph had been extended from Bucharest to Varna. On April 26 telegraphic communication was established from London and Paris to the Crimea; from this date, telegrams began to flow both ways and took from twelve to twenty-four hours as they had to be relayed a number of times along the route.

The very early telegrams, or telegraphic communications as they were called, were written without any economy of words. 'The allied expedition arrived off the Straits of Kerch at early dawn on Her Majesty's birthday, and steamed rapidly up to Kamiesh, where the army landed under the cover of steamers' guns, and immediately ascended the heights', reported Sir Edmund Lyons, the new naval Commander-in-Chief to the Secretary of the Admiralty on May 25. Brevity soon became the fashion, however, and only three weeks later, Admiral Lyons reported, 'Expedition returned, after leaving garrison in the Straits of Kerch. No enemy at Taman. Garrison of Anapa crossed the Kuban and gone to the northward'. The Admiralty could not resist using the telegraph to interfere with the Commander-in-Chief rather than to send him directions.

On June 12, Sir Charles Wood, the First Lord, sent a peremptory message to Sir Edmund Lyons on what can only be described as a tactical matter. 'If the Russian garrison of Anapa has retired to Taman, attack that place, and drive them out' and on June 29 'Destroy the sea fortifications of Anapa'. The Generals in the Crimea were exasperated by this kind of 'back-seat driving'. The French Commander-in-Chief General Pelissier, regarded the telegraph as 'their greatest enemy – worse even than the newspapers'. In a telegraphic dispute with Napoleon III about strategy he wired 'Let Your Majesty free me from the restriction imposed on me or permit me to resign a command impossible to exercise . . . at the extremity, sometimes paralysing, of an electric wire'. General Simpson, who succeeded Lord Raglan, said the telegraph caused 'infinite confusion'.

The telegraph proved, however, of great value on occasion. On July 20, Sir Charles Wood sent to Sir Edward Lyons: 'The French Government require transport for 15,000 from Marseilles in the first week in August. Send as many transports as you can spare, and let me know how many men you can convey.' Four days later the Commander-in-Chief sent: 'In reply to your telegraphic message of the 20th instant, I can furnish three-fourths of the means required, at the time and the place appointed – probably the remaining fourth about a week later.' An important administrative matter which would have taken some six weeks by letter was thus concluded in five days. The continued dependence of the telegraph on the co-operation of despatch vessels was demonstrated when, after the fall of Sebastopol, the scene of action shifted to Kinburn. News of the successful bombardment had to be sent to Varna in H.M.S. *Banshee* for despatch by telegraph to London (Note 7).

It was in the Crimean War of 1854–5 that the telegraph was first used during hostilities. It cannot be claimed that it made very much difference. No great strategic move was achieved by its existence and its influence on plans was marginal. Indeed there were many who claimed that the interference it caused was an actual disadvantage. Nevertheless it greatly increased the control of the central governments and made communication with the theatre of war very much more rapid. It is probable that in administrative matters and logistics it paid greater dividends.

In distant places where the telegraph still did not reach, communications were carried on much as before. In the Second China War of 1856–60 there was no telegraph at all. War was in fact declared by the local authorities and carried on for four months before they even knew that London approved. This period was, however, one in which a great effort was put into the extension of the cable system. In 1857 the first attempt was made to lay a transatlantic cable using the British battleship *Agamemnon*, but the cable broke before it was completed and could not be recovered. Next year a new one was laid successfully from Ireland to Newfoundland but it lasted only three months and was then found to be irreparable. In 1859 an attempt was made to lay a cable from Suez to Karachi via the Red Sea and the Arabian coast. It was in six sections and all of them worked when it was completed. Defects soon became apparent, however, and within a year only two of the sections were working. Indeed the degree of success of all submarine cables was very low: by 1861 some 11,000 miles had been laid and of these only 3,000 were in working order.

The inland telegraph system in the British Isles spread rapidly too and this led to increased use by the Admiralty. It was used frequently to pass orders to ships in the Fenian troubles of the late sixties off the coast of Ireland. In 1867, for example, H.M.S. *Helicon*, when at Valencia, received orders by telegraph to return to Portsmouth.

In the war between Italy and Austria in 1866, the telegraph was first used for what could be called a tactical as opposed to a strategic purpose. In July of that year, the Italian fleet, of which some action had been demanded by the Government, sailed from Ancona to try to capture the fortified island of Lissa off the Dalmatian coast. Lissa was connected by cable with the mainland and at once reported the position of the Italian fleet to the Austrian naval Commander-in-Chief at Pola. A number of amplifying messages got through before the Italians cut the cable. The Austrian fleet sailed at once and on 18 July 1866 completely defeated the Italians at the Battle of Lissa. Without the telegraph it is unlikely that this famous battle would ever have been fought.

In the same year as Lissa the transatlantic cable was relaid successfully by the *Great Eastern*, then the largest ship in the world, and reliable communication was at last established. Shortly afterwards a second cable which had been partly laid the year before was also completed. The Royal Navy had shown great interest in the laying of the transatlantic cable and had provided H.M.S. *Terrible* and *Niger* to assist. The transatlantic cable connected the Admiralty with Halifax, which was the northern base of the America and West Indies Station, and as a result of the transcontinental telegraph having been completed five years before, with the British Pacific fleet base at Esquimalt in British Columbia. The political situation in the Pacific at the time was uncertain and the Admiralty were so enamoured of this new way to control a distant Commander-in-Chief that they kept H.M.S. *Zealous*, the flagship on the station, in harbour at Esquimalt 'on the end of the line' from July 1867 until April 1869.

By 1870 a British cable had been laid from Falmouth via Lisbon, Gibraltar and Malta to Alexandria. Two years later a cable from Karachi had been connected to Persia and so by land-line to London. This connected the British East Indies Squadron base at Bombay with the Admiralty. Throughout the seventies there was great commercial pressure to lay cables and by 1875 the majority of important outlying islands were connected. There were six transatlantic cables, including one from Lisbon to Pernambuco, and the cables from Great Britain to India through the Red Sea were in working order with extensions to Australia, China and Japan. In the Ashanti War of 1873–4, however, the main communication between the Admiralty and the Senior Naval Officer on the coast was still by letter by the mail steamer. On occasion the S.N.O. sent telegrams for the Admiralty by the mail steamer to be transmitted as soon as she reached Lisbon. Telegrams were also collected and transmitted from the Cape Verde Islands and Madeira, using ships which happened to be calling there.

In the late seventies the use of the telegraph wherever it existed was fairly common, yet in 1879, after sending a telegram on an administrative subject from the coastguard ship at Leith, her captain was admonished and told that the telegraph was only to be used for urgent or important messages (Note 8). Abroad the use of the telegraph was not always possible as some countries, such as Turkey, refused to accept messages in code or cipher. Confidential messages were normally sent by cipher, which was also used for letters destined to pass through foreign countries. The system used by the British in 1877 was Cipher N which was similar to a dictionary with a three, four or five figure number alongside each word. To give extra security the groups could be reciphered by adding a secret number, the value of which was indicated by the first group, to all the remaining groups. There was a choice of ten secret numbers and so a reciphered message could appear in any of ten completely different forms.

By the end of the seventies the telegraph connected all the main British naval stations with the Admiralty (Map 1). Where there was no telegraph matters remained much as before, and naval officers often had to assume heavy responsibilities both naval and diplomatic when out of touch with senior officers. The cable was often used in conjunction with written orders. For example in 1877, when H.M.S. *Egeria*, on the China Station, was sent to Japan she was given the ordinary written sailing orders but also sealed orders which were to be opened when ordered by telegraph. On reaching Japan, a telegram duly arrived from Hong Kong and the sealed orders were opened.

These directed her to proceed to Petropavlovsk in Kamchatka. In 1878 when at Nagasaki, the *Egeria* received a telegram from the C.-in-C. at Hong Kong telling her to be at immediate notice for sea when the next mail steamer arrived as it contained important orders for her. On the other side of the world at this time the C.-in-C. America and West Indies still had no cable communication between his base at Bermuda and the Admiralty. One of the principal duties of the paddle sloop *Argus* was to take letters and telegrams to Halifax for despatch and to collect the mail and any incoming telegrams.

The invention of the telegraph therefore provided the first real effect of the electron on sea power. It enabled ocean strategy to be controlled centrally in a way which had not been possible before. Messages reporting the situation could be received within hours at the seat of government, and orders could be despatched in a fraction of the time taken by despatch vessels. Sir William Preece, the Chief Engineer of the Post Office, said in a lecture at this time that the telegraph had revolutionized warfare. 'It is now possible,' he said, for 'the strategist to grasp a continent in his combinations.' [*sic*] The despatch vessel, however, had not been entirely replaced and was still an essential adjunct to the telegraph, particularly whenever the fleet was at sea or away from a telegraph station. It is of interest that Great Britain built two large and very fast despatch vessels towards the end of the seventies (Note 9).

Telegraphic communication was, without question, of most value to the British with their far-spread Empire and distant naval stations. The world-wide cable network was almost a British monopoly, and they manufactured and owned most of the cables of the world. Other countries could, of course, also use these cables to control their ships stationed abroad. The inland telegraph, too, connected the U.S. Atlantic and Pacific fleets with the Navy Department in Washington. The French Atlantic and Mediterranean fleets were in touch with the Ministry of Marine in Paris, who also had a cable to Algeria.

We must now turn to some of the other uses of electricity at sea during this period, the first of which had a profound effect on night actions. In the preceding three centuries of naval warfare, the vast majority of sea battles were fought by day. It is difficult to find more than a dozen examples of fighting at night, and of these all except a handful (Note 10) were actions begun by day and continued after dark. It was more normal for actions to cease at sunset and the reason is clear enough. There were no means of illumination to enable the contestants to see what they were doing. Candles or oil lanterns of about eight candle-power were useless except for lighting up the interior of ships or for providing a mark to show where ships were. Night actions were therefore a very chancy business (Note 11) in which the superior fleet was reluctant to indulge and in which the inferior fleet preferred to slip away rather than fight.

In 1868 the Whitehead locomotive torpedo was offered for sale by its inventor, Captain Luppis of the Austrian Navy. Two torpedoes were purchased by the Royal Navy at the end of 1870. In trials one of them blew a huge hole in an old corvette and satisfied its purchasers that it was a weapon of the future. Its range was, however, only 800 yards at six knots and it was evident that by day quick-firing guns should be able to sink the attacking vessel before it could get within range. It would clearly be most effective when used against ships lying in open anchorages at night.

Night action therefore seemed by now to be something which even the strongest fleet might be unable to avoid in the future and so received serious consideration. In 1873 the British Admiralty set up a Torpedo Committee to investigate the whole question and among other defensive measures they considered the use of illuminants. Before them they had the proverbial lime light, various pyrotechnics such as rockets and parachute flares and finally the electric arc light. The electric arc had been discovered by Sir Humphrey Davy in the early years of the century, but the high current required soon exhausted the primary batteries of the day. Arc lights were, however, used at some expense for Dungeness Lighthouse in 1857 and in an exhibition at South Kensington in 1862.

With the development of Gramme's 'electro-magnetic induction machine' or what we would now call a dynamo, the arc light became a practical proposition. The dynamo was the result of research by many eminent scientists during the first half of the nineteenth century and was brought to a practical form in the late sixties. In 1874 Mr Wilde's 'electric light' was tried in H.M.S. *Comet*, a corvette. It consisted of an arc light enclosed in a directional case, 22 in. in diameter, the beam

being concentrated to 3–4 degrees by lenses. Current was
supplied by a Wilde dynamo driven by a small steam engine
of 6 h.p. The result was an intense light of about 11,000 candle-
power (Note 12). In the trials it was found that, although the
arc light did not meet the committee's requirement to floodlight
the entire area round a ship to beyond torpedo range, it was far
superior to the other illuminants. The gunboat *Skylark*, painted
black with a yellow funnel, was picked up a mile away. A white
gig was clearly visible at the same range but a black gig could
only be seen at half the distance. The committee complained
that the beam was too narrow but it was noted that ships could
be seen crossing it and silhouetted against it. The ship using the
'electric light', although it gave away its position by doing so,
could not itself be seen by the attacking ship through the glare
of the light, thus its course and movements could not be ascertained. 'The value of the light is decided and considerable,' the
committee reported, and the next year an improved 'electric
light' was fitted in the battleship *Minotaur* of the Channel
Squadron. In the next few years a 'searchlight', as it came to be
called, was fitted in all new ships, the first being H.M.S.
Alexandra completed early in 1877 (Diagram 2). With the fully
rigged ships of the 'up funnel, down screw' variety it was found
very difficult to position the searchlight both clear of rigging or
other obstructions and where it would not be smashed by gun
blast. To obtain all round arcs of training it was soon found
necessary to fit two searchlights in each ship. By 1880 eighteen
ships had two searchlights as well as four ships with a single
searchlight, and this included most of the large ships in commission, except the *Iron Duke* on the China Station.

To date all the searchlights were of the Wilde type, but in
1880 it was decided to fit the *Sultan* and *Inflexible* with Gramme's
and the *Triumph* and *Repulse* with Siemen's searchlights. Both
of these types produced a brighter light, the Siemen's of 18,000
and the Gramme's of 20,000 candle-power. This was done by
using a direct instead of an alternating current which allowed a
better arrangement of the carbons. The Siemen's lights were,
however, found to be too fragile and so the new battleships
Ajax and *Agamemnon* were given Gramme's lights. A committee
of 1882 recommended that all ships should have two searchlights of 25,000 candle-power but these two ships were completed with three searchlights each, two side by side on a small

2. Searchlights in the Royal Navy 1875 - 95

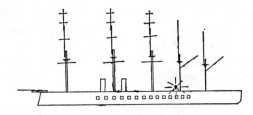

Minotaur 1875.

One 22 inch S.L.

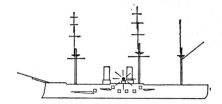

Alexandra 1877.

Two 24 inch S.L.
(One each side.)

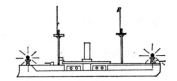

Ajax 1883.

Three 24 inch S.L.
(Two side by side in bow.
One aft.)

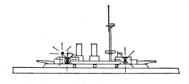

Rodney 1888.

Five 24 inch S.L.
(One on bridge.
Four in sponsons at corners
of superstructure.)

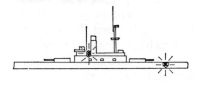

Trafalgar 1890.

Four 24 inch S.L.
(Two in sponsons in superstructure.
Two with ports
in hull aft.)

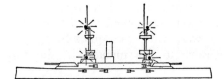

Majestic 1895.

Six 24 inch S.L.
(Four on wings of fore and after
bridges. Two at mastheads.)

platform right forward and a third on another platform right aft (Plate I). This arrangement gave better all-round arcs and kept the lights away from the heavy guns, which in these ships were mounted in turrets *en echelon* amidships. These more powerful searchlights replaced the older type in battleships, and the original Wilde type were then transferred to corvettes and sloops.

The main use of the searchlight at this time was to protect ships at anchor in open roadsteads, and some experience with it was obtained in night exercises. The limitation of the narrow beam was confirmed and it was decided that the searchlight must be used to sweep constantly. The searchlight was excellent when it picked up a torpedo boat which it could hold in its beam without difficulty. There was a danger, however, that meanwhile other torpedo boats could approach unseen from other directions. The disadvantage of giving away a ship's position by using searchlights was realized and it was put forward that ships could best be defended when at anchor by searchlights in boats or small ships illuminating the area round them while the ship herself kept her searchlights in reserve. The possibility of searchlights being destroyed by gunfire from a torpedo boat was also discussed, but it was realized that it would be very difficult to estimate the range of a searchlight at night. Some of these problems could be alleviated by fitting more searchlights as in the *Ajax* and *Agamemnon*.

Searchlights were first used in war during the operations which led to the bombardment of Alexandria in 1882. It was the searchlights of the fleet which detected that the Egyptians were strengthening the fortifications at night and mounting additional guns. After the bombardment which was carried out by day, searchlights were used to try to assist the landing parties at night by illuminating the shore. This proved a mixed blessing, and it was commented that they blinded the sentries and gave away their positions. The searchlight was not a British prerogative and other nations developed and fitted it simultaneously. Indeed, in 1880 the British believed that the French and Russians were ahead of them.

The searchlight was therefore the second important effect of the electron upon sea power. It opened up the possibility of fighting at night and was, with the quick-firing gun, an important counter-measure to the menace of the torpedo.

Whilst the searchlight was being introduced, electricity began to be used for a number of other purposes in naval warfare. In 1860 when the otherwise revolutionary warship *Warrior* was completed, she had no electrical equipment on board of any description except her lightning conductors. In the early seventies the firing of guns by electricity using primary batteries was introduced into the British Navy and was well established by 1874. Originally too high a voltage was used but this was reduced in 1875–6 to a low voltage which proved much more satisfactory. The main advantage of electric firing was that it was practically instantaneous, whereas various forms of percussion firing suffered from delays which although measured in fractions of a second made gunlaying at sea difficult. By 1880 some forty-three ships in the Royal Navy, including all the battleships, had electric firing for their guns.

Electric light obviously had possibilities for lighting ships internally. Illumination by candles and oil lanterns, as heretofore, was expensive, and there was a great danger of fire. Furthermore electricity gave a brighter light and did not use any oxygen or foul the air. The new battleship *Inflexible*, completed in October 1881, was the first ship in the Royal Navy to have electric lighting. The Brush system of low intensity arc lights employing an alternating current at very high voltage (600 volts) was used, about twelve lights being in series with no local switches. This system resulted in the electrocution of a stoker by an 'earth' leak but was otherwise a success. With the development of the carbon filament incandescent lamp in 1879, a superior system of lighting for ships had obviously been produced. Its first commercial application was, in fact, in an American merchant vessel. With such a system it was possible to lower the voltage to 60 volts which was very necessary for safety. Candles and oil lanterns had however to be retained as well as electric lighting for use when the boilers were allowed to die out in harbour. In the *Inflexible* the lighting system, with its generators and switchboards, was quite separate from the searchlight installation. The committee of 1882, however, recommended that a single electrical system for both lighting and searchlights should be fitted in future. The first ship with incandescent lights and a system which included the searchlights was H.M.S. *Colossus*, a battleship completed at Portsmouth in 1886. She had 264 lamps of 20 and 12 candle-power and three searchlights all worked from a common system of 60 volts d.c. There were three Gramme type dynamos, two of which were sufficient to light the ship fully inside, leaving one for a searchlight. At general quarters at night lighting had to be reduced to allow a second generator to be used for the search-lights. Ships built subsequently had similar electrical systems.

In the middle of the nineteenth century the sea-mine came into use as a weapon in naval warfare. It was employed by the Russians in the Crimean War of 1854–6 without any great success, the mines being fired by mechanical means similar to a gunlock or by chemical means in which the contact of the ship broke a glass phial and allowed acid to mix with another chemical. There is indication that the Russians had some mines which were fired electrically and this method was definitely used ten years later in the American Civil War. In 1865 the Federal armoured gunboat *Commodore James* was sunk in the Roanoke River by a 1,000 pound mine fired electrically from the shore. Mining of this type had the great advantage that the mines could be made safe while friendly ships passed and they could be raised, maintained and repaired; this was not so for the older type which, once laid, remained dangerous alike for friend and foe. A similar type of mine was used by the Germans to defend their ports in the Franco-Prussian War of 1870–1. They sank no ships, but the vastly superior French fleet kept its distance and contented itself with a blockade.

The attack by ships on forts and defended harbours had become easier with the introduction of the powerful steam-propelled armoured ship. In the past the superiority of forts against wooden ships of the time had depended on the use of red hot shot and more recently on explosive shells, which set them on fire. Now ships' armour made them proof against shells, and at the same time their heavy armour-piercing guns were more effective against forts. Booms were also less effective as they would now have to be very strong to withstand ramming.

In the early eighteen-seventies, therefore, the British Navy began to take an interest in mines for harbour defence. In 1873–4 they conducted a number of experiments against H.M.S. *Oberon* with parts of her hull strengthened to represent the modern battleship *Hercules*. From these experiments two types of mine resulted: the first of them was the observation mine, which could be either a moored or a ground mine, laid either singly or in lines of up to half a dozen. It was fired electrically with a primary battery by an observer on shore when the ship passed the line of his sight which was set along the line of mines. The mines were laid deep so that friendly ships would pass over them without damaging them or fouling their screws, and they therefore had to have a heavy charge weighing from 500 to 1,500 pounds of guncotton. The mines were immune from counter-mining, which was the principal counter-measure of the day, unless the counter-mine was very close. On the other hand the observation hut was liable to attack and the mines were no use in fog or low visibility.

The second type of mine was much smaller, with a charge of only 76 pounds of guncotton and was designed to go off when hit by a ship. It was still controlled from the shore to a certain extent as the circuit could be switched off and so made safe. This type of mine would therefore work in fog or low visibility and did not need an observation station overlooking the field; the mines, however, had to be set shallow and could not be used in a main channel without risk of damage to their structure. In Great Britain, responsibility for the defence of ports and naval bases rested with the Army. These mines were laid and operated by the Royal Engineers in close co-operation with the shore batteries; but the Royal Navy also took a number of these mines with it in the fleet for the defence of open anchorages and temporary naval bases. The torpedo depot ship *Hecla* carried 168 mines and most battleships a few. For example H.M.S. *Alexandra* carried twelve and the *Lord Warden* and *Repulse* had six each.

Controlled defensive minefields are one of those weapons which succeed by not being used. If the enemy decides not to attack because of their existence they have won. Nevertheless in October 1877 in the Russo-Turkish War, the Turkish gunboat *Suna* was sunk by one when reconnoitring Soulina. Electricity therefore combined with the mine made it possible to defend ports and naval bases against modern ironclads (Note 13)

We must now return to the telegraph. If the seventies were the period in which the telegraph cable spread all over the world, the eighties were one of consolidation. The majority of seaports were connected to the telegraph and it was possible to contact ships whenever they were in a port of any size. Cables were laid almost entirely by commercial interests but strategic influences began to be felt. It was obvious that telegraph lines which passed through foreign countries would be of doubtful value in wartime. If the country was hostile they would obviously stop any communication, but even if it was neutral they might refuse to pass messages in code or cipher. From this point of view the British cable to Alexandria through the Bay of Biscay and the Mediterranean was of greater strategic value than an overland line through some five countries. Steps had also to be taken to defend existing cables at vulnerable points and to repair them if they were cut. Although South Africa was now connected by cable, this was routed from Aden by the east coast; consequently there was pressure to lay a new cable by the west coast to the Cape which would be easier to defend, and which could also be used for communication with India, the Far East and Australia if the Mediterranean cable were cut.

By 1880 telegrams were in fairly general use for operational signals in the Mediterranean. In the period preceding the bombardment of Alexandria in 1882, telegraph communication between London and Egypt was continuous. In May of that year when the situation was becoming tense the British Mediterranean fleet was cruising in Greek and Cretan waters. Their mails and despatches were being sent overland to Brindisi, where they were picked up by a despatch vessel. Suda Bay in Crete was in touch, via Alexandria and the British cable through Malta and Gibraltar, with the United Kingdom. On arrival at Alexandria on May 20, Admiral Sir Beauchamp Seymour, the Commander-in-Chief Mediterranean, reported his proceedings by telegraph to London. To do this he had to send the message ashore to the telegraph office. Two days later he heard by telegraph from Suda Bay that the despatches just received from Brindisi in H.M.S. *Helicon* had nothing of importance in them. On June 2 the Admiralty, in consultation with the Eastern Telegraph Company, ordered the Commander-in-Chief to grapple the telegraph cable to ensure that his communications would not be cut if the situation ashore deteriorated. H.M.S. *Cygnet* dragged for the cable from June 7 to 10 and finally found it two and a half miles off shore and buoyed it. Next day the massacre of Europeans ashore occurred. On June 16 the Telegraph Company's cable ship *Chiltern* arrived and grappled the cable but moved to four miles off shore to be out of gun range from the forts. She then connected the cable and set up a telegraph office direct with London. The British Government in London were therefore in close touch during the days preceding the bombardment. They knew that the Egyptians were strengthening the batteries as a threat to the fleet and on July 3 instructed the Commander-in-Chief that if work on the fortifications was not stopped he should destroy the earthworks and silence the batteries. Admiral Seymour asserted his independence to a small extent after a council of war. He exceeded his instructions slightly by sending an ultimatum to the Egyptians that unless the batteries at Ras el Tin were temporarily surrendered so that they could be disarmed, the fleet would attack them. There being no satisfactory answer, the bombardment began at 0700 on July 11. Close telegraph communication continued with London even on such minor problems as the capture of a midshipman by the Egyptians on July 31. The bombardment of Alexandria was therefore the first time that the commander-in-chief of a foreign station was in really close touch with the central government during a war situation.

In the 1887 manoeuvres in home waters the telegraph was used tactically to pass information. Ships put into port to send messages and the admirals kept touch with the telegraph system by despatch vessels. The first attempt was also made to deceive the 'enemy' by a bogus telegram. In these manoeuvres the Channel fleet was divided into two sides. One was to defend the Channel and the other to attempt to raid the Thames estuary. The raiding side landed an officer to send a telegram to the opposing admiral giving a false position of the 'enemy' battle-fleet and purporting to have been sent by one of his own cruisers. The ruse nearly succeeded but was discovered when the ship which was supposed to have sent the telegram came in sight from the flagship and was able to deny it. For all normal administrative and operational purposes, however, despatches by mail steamer were still the main method of communication, and the telegraph was confined to important messages in which speed was important. In 1888, for instance, the Commander-in-Chief in the East Indies was required to send a report of proceedings by every mail steamer. Telegrams were freely used during 'trouble' in East Africa, not only from England to Zanzibar but from Zanzibar to the Government of

India at Calcutta. In January 1890 a concentration of fourteen ships off Mozambique under the C.-in-C. East Indies was organized entirely by the telegraph. The ships came not only from the East Indies Station but from the Cape, China and Australian Stations as well. Thereafter in the nineties, the telegraph was in almost continuous use for operational and other important messages, not only between the Admiralty and the commanders-in-chief but from the commanders-in-chief to the ships on their stations.

In the Spanish-American War of 1898 both governments depended upon the cable systems of the world for communication with their outlying squadrons of warships. The U.S. Navy Department at first believed it best not to cut any cables but to declare them neutral for use by both belligerents. Commodore Dewey with the U.S. Asiatic Squadron was at Hong Kong when war broke out and remained there in touch with Washington by cable. This communication was by the transatlantic cable, thence through the Mediterranean and Red Sea and so to the Far East. Most of the route was British controlled and Spain was using the same cable with its extension from Hong Kong to Manila. After the American naval victory in Manila Bay, Commodore Dewey tried to arrange with his enemy for both sides to use the cable to Hong Kong. When this was refused he cut it. He was then forced to use a dispatch vessel to take his messages to Hong Kong. His adversary, however, was isolated altogether, much to the advantage of the United States; shortly afterwards the Navy Department changed its policy and ordered the cables to Cuba to be cut, thus isolating the Spanish forces on the island. Subsequently the U.S. Government took care that the new cable to be laid from the Pacific coast to the Philippines touched land only at places where the U.S.A. had sovereignty. Wake Island, at the time unclaimed, was annexed by the U.S.A. for this purpose.

By the end of the century the cable network had spread throughout the world. It was now possible in peacetime for all countries to communicate with their warships whenever they were in port except in very out-of-the-way places. The network was such that messages could generally be routed clear of hostile countries. Great Britain, owning most of the cables, was in a good position to protect them with her world-wide disposition of the Royal Navy. Other countries were not so well

placed when at war but often contrived to maintain communication.

Other electrical matters besides the telegraph progressed during
the last twenty years of the century. The standard searchlight
in the Royal Navy in the eighties was of 24 in. diameter with a
reflector instead of a lens. The carbons were hand-adjusted and
there was no form of shutter. Each searchlight required a
current of 100 amps at 80 volts giving a light of 25,000 candle-
power, which could normally illuminate a ship at over a mile.
To protect them from gunfire in a day action, the searchlights
were normally unshipped and stowed away behind armour.
Smaller types of ships also carried searchlights; even torpedo
boats had one of 20 in. diameter.

In 1886 a 'Squadron of Evolution' was formed to test the
practical efficiency of the material of the Royal Navy. These
ships were mostly of the 'up funnel, down screw' type fitted
with one or two searchlights. They concentrated on the problem
of defending a fleet at anchor in an open roadstead against
attack by torpedo boats. At Berehaven the torpedo boats were
decisively repulsed by the use of searchlights which were kept
on all the time. At Blacksod Bay, also on the west coast of
Ireland, the ships kept their lights off but corvettes and gunboats illuminated an area round them continuously. Again the
torpedo boats were decisively repulsed. It was not many years
before the attack on ships at anchor was completely countered
by the building of breakwaters such as those at Portland, Dover
and Gibraltar. Searchlights were then mounted in the forts
which defended the entrances to the harbours. The main use
of searchlights thus became the defence of ships at sea.

By the end of the eighteen-eighties, when the battleships of
the 'Admiral' class were completed in Britain, electricity was
well established in ships of the Royal Navy. New ships had
electric light consisting of some 300 incandescent lights of 10,
20 or 40 candle-power. The distribution was generally divided
into five separate circuits with two steam generators supplying
electricity at 80 volts d.c. Searchlights were still 24 in. in diameter and of 25,000 candle-power, and their power supplies
were combined with those for electric light. The 'Admiral'
class (Diagram 2) had six searchlights, four of which were
mounted low down in sponsons at each corner of the super-

structure. It had been found in exercises that if the lights were mounted too high torpedo boats could pass at close range under the beams without being seen. The sponsons also gave better arcs of training and some protection to the lights from gunfire. The remaining two searchlights were mounted on the centre line on the fore and after bridges and were fitted with venetian blind type shutters for signalling. It had been found possible to signal at visibility distance at night and even beyond the horizon with the beam pointed in the air to reflect off clouds, a range of thirty-one miles being obtained on one occasion.

By the early nineties, when the 'Royal Sovereign' class battleships were built, they were fitted with a number of electric bells and the guns and torpedoes could be fired remotely from the conning tower. There was also an electrical system to ensure that the guns were fired when the ship was upright. Telephones and step-by-step range transmitters were in an experimental stage but the main system of internal communication in ships was still by the more reliable voice pipe.

In 1893 the French yard at La Seyne completed a small second-class ironclad for Chile (Note 14), in which electricity was used extensively for power for the first time. All her guns were laid and trained and all her ammunition hoists were operated by electric motors. Auxiliary steam and hydraulic systems were almost entirely replaced, but manual methods were retained in case of breakdown. The French Navy soon followed this policy and the battleship *Brennus*, completed in 1895, had electric hoists for ammunition and electric motors for laying and training her guns. With one exception the eight other French battleships completed before 1900 were similarly fitted. This policy was also followed in the U.S. Navy which went 'electric' in the 'Indiana' class battleships completed in 1895–6. The system had been tried out on a smaller scale in the armoured cruiser *New York*, completed in 1893. Thereafter all U.S. battleships' guns were operated by electricity. The German Navy were more cautious and tried electricity for some purposes but retained hydraulic power in addition.

The British Navy on the other hand did not produce any ships with more than a few fans using electric power until the completion of the two large cruisers *Powerful* and *Terrible* in 1898 (Plate I). In these ships the 9·2-in. guns were laid and trained electrically and all ammunition hoists for both 9·2 in. and

6 in. guns as well as the boat hoists and cranes were electrically operated. The vessels were lighted by some 800 electric bulbs and had six 24 in. searchlights. Electric lighting and searchlights were fed from a single electrical system powered by three 48 kw. steam-driven dynamos. Two of the searchlights were now mounted in the fore and main tops at a height of about a hundred feet above the sea. This position was found to be satisfactory for the gunlayers as it enabled them to see the target much better. The other four searchlights were mounted at each side of the fore and after flying bridges, considerably higher than the sponsons of the 'Admiral' class ships which had been found very wet in a seaway. These four searchlights were designed to be dismantled and stowed below by day. Such a searchlight arrangement was also used in the 'Majestic' class battleships, completed between 1895 and 1898, and remained standard in subsequent classes for some years. Electric power for gun turrets however did not find favour in the Royal Navy and subsequent ships had hydraulic systems. Electric ammunition hoists for the secondary armament continued to be used, and together with a third dynamo to supply the power they were fitted retrospectively in the 'Majestic' class as they came in for refit. Whereas electric lighting, bells and remote firing circuits contributed to the efficiency of warships in action, the spread of electric power in such vessels cannot be claimed as very significant. Opinion varied widely on whether it was better than hydraulic or steam power which were certainly complete substitutes.

While the use for electricity on board ships was being extended in these ways, the electrical storage cell or secondary battery was also being developed. These batteries could be charged by a current from either a dynamo or a primary battery and would subsequently release the energy and could then be charged again. Such batteries could be used in place of primary batteries on board ship with advantage, but it was for the propulsion of submarines that they had their greatest influence on sea power. The development of submarines before 1885 had not been attended with any degree of success, one of the reasons being the lack of any way of propelling them submerged other than by manpower. An electric motor with a secondary battery to drive it provided a propulsion system independent of the atmosphere; although limited in endurance, this was thousands of times greater than could be exerted manually.

In 1887 the French laid down a small submarine of thirty tons at Toulon called the *Gymnote*. She was propelled by a 55 hp electric motor with current supplied by 564 accumulators weighing 9·8 tons altogether. The battery therefore constituted roughly one-third of the weight of the whole submarine. The *Gymnote* had many problems but her propulsion system was not one of them and was able to propel her at seven to eight knots for several hours. The *Gymnote* was so small that she was only of use for trials and training, but in 1890 a much larger submarine, the *Gustave Zédé*, was laid down, also at Toulon. The *Gustave Zédé* was of 266 tons driven by a pair of electric motors of a total of 720 hp, the current being supplied by a battery of 720 cells weighing 130 tons or half the total weight of the submarine. The *Gustave Zédé* was launched in 1893 but suffered many set-backs which delayed her completion for years. The first battery collapsed internally and it was eighteen months before a replacement was provided. The second battery then exploded and a lot of damage was done. She finally put to sea on trials with a third battery which was only half the size of the earlier ones. At sea she proved very difficult to control and had to return for considerable modifications. Finally, after four years and with her fourth battery, her trials were successful. She reached twelve knots on the surface and eight knots submerged. Subsequently she made the voyage from Toulon to Marseilles, a distance of forty-one nautical miles, under her own power. These early French submarines were propelled solely by electric motors deriving their power from batteries and so had a very short range. They had to return to harbour to have their batteries recharged and so could only be used for local defence.

In 1896 the French Minister of Marine opened a competition to design something better which he defined as a submersible torpedo boat. A large number of entries were received; the competition was won by a M. Leubeuf, and the *Narval* was laid down at Cherbourg to his designs. The *Narval* had two systems of propulsion; steam for use on the surface and electric power when submerged. To make room for the boiler and steam engine, the battery capacity had to be halved which greatly reduced the submerged endurance. The steam engine, however, could be used to drive the electric motor as a dynamo and so recharge the battery without returning to harbour. The *Narval* had a similar endurance on the surface under steam to a second-class torpedo boat and so could be used for coast defence. Completed in 1899, she was the first of the 'submersible' type of submarine as opposed to the 'sousmarin' type such as the *Gustave Zédé*.

In the U.S.A. a similar development was achieved which also relied on batteries and electric motors for submerged propulsion. The 'Adder' class, designed by Mr Holland, used a petrol engine for surface propulsion and recharging the battery rather than steam. The internal combustion engine had many advantages over steam but petrol was found to be dangerous in a confined space. The electric accumulator or storage battery driving an electric motor can claim to be one of the developments which made the submarine possible – steel hulls, the torpedo and the screw propeller must all take their share of the credit – but no other practicable method of submerged propulsion emerged during the next fifty years.

During the nineteenth century, therefore, especially in the second half of it, the electron had a very distinct influence upon sea power. Without doubt, its most important effect came with the invention of the telegraph, especially in the form of the submarine cable. The second most important effect was in the invention of the searchlight which made night fighting, especially to repel torpedo craft, a practicable proposition (Note 15). The controlled mine, by greatly increasing the effectiveness of harbour defence, also made its contribution. If from 1870 onwards many minor uses for electricity in warships were developed, including electric firing for guns, electric lighting and electric power for laying and training guns and supplying ammunition, these were not essential; there were reasonably efficient alternatives and the innovations can only be classed as minor improvements. On the other hand electric power, in the form of accumulators and electric motors, made the development of the submarine possible. Although by 1900 it was little more than a toy, it was to become one of the major developments in maritime war of the twentieth century.

II

The Invention of Wireless

WHILE THE DEVELOPMENTS with electricity, described
in the last chapter, were being put into practice in the
fleets of the world, scientific experiments continued.
Not only were existing practical uses for electricity improved
but scientists broke entirely new ground. In the sixties and
early seventies, a brilliant British mathematician and physicist,
James Clark Maxwell, building upon the ideas and theories of
Faraday and others, predicted the propagation in space of
electro-magnetic waves and asserted that they would travel
with the speed of light. His mathematical equations were by
no means accepted universally and indeed were known only to
mathematicians and physicists. It was a decade before the
German scientist Heinrich Hertz actually propagated electro-
magnetic waves in his laboratory and proved the accuracy of
Clark Maxwell's theories. Hertz's apparatus was, in fact, the
first radio transmitter but it had a range of only twenty-five feet.

In a remarkable series of experiments he confirmed that
electro-magnetic waves were radiated in all directions and
moved with the speed of light. He showed that they could be
reflected and refracted and would penetrate some materials
opaque to light. Hertz's experiments set many other scientists
working in this field of research but most of them seem only to
have been interested in the pure physics of the subject. Although
the results of Hertz's experiments were published in 1888, no
suggestion that electro-magnetic waves would be useful for
communication or any other purpose was made for four years.
Then a noted British scientist, Sir William Crookes, published
an article in which he forecast the use of electro-magnetic
waves for communication. Hertz had made his experiments on
a wavelength of about 4 m., that is a frequency of 75 million

cycles per second, which is in the middle of what we now know as the V.H.F. band. His conclusions that radio waves behaved like light were correct for this frequency, but the conclusion was drawn that communication by any electro-magnetic waves could only be established by stations which could 'see' each other and so was bound to be of very limited range. At the time of the publication of Sir William Crookes' article, Captain H. B. Jackson, a torpedo and electrical specialist in the Royal Navy, had become interested in 'Hertzian waves' as they were called, not as a general means of communication but for solving the problem of distinguishing friend from foe during night attacks by torpedo boats. This seems to us today to have been an extraordinarily limited objective, but it was a direct result of Hertz's findings which indicated that his waves would never, because of the curvature of the earth, be received much beyond the horizon. The six years following the publication of Hertz's experiments were however not wasted. Many scientists working independently and in the interests of pure science made contributions which were to prove most valuable. Of these the experiments of Sir Oliver Lodge, with the tuning of circuits or 'syntony' as it was called, were probably the most important.

In 1895 Captain Jackson was appointed to command H.M.S. *Defiance*, the torpedo school at Plymouth. This gave him the time and the means to make experiments. He had constructed a wireless set by the end of the year and had soon sent messages from one end of the ship to the other. During 1896 he made steady progress and sent radio signals between two ships in harbour, ringing an electric bell. In September of that year he met Signor Marconi in a demonstration on Salisbury Plain. In the demonstration Signor Marconi's apparatus, for which he had applied for a patent three months earlier, obtained a range of one and three-quarter miles and was clearly ahead of that produced by Captain Jackson. Signor Marconi had devoted himself to the development of radio in Italy for the previous two years. He had increased the range of a Hertz-type transmitter from a few metres to nearly two miles by combining it with an aerial system devised by the Russian scientist Popoff for experiments with lightning. He made a number of other minor improvements and added a telegraph recorder. He then offered the Italian Government a demonstration. When they declined he moved to England, partly because of family connections but also because he foresaw that the greatest need for wireless was at sea.

At this time the telegraph had already made communication between any part of the civilized world rapid and reliable. The development of wireless as a rival would merely be another way of doing the same thing. For ships at sea, however, it was a very different matter. Once they were out of sight of land they were completely isolated. Merchant ships could not report if they were delayed or in distress and could not receive news, weather reports or any other information. Warships could not be given instructions or report the enemy until they contacted a shore signal station. The need for some such communication system as wireless at sea was therefore urgent and seemed promising, as experiments already showed that electro-magnetic waves travelled better over the sea than over the land. Great Britain, with the greatest navy in the world and by far the largest merchant fleet, was the obvious place for Marconi to go to sell wireless as a system of communication.

Marconi was more of a practical engineer and businessman than a scientist. He was not interested so much in extending the work of Clark Maxwell and Hertz as in making the predictions of Sir William Crookes come true. In this quest he does not seem to have been in the least deterred by the inherently short ranges which followed from an acceptance of Hertz's findings. Captain Jackson and Marconi both benefited from their meeting on Salisbury Plain and their exchange of views. Captain Jackson soon obtained a range of 5,300 yards between the *Defiance* and the gunboat *Scourge* underway in the Hamoaze, and later a range of three miles between the *Defiance* and Admiralty House at Plymouth. In March 1897 Marconi obtained four and a half miles between two stations on Salisbury Plain. It was at this point that the British Admiralty made a financial grant to the torpedo school to enable them to make wireless sets for trials in the fleet at sea. Unfortunately at the same time they appointed Captain Jackson to be Naval Attaché in Paris and he was unable to continue his experiments. Signor Marconi however greatly improved his apparatus and in July 1897 demonstrated it to the Italian Ministry of Marine. He communicated from the dockyard at La Spezia with the armoured cruiser *San Martino* eleven miles away at sea. In the following month the Italian Navy announced that it would adopt the Marconi apparatus. They confirmed the decision in May 1898 but were slow to follow it up and only purchased four sets.

At this point with the British and Italian Navies interested in wireless and apparatus of practical use emerging, it is difficult to proceed much further without some idea of the principles upon which these work. Wireless waves are propagated by applying a high voltage alternately of opposite polarity very rapidly to an aerial. When a high voltage is applied to an aerial, electro-magnetic and electro-static fields are built up and remain in place so long as the voltage is maintained. If the voltage is removed the fields simply collapse, but if the voltage is reversed rapidly enough, that is at the rate of over ten thousand times a second, successive opposite poled fields are formed which have not time to collapse before the subsequent ones begin to form. The fields therefore continue outwards in the form of electro-magnetic waves travelling at the speed of light. So a wireless transmitter is basically an electrical device capable of imparting a high and rapidly alternating voltage to an aerial. The very high frequency at which the alternating voltages had to be applied made any form of mechanical switching out of the question, and the only way known at the end of the nineteenth century to do this was to utilize the discovery already made, that when a condenser was discharged into a circuit containing an inductance, the current oscillated backwards and forwards extremely rapidly but with gradually decreasing force until it came to rest. The early transmitters, from Hertz onwards, used this principle with a battery to supply the power, the voltage being stepped up with an induction coil. The properties of a spark gap (Note 1) were utilized to discharge the condenser into the oscillating circuit resulting in the propagation of a series of damped electro-magnetic waves following rapidly one after the other (Diagram 3, Fig. 3). The power used was small, about ¼ kw., and the result was the transmission, whenever the key was pressed, of an unmusical noise similar to atmospherics over a very broad band of frequencies. In those days there was no practical way to measure the wavelength, and tuning or 'syntony' was in its infancy. In fact, the major frequency transmitted was mainly dependent on the size and configuration of the aerial. The result was that there was virtually only one wireless channel, and transmissions

3. Diagram of Wireless Waves

Fig. 1 Damped Waves Produced by Spark Transmitter.

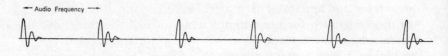

← Audio Frequency →

Fig. 2 Waves Produced by Quenched or Rotary Spark Transmitter. (Higher sparking rate, waves less damped.)

← Audio Frequency

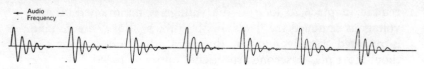

Fig. 3 Waves Produced by Marconi's Timed Spark Transmitter. (Still higher sparking rate, damped waves overlap to give a form of continuous wave.)

← Audio Frequency

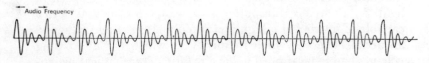

Fig. 4 Continuous Waves Produced by Poulsen Arc or Alexanderson Alternator. (and later by Thermionic Valve Transmitter.) (Waves are not audible in headphones.)

Fig. 5 Reception of Continuous Waves by Interruption at Receiver. (as in Poulsen Tikker.)

← Audio Frequency →

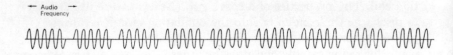

Fig. 6 Reception of Continuous Waves by Heterodyne Method.

——— Continuous waves as received.　　- - - - - Heterodyne frequency superimposed by receiver.

← Audio Frequency →　　—·—·—· Resultant wave audible in headphones.

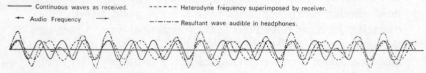

blanketed the whole usable radio spectrum. Once the waves were transmitted, the attenuation caused their strength to fall off rapidly with distance.

The wireless receiver consisted of an aerial similar to the transmitter and the use of a 'coherer' (Note 2) which detected the presence of the electro-magnetic waves. A circuit powered by batteries then operated a telegraph 'inker' which displayed the signal visually on a tape. There were no means of tuning a receiver except to make its aerial the same general size as that of the transmitter. The receiver could not discriminate at all between atmospherics and signals, and if two stations transmitted at once the result was a jumble of unintelligible marks on the tape.

In 1897 Professor Slaby from Germany attended one of Signor Marconi's demonstrations on Salisbury Plain. His experiments had not so far produced ranges of more than a hundred metres. Again, both he and Marconi benefited from this meeting and thereafter Professor Slaby's sets worked much better. This may be taken as the point at which practical radio development began in Germany. In 1897 Marconi established a station at Alum Bay in the Isle of Wight to work with the local paddle-steamers in which he installed sets when necessary. Before long he was getting ranges of eighteen and a half miles and he then set up another station at Bournemouth. The next year he obtained considerable publicity by reporting the Kingstown Regatta for the Dublin *Daily Express*, sending some 700 messages at ranges up to twenty-five miles. In 1899 he succeeded in sending messages across the Channel from the South Foreland to Wimereux, a distance of thirty miles. The French Government became interested and he made further demonstrations for them in the gunboat *Ibis* and a store ship.

Meanwhile the torpedo school at Plymouth persevered but had much less success than Marconi. The principal reason for this was probably the absence of Captain Jackson, but they also had manufacturing problems and their sets did not prove to be robust enough. The results obtained were not consistent either, and by the spring of 1899 they had to report that the sets were not ready for trial in the annual manoeuvres. The Admiralty therefore approached Signor Marconi and asked him to fit two ships. He said that he had three sets available and these were installed in the old battleship *Alexandra* and the cruisers *Europa* and *Juno*. Signor Marconi embarked in the *Juno* which was under the command of Captain Jackson for the period of the manoeuvres. The sets provided by Marconi embodied a substantial improvement in their receivers, called a 'jigger' (Note 3). Preliminary trials with the *Juno* in Torbay obtained a range of no less than eighty-seven miles with the Marconi station in the Isle of Wight.

The 1899 manoeuvres took place to the west of the British Isles, the Reserve fleet was mobilized and together with the Channel fleet there were seventeen battleships and forty-two cruisers involved, as well as many destroyers and torpedo boats. The principal object of the manoeuvres was to investigate the best way to use a large number of cruisers with a fleet. There were, as usual, two sides. Side 'A', which was 'hostile', had Ireland as its territory with the weaker of the two battlefleets based on Belfast and with torpedo boats at Kingstown and Waterford. Side 'B' represented the 'British' with the superior but slower battlefleet based on Milford Haven with torpedo boats and destroyers at Holyhead and Lamlash.

The situation at the start of the exercise was that a convoy belonging to 'B' was on its way across the Atlantic from Halifax to Milford Haven. This convoy, represented by two old cruisers escorted by a third, had been given a rendezvous at which to meet 'B' fleet. As soon as the exercise began, 'A' fleet left Belfast and passed through the North Channel to search for the convoy west of Ireland. It was seen by 'B' fleet's destroyers from Lamlash who reported to a shore signal station and the message was relayed by telegraph to the Admiral commanding 'B' fleet at Milford Haven. On rounding the Bloody Foreland, 'A' fleet threw out sixteen of its cruisers in a search for the convoy with orders to rendezvous on its completion for further instructions. Three cruisers had to be kept back for contacting shore signal stations to obtain any information arriving by telegraph. The first search drew blank and was renewed, the orders being sent by visual signal at the rendezvous. The second search also failed but H.M.S. *Minerva* returned from the signal station at Blacksod Bay with the news that 'B' fleet had left Milford Haven for the westwards. This information came from the torpedo boats at Waterford and was relayed by land-line to Blacksod Bay. 'B' fleet had, in fact, sent a squadron of fast cruisers ahead to meet the convoy at the rendezvous and was following as fast as it could. H.M.S. *Europa* with wireless was in the advanced squadron, and to keep touch with H.M.S. *Alexandra*, the flagship with the main body, H.M.S. *Juno* was stationed half-way to relay the messages. The *Europa* had instructions to steam back and report as soon as the convoy was located. This she did and contacted the *Juno* at a range of sixty miles, the *Juno* relaying the message to the *Alexandra* at forty-five miles (Note 4). The convoy was subsequently safely escorted to Milford Haven by 'B' fleet.

The 1899 manoeuvres have been described in some detail to compare the easy exchange of wireless messages with the cumbersome older methods of visual signalling, shore signal stations and the telegraph. To search the maximum area cruisers had to be twice visibility distance apart. If they sighted the enemy they had to make up their mind whether to shadow or to return to the fleet to report. In any case, all the other cruisers of the search line would continue on their courses ignorant that the enemy had been sighted and would not get any new instructions until they made the rendezvous on completion of the search. Wireless was obviously going to make a great difference to all this. Yet it was still far from perfect: only one ship could transmit at a time, and it was realized that the enemy would be able to intercept the messages and might well be able to jam them. On the other hand there were very hopeful signs too. The ranges obtained in the manoeuvres were much greater than should have been possible if Hertz was right and electro-magnetic waves behaved like light. Without doubt they were not only being projected tangentially into space, but were following the curvature of the earth. Whatever the scientific explanation of this might prove to be, longer ranges still were now a distinct possibility. Experiments with tuning gave promise that it would be possible to use more than one radio channel and to tune sets to a secret frequency which it would be difficult for the enemy to discover. The use of wireless in the 1899 manoeuvres was a great milestone in its development and was adjudged at the time to have been a great success.

After the 1899 manoeuvres the Admiralty wished to purchase a number of Marconi sets but they found the financial conditions, especially the payment of royalties, unsatisfactory. They therefore did not place an order with Marconi straight away, indeed the three sets used in the manoeuvres were returned to the company. Fresh impetus was however given to experiments with the 'service' sets of the type designed by Captain Jackson in the torpedo school in the hope that they could catch up Marconi's lead. Towards the end of the year, components for eight of these sets were purchased from a number of firms and the sets were assembled in H.M.S. *Vernon*. After making sets for both *Vernon* and *Defiance*, the battleship *Canopus*, under orders for the Mediterranean, was fitted and obtained a range of twelve miles on trials. Two more sets were sent to the Mediterranean to H.M.S. *Vulcan*, where Captain Jackson was now stationed so that he could continue to experiment. At about the same time the battleships *Majestic*, *Magnificent*, *Jupiter* and *Hannibal* of the Channel Squadron were also fitted.

After the manoeuvres the U.S. Naval Attaché in London was instructed to see if Marconi could give a demonstration to the U.S. Navy. Marconi was already on his way to the U.S.A. where in September he reported the America Cup Races by wireless for the *New York Herald*. After the races he agreed to give a demonstration to the U.S. Navy but warned that the sets he had with him were inferior to those used in the British manoeuvrres. The sets were installed in the armoured cruiser *New York* and the battleship *Massachusetts*, and messages were exchanged in a gale at thirty-six and a half miles and received by one ship at forty-six miles. When one set was transferred to the torpedo boat *Porter* however only seven-to-eight miles' range was obtained. The U.S. Navy were impressed, and although they realized that the British, Italian and French Navies were all interested in wireless and were already ahead of them, they too found Marconi's conditions of sale quite unacceptable and decided to await developments.

With the outbreak of the South African War, the British War Office asked Marconi to supply five sets of apparatus which were used for the communications of the Army in the field (Note 5). The sets were carried up country in horse-drawn wagons of the telegraph section of the Royal Engineers but were operated by Marconi personnel. The sets proved a failure: the aerials were unsatisfactory, atmospherics were very bad and the hills interfered with communication. The Army therefore dispensed with their services and the sets were taken up by the Navy in February 1900.

The Royal Navy had three functions in South Africa: the

first was to defend the ports, the second was to provide naval brigades to work with the Army and the third was to blockade Portuguese Mozambique and to a certain extent German South-West Africa, to prevent any contraband of war reaching the Boers. It was for this last task that the Commander-in-Chief at the Cape needed wireless. Sets were installed in the cruisers *Forte*, *Thetis* and *Magicienne*, which were busy blockading Lourenço Marques. One of the Marconi engineers is on record as saying that wireless proved useful to the officers for making private arrangements when returning to port! No doubt this was true but it was of great value for operations too. The Portuguese had not declared their neutrality and a British cruiser normally lay in Lourenço Marques itself while other warships patrolled outside territorial waters to search merchant ships for contraband. Wireless was used a great deal between the cruiser in harbour and the ships on patrol, also much information about the expected arrival of merchant ships was passed out. At the same time it enabled communication to be maintained by telegraph through the cruiser in harbour in Lourenço Marques with the Commander-in-Chief in Simonstown. On occasion when two of the ships with wireless were on patrol together, they were able to co-ordinate their operations and head off ships which would otherwise have escaped.

In May 1900 an attempt was made to land a cavalry regiment at Kosi Bay to help in the advance on Pretoria. For this operation the C.-in-C. was present, flying his flag in H.M.S. *Doris* which had also been fitted with a Marconi set. The operation was called off because intelligence was sent by wireless from the Consul-General at Lourenço Marques to say that the plan was compromised and the Boers had diverted forces to deal with it (Note 6). While on the subject of the Boer War it is of interest to note that communication between the Admiralty in London and the naval C.-in-C. at Simonstown was by cable and was constant and effective. It dealt even with such details as what articles were to be considered contraband, with particular cases of the seizure of cargo or ships and with how many men were at the front in the naval brigades. Cable communication between Great Britain and South Africa followed the sea route and did not pass through a foreign country and so was not only reliable but secure.

The British 1900 manoeuvres were on a large scale and

similar to those of the year before to the west of the British
Isles. Seven wireless sets of the type developed by H.M.S.
Vernon were sent to sea. On one side the battleship *Majestic*,
which was the flagship, and the cruisers *Diadem*, *Edgar* and
Blake had service sets of apparatus, the last ship being fitted up
from spare parts in the torpedo school. On the other side the
veteran battleship *Alexandra* and the cruisers *Ariadne* and *Hawke*
had 'service' sets too. The *Majestic* was able to communicate
with her three cruisers successfully throughout the exercises
with varying results, the set in the *Diadem* proving excellent
but that in the *Edgar* indifferent. There was some interference
from Marconi's shore stations and from atmospherics, while the
ranges obtained were poor compared with those of the manoeuvres of the previous year. Communication was often only
possible at twelve to fifteen miles and the longest range obtained
was twenty-two miles, nevertheless the cruisers were able to
report the approach of the enemy on several occasions. The
operating procedure laid down just before the exercises as well
as the instructions issued by this side to prevent all ships transmitting at once proved adequate. On the other side, the cruisers
Ariadne and *Hawke* had continual technical trouble and the use
of wireless had to be abandoned altogether. Nevertheless the
C.-in-C. of the Channel Squadron reported that wireless was
extremely valuable.

By the midsummer of 1900 and before the manoeuvres, the
superiority of the Marconi sets to the 'service' sets was so
obvious that the Admiralty accepted Marconi's terms and purchased thirty-two of them including those which had been
installed in the three ships on the Cape Station. The majority of
these sets were installed in ships of the Channel Squadron but
six of them were allocated to the Mediterranean, four to the
Reserve fleet and six for shore stations along the south coast of
England and Ireland (Map 4). The sets for the Channel Squadron were fitted by October, having passed the test of communicating between Portsmouth and Portland, a distance of fifty-two
miles, using naval personnel at a speed of ten words a minute.
By the end of the year there were eight shore stations and forty-
two British warships fitted with wireless.

During the autumn and winter Captain Jackson began to
have better results with the 'service' sets in the Mediterranean
and by December had achieved sixty miles. He developed a

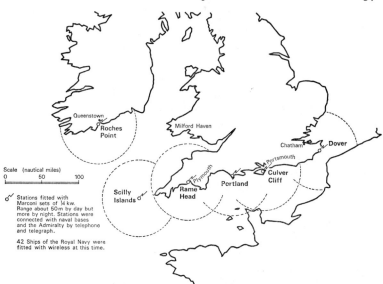

4. Shore Wireless Stations of the Royal Navy 1901.

system of 'syntony' which gave a finer degree of resonance between transmitters and receivers. This was in effect the tuning of all sets to the same wavelength, and he pointed out that this was the secret of Marconi's success. In January 1901 the Admiralty sent for Captain Jackson to confer with the *Vernon*, as a result of which they decided to continue with both Marconi and 'service' sets. While he was away a range of 134 miles was obtained between the shore station at Gargur in Malta and the storeship *Tyne*. In April the Admiralty ordered another fifty 'service' sets so as to equip all the battleships and cruisers in commission on the Home, Mediterranean and China Stations. In the British naval manoeuvres of 1901 most of the ships taking part had wireless. Wireless was found to be very useful but now that it was employed by both sides, the danger of interception by the enemy received confirmation. There were two cases in which this occurred during the manoeuvres and the need always to use a secret code was realized.

The development of wireless was not, of course, confined to the British and Italian Navies. In the latter part of 1900 the Marconi Company built seven shore stations to communicate

with merchant ships which were now beginning to be fitted
with wireless. French interest had shifted from Marconi to the
Popov Ducretet system for their Navy which was made in
France. In 1901 the first wireless station in Germany was
established on Borkum Island by Marconi and the liner *Kaiser
Wilhelm der Grosse* was fitted. Shortly afterwards another German
liner, the *Deutschland*, was fitted with a German Slaby-Arco
wireless set. Admiral Tirpitz, the head of the German Navy,
had followed a policy for some years of no new equipment of
any kind being introduced into the fleet until it had been
thoroughly proved to be reliable. Although he realized the value
of wireless to a fleet, he was opposed to its introduction in its
present primitive form. Early in 1902, while he was away in
America for the launching of the Kaiser's new racing yacht
Meteor, his deputy was subjected to pressure to adopt wireless
from many quarters, among them the Slaby-Arco Company and
the Emperor. As a result Slaby-Arco sets were purchased and
fitted in the fleet in 1902 and, as feared by Admiral Tirpitz,
proved unreliable and gave much trouble. What was worse,
experiment by the company had to give way to production and
so development was slowed down.

The development of wireless over this period was dominated
by Marconi's astonishing achievement in December 1901 in
sending a message across the Atlantic. With most pure scientists
clinging to Hertz's findings that radio waves travelled in straight
lines, they believed that the curvature of the earth made any
really long-range communication out of the question. The
Atlantic can be visualized as a mountain a hundred miles high
and so, they maintained, masts two hundred miles high on both
sides of the ocean would be necessary to establish communication by electro-magnetic waves. Undaunted by such theories,
Marconi built a new and powerful wireless station at Poldhu in
Cornwall and a similar station at Cape Cod in Massachusetts.
After serious set-backs, when both aerial arrays were blown
down in storms, success was achieved and faint signals from
Poldhu were picked up by a portable receiver in Newfoundland.
The Poldhu transmitter was a 25 kw. alternator driven spark
set coupled to a very large umbrella-shaped aerial working on a
wavelength of about 366 metres. Marconi's claims were simply
disbelieved in many scientific circles, but in January 1902 he
arranged for the Cunard liner *Philadelphia* to embark a wireless

set and to listen to Poldhu during her voyage to the U.S.A. To give credence to the trial, the reception of the messages was to be certified by the Master. Poldhu was received out to 700 miles by day and 1,550 miles by night.

We now know that Hertz's experiments were correct for the very high frequency which he used but they do not apply to low-frequency transmissions. Transmissions on this band are propagated in the form of a ground wave which follows the curvature of the earth out to a distance of about a thousand miles. There are also reflections between the troposphere and low ionosphere and the earth's surface which have much the same effect as a modern wave-guide. The ground wave has a greater range over sea than over land, but the wave-guide effect means that transmissions can be heard at any distance providing they are sufficiently powerful. To get sufficient power into the aerials these had to be very large and so the frequency had to be low. Marconi had long realized that high power and low frequency were the secret of long range and it is probable that his faith and perseverance in proving that wireless could be used world wide was the most important success of his whole career.

Marconi produced two other important developments in this period. The first of these was a transmitter with a separate oscillating circuit coupled by a transformer to the aerial circuit. His aim was to produce higher power than was possible with the old 'plain aerial'. Not only was he successful in this but the resulting transmissions were found to be on two separate wavelengths. These were known as Tune A and Tune B, the first being on a wavelength of about 100 m. with a range of 50–70 miles and the second on 270 m. with a range of 80–150 miles. Separate sets were at first produced which could be used on Tune A and others on Tune B and they could be used at the same time without interfering with each other. Later combined sets were developed which could work on either Tune A or Tune B. It was also found that Poldhu on 366 m. would not interfere with either of these tunes. The second advance produced by Marconi was his magnetic detector or 'Maggie' which replaced the coherer as a receiver and which could be used with headphones. It proved much more sensitive and it was found possible to raise the speed of communication from ten to twenty words a minute. The British Admiralty at first turned down the 'Maggie' as they were reluctant to rely on the ears of a single

young signalman and preferred the 'inker' which recorded a
message which could be checked by others later.

In the 1902 British manoeuvres in the Mediterranean the
problem was to investigate the blockade of a fleet in harbour
using cruisers which were to call up their own battlefleet by
wireless if the 'enemy' tried to escape. Most of the large ships
were fitted with wireless and the danger of interference with
each other was appreciated. Instructions were issued that wireless was only to be used if the intelligence to be reported was
really important and that all reports were to be addressed to
the flagship. Cruisers were told not to answer wireless signals
unless they were actually addressed. Ships were still fitted with
semaphore at the top of their masts and the cruisers on blockade
duty were stationed within touch of each other. In these exercises, jamming was used extensively. When the blockaded
squadron escaped to sea it effectively jammed all the enemy
reports made by the blockading cruisers. Considerable trouble
was also experienced with vibration and atmospherics and, in
spite of the instructions issued before the exercise, with interference by ships of the same side with each other. One report
complained, 'In most ships the Marconi Room is between
decks. An operator, often a young signalman, is shut up in this
room alone. What he does there no one but himself knows: he
is told to send a certain message, and, regardless of other messages passing, he at once commences, thus stopping all signalling.
Another report said, 'Apparently every ship was at the same
moment calling up some other ship, and the only result was
miles of tape run off the instrument which no one could make
any sense of.' With spark transmitters that blanketed a wide
band of frequencies and only the 'inker' type of receiver, the
difficulties were immense. There is no doubt, however, that
many ships disregarded the instructions that wireless was only
to be used to report the enemy. One exasperated admiral actually said that what was really required was more despatch
vessels!

During 1902 Marconi was engaged almost entirely in his
transatlantic experiments in which his aim was to rival the
cable system of the world for long-distance communications.
He lengthened the wavelength of Poldhu to 1,100 metres and
built a new and more powerful station at Glace Bay in Nova
Scotia, but the system was not reliable enough to use commerci-

ally. The Italian Navy lent Marconi the cruiser *Carlo Alberto*; she received Poldhu 1,600 miles away in Kronstadt and subsequently right across the Atlantic. Although Marconi had built Poldhu to establish transatlantic wireless communication, the British Admiralty wanted to use it for a different purpose. They were not interested in it as a means of sending a message from one station to another — they had cables for that. They wanted it as a way to broadcast messages simultaneously to all their ships within a large area of the eastern Atlantic. In October 1903 H.M.S. *Duncan* sailed from Portsmouth to Gibraltar and was able to receive Poldhu's transmissions the whole way.

The U.S. Navy was content simply to watch wireless development during 1900 and 1901. The only confidence they showed in its future was to discontinue their homing pigeon service from ships at sea. Then, early in 1902, they decided to buy a number of sets from various companies for trial. Although they were fully aware that the Marconi sets were the best, they could see no hope of a satisfactory financial agreement with the company and so these did not take part in the trials. Two sets were bought from the German companies Slaby-Arco and Braun Siemen's Halske, two sets from the French companies Popoff Ducretet and Rochefort and two sets from the American companies of De Forest and Shoemaker. Later they ordered two sets from the British Lodge-Muirhead concern. By April 1903 they had decided that the Slaby-Arco sets as fitted in the German Navy were the best and ordered twenty of them. In September they ordered another twenty-five sets making fifty-seven sets in all counting all the sets used in the trials (Note 7). Five shore stations on the Atlantic coast and five ships were hastily equipped before the 1903 summer manoeuvres in August, for which the fleet was divided into White and Blue sides. White was the 'enemy' and starting 500 miles east of Cape Cod was to attack and try to land on the New England coast. U.S.S. *Texas* was the only 'white' ship to have wireless. The Blue fleet was to find and destroy the White fleet before it could establish its landing force ashore. U.S.S. *Kearsage, Olympia, Illinois* and *Prairie* of this fleet were fitted with wireless. The main body of the Blue fleet took up a central position and threw out scouts. For three days they searched in rain, mist and fog and then U.S.S. *Olympia* found the White fleet and reported its position by wireless. The Blue fleet closed in and brought it to action before it could put its landing party ashore. U.S.S. *Texas* on the White side had intended to jam any enemy reports but missed the chance to do so (Note 8). In this exercise, therefore, wireless proved an outstanding success and the C.-in-C. Atlantic reported 'the problem had demonstrated to my satisfaction that wireless had come to stay; that it was capable of development and would be of great use in time of war and in peace'.

This was by no means the universal opinion in the U.S. Navy, however, and other senior officers were opposed to its introduction. Apart from the natural dislike of being told what to do at sea from the shore and the consequent curbing of their initiative, they were worried about the interception and counterfeiting of messages by the enemy; by the fact that wireless gave away one's own position and that jamming would probably stop messages getting through. In short they believed that wireless, although possibly a convenience in peace, would prove useless under war conditions. Their fears had some justification; in the British 1903 manoeuvres an attempt was made by one side to use H.M.S. *Minerva* to try to confuse their opponents by making false wireless reports.

The Admiralty continued with their own wireless development in the torpedo schools and were without doubt infringing Marconi's patents. In July 1903 they signed an agreement with the Marconi Company in which, on payment of an annual sum, they were granted the use of all his patent rights for a period of eleven years and also the use of the high-power station at Poldhu for twenty minutes each day. The Admiralty were particularly keen to use his new transmitters with the two Tunes A and B. The Royal Navy at once began to fit transmitters using Tunes A and B and during 1904 all sets were converted or replaced. In 1903 the Royal Navy was represented at a demonstration by De Forest between Howth and Holyhead. De Forest, as Marconi had for Poldhu, used a transmitter powered by an alternator and transformer instead of a battery and induction coil which was more powerful and gave a more musical note. Used in conjunction with telephones for reception, this meant that signals could be picked out through atmospherics or other transmissions and that reception was possible at thirty words a minute.

In 1904 a wireless experimental section of H.M.S. *Vernon*,

the torpedo school at Portsmouth, was formed under the direction of Mr H. B. Madge, a former employee of Marconi, to develop wireless equipment for the fleet. Naval requirements were now adjudged to have diverged from commercial practice so much as to need specialized designs. The Royal Navy decided to try to use aural reception and to train signalmen to read morse by ear. During the year the experimental section studied alternators and telephone reception as well as problems of tuning and using different wavelengths. By the end of 1904 they had designed a naval wireless set using an alternator in the transmitter and the 'Maggie' and telephones for reception. They also produced a wavemeter to measure the wavelength of transmissions, improved the selectivity of receivers and produced a 'roof' aerial slung between the masts for use with lower frequencies. In 1904 wireless in the Royal Navy ceased to be a new toy and took up its position as a reliable communication system in the fleet.

In February 1904 the Russo-Japanese War broke out. The Russian Navy had adopted the Popoff Ducretet system of wireless telegraphy a few years previously and a wireless station was installed at Port Arthur in the autumn of 1903. On February 8, just before war broke out, the Russian cruiser *Variag*, which was at Chemulpo as guardship, was recalled by a wireless message from Port Arthur but this was never received, which was not altogether surprising as Chemulpo is 180 miles away. However, the signal was taken in by the Japanese. All ships of the Japanese fleet larger than destroyers were equipped with wireless made in Japan. The name of Professor Kimura is connected with it but there is little doubt that it was basically a copy of the Marconi apparatus of the turn of the century. One report of a naval attaché describes it as Marconi equipment 'improved by the Japanese'. The sets were, however, certainly inferior to Marconi equipment of 1904 and still employed a single frequency and plain aerial. The Japanese used their wireless virtually without restriction and were generally able to communicate at a range of sixty miles. Whenever they required a longer range they stationed linking ships to relay the messages. Their advanced naval bases in Korea and the Elliot Islands were however connected to Japan by cable. The strategy by which they blockaded the Russian fleet in Port Arthur was made possible by wireless. Scouting cruisers were kept in the offing and were in a position to summon the main Japanese fleet if the Russians made a move. The Russian sortie of 23 June 1904 was first seen at 0600 by a Japanese destroyer which had no wireless. She had to steam away and find the cruiser *Yakumo* and this took two hours; nevertheless Admiral Togo received the report at 0820.

Wireless proved of most value to the Russians during the siege of Port Arthur from the warning it gave of the approach of Japanese ships. The Russian receivers were always able to pick up the Japanese radio before they sighted the ships from the shore signal station, which was particularly valuable in low visibility. This was not the only use of radio warfare by the Russians; on April 15 they were able to jam the Japanese wireless signals when they were trying to spot their fall of shot during a bombardment. On 24 April 1904 the Vladivostok Squadron under Admiral Jessen put to sea to attack Gensan. It passed a Japanese Squadron under Admiral Kamimura quite close in fog on an opposite course. The Russian Squadron realized what was happening by listening to the Japanese wireless transmissions while the Japanese were quite unaware of the situation. As a result Admiral Jessen met no opposition off Gensan and his raid was a success. On another occasion, when the Vladivostok Squadron set out on a raid, it was able from the Japanese wireless traffic to deduce that the sortie had been detected and to avoid running into a trap. The active use of Russian wireless was of value too. It warned Admiral Makaroff when he was at sea on one occasion that Japanese ships were in sight from the signal station at Port Arthur and on another warned the Vladivostok Squadron that mines had been laid off the port during their absence.

When the Russian fleet sortied from Port Arthur on August 10 with the intention of proceeding to Vladivostok, it was seen and reported by wireless by the Japanese cruiser *Kasagi*. As a result it was brought to action by the main Japanese fleet later in the day. Throughout the Japanese concentration they used their wireless freely. The Russians on the other hand do not seem to have used it at all. When the Russian flagship *Tsarevitch* was hit in the conning tower and Admiral Vityeft was killed, the helm jammed hard over and the fleet was thrown into confusion. Both the masts of the Second-in-Command's flagship had been shot away and he was unable to hoist any signals to rally the

fleet, indeed there was doubt that he was still alive as his flag
was not flying. His wireless aerials were shot away too. Admiral
Reitzenstein, next in command, in his flagship the *Askold* was
undamaged but had no more success in rallying the fleet by
visual signals. In this emergency it does not seem that any
attempt was made to use wireless, but it seems unlikely that,
even had this been done with the state of wireless communications in the Russian Navy, the signal would have been received
by more than a few ships. As a result the Russian fleet disintegrated, most of the ships returning to Port Arthur in dis-
order, some making for neutral ports and only one trying to
get through to Vladivostok. There was some delay in the Japanese fleet in pursuing the scattered ships as it was their practice
to dismantle their wireless sets in action and stow them below
the armoured deck. Many detached ships who called up the
Mikasa for instructions could therefore get no answer. Wireless
was subsequently used freely to try to round up the escaping
ships but there was great difficulty in getting through on a
number of occasions and operations were much handicapped.
Some ships had to put into harbour to use the telegraph.
Nevertheless Admiral Kamimura, using wireless, did succeed
four days later in concentrating against the Vladivostok Squadron which had come out, and defeating it at the Battle of Ulsan.

The Second Pacific Squadron which sailed from Libau for
the Far East in October 1904 under Admiral Rojestvensky, was
equipped with German Slaby-Arco apparatus. This system was
undoubtedly an improvement and was by now standard in the
German and American Navies. The Slaby-Arco equipment was
by no means perfect however, as was soon demonstrated in the
Great Belt when the tug *Russ* with a Marconi set had to tell the
battleship *Orel* that she was being called by the flagship and
had to act as wireless link for her. The main communication
between the Russian Admiralty and the Second Pacific Squadron, and indeed the Third under Admiral Nebogotoff which
followed it, was by the international cable system at the various
ports at which they called. The fleet was in fact cut off from the
world between ports; for instance, no news was received from
the time it left Libau on the 15th until it arrived at Vigo on
October 26. During the long stay at Nossé Be in Madagascar,
while waiting for the Third Squadron, the ciphered telegrams
had to be sent by destroyer to a small port near Diego Suarez

where there was a telegraph station. Wireless was really only of use for tactical purposes within the fleet. Not all of the Russian fleet was fitted with standard Slaby-Arco equipment: the armed merchant cruiser *Ural* had a specially powerful Slaby-Arco set which was supposed to work up to 500 miles, and the auxiliaries *Korea* and *Kitai* had commercial Marconi sets. Admiral Rojestvensky complained that no ship was able to receive messages at a greater distance than sixty-five miles except the *Korea*, which picked one up at ninety miles.

In February 1905 at Nossé Be in Madagascar, Admiral Rojestvensky directed the *Ural* to get into touch with the cruiser *Oleg*, which was joining the fleet from Russia as a reinforcement. The *Ural* failed to establish communication at all and it was the *Korea* with her Marconi set which first picked up the *Oleg*'s signals. In April, in Kamrahn Bay, Admiral Rojestvensky complained that after strenuous efforts over eight months to perfect wireless telegraphy in the fleet, the results were hopeless. When at sea exercising he wished to send a message to a ship in harbour and called her for an hour and a half without reply although she was only fifteen miles away. He then tried another ship without success while four more ships which were supposed to be keeping wireless watch failed to relay the message. At the same time three armed merchant cruisers returning from scouting failed to get messages through as they rejoined the fleet. Finally the flagship tried to call the armed merchant cruiser *Rion* on patrol and could get no answer at all. Admiral Rojestvensky asked in a general order on April 20, 'Is the Captain of the *Rion* quite clear in his mind as to how useless his patrolling service is if his wireless apparatus is not in working order?' Three weeks later at Van Fong there was similar trouble communicating with ships on patrol. Exasperating as these deficiencies must have been to Admiral Rojestvensky, too much blame cannot be put on the Slaby-Arco equipment which did not claim a range of more than seventy miles and with which the U.S. Navy trials only obtained sixty-two miles. The company's representatives sailed with the fleet but returned to Germany from Madagascar. It is probable that maintenance of the equipment suffered during the long voyage and there is no doubt that the officers failed to supervise the operators sufficiently.

Admiral Rojestvensky made a final effort to use wireless in his fleet as it passed north between Formosa and the Philippines. He tried to push his advanced screen ahead and to keep touch with it by wireless. After almost total failure to communicate he had to withdraw it back into visibility distance. He himself had a clear idea of the advantages and indeed the disadvantages of wireless. In his final approach to the Straits of Tsushima, his object was to try and get through to Vladivostok without a battle. He prohibited the 'sending of all telegrams' or in modern parlance imposed strict radio silence on his whole fleet. As he approached the Straits of Tsushima his ships reported they could hear fragments of signals which they took to be Japanese wireless messages. On the evening of May 25 many ships in the Russian fleet heard the Japanese scouts talking to each other. The *Ural*, with her powerful wireless set, asked permission to jam the transmissions but Admiral Rojest-vensky rightly refused. The Japanese in consequence were unable to get any information of the Russian approach by radio intelligence.

The Japanese, with their aim of finding and bringing the Russian fleet to action, had an entirely different policy. There were three routes by which the Russian fleet could get to Vladivostok. The first was by the Straits of Tsushima which had the advantage that they were the most direct and the widest route. The other two routes were by the Tsugaru Straits between Honshu and Hokkaido and the Straits of La Perouse between Hokkaido and Sakhalin. The distance from all of these straits to Vladivostok was approximately the same. Admiral Togo therefore based his fleet at Mesampo Bay in south-eastern Korea, from which place with his superior speed he would be able to engage the Russian fleet before it could reach Vladi-vostok by any of the three ways into the Sea of Japan. For this plan to succeed, however, it was essential that reports from his patrols in these defiles should reach him without delay. For the Straits of Tsushima he relied entirely on wireless and for the two northern straits upon a combination of wireless and the telegraph. His outer line of scouts in the Straits of Tsushima consisted of four armed merchant cruisers spaced at twice the visibility distance apart. They advanced south-westwards by day and at sunset turned back to the north-eastwards to avoid missing the Russian fleet during the night. This line was backed up by six protected cruisers patrolling fixed beats on a line across the Straits sixty miles south-west of the Island of

Tsushima. The old battleship *Fuso* was stationed just south of Tsushima to act as a wireless link between the scouts and Admiral Togo in Mesampo Bay. Admiral Togo's strategy therefore depended entirely on wireless and telegraphic communication, without which he would have had to adopt a different and far less satisfactory plan such as a close patrol with his whole fleet off Vladivostok or an advance into the South China Sea to meet the enemy.

Early on the morning of May 27 the armed merchant cruiser *Shinano Maru* sighted the Russian fleet and reported its position by wireless. The message was at once relayed and within minutes was received not only by Admiral Katoaka at the advanced base at Takeshiki on Tsushima Island and Admiral Togo at Mesampo Bay but by all the ships of both scouting lines. The Russians also received this report and heard it being repeated farther and farther away into the distance. Although now fairly certain that he had been sighted, Admiral Rojestvensky stuck to his policy and still refused to jam in the vague hope that he was still undetected. The main Japanese fleet at once put to sea and the cruisers closed in on the Russians. During the forenoon the Japanese cruisers and other ships which had left Takeshiki made contact and gave Admiral Togo an accurate position, course and speed of the Russians and also a description of their formation. As a result the Japanese fleet was able to bring the Russian fleet to action during the afternoon. The Japanese battle orders were clear and well understood and few directions were needed. Admiral Togo did, however, use wireless to tell Vice-Admiral Katoaka that he intended to cover the eastern channel and he in his turn directed the elderly Seventh Squadron to cover the western side of Tsushima in case any Russian ships attempted to get through that way. During the approach Admiral Togo also asked which side the enemy main body was stationed and ordered the shadowing cruisers to report at once should the Russians alter course.

On sighting the enemy, Togo ordered his Fifth and Sixth Squadrons to attack the enemy rear. In general, while the Russians maintained strict wireless silence, the Japanese used this new method of communication with great skill, not only to report the position and course of the enemy but to give essential tactical direction to their fleet. All this was done without any important signal going astray or any confusion due to too many ships trying to send messages at once. The manoeuvring and action signals during the battle were made by visual signals by both sides and after the action became general, wireless was little used. At sunset all the large Japanese ships broke off the action automatically in accordance with the battle orders so as to leave the field clear for torpedo craft to attack. The disintegration of the Russian fleet after sunset could have been prevented by efficient wireless communications.

It is not known why Admiral Nebogotoff did not use it to rally the fleet, especially after what had happened on August 10. Nevertheless had he done so, the defeat of the remnants of the Russians next day was virtually certain whether concentrated or dispersed. At sunset Admiral Togo then used his despatch vessel, the *Tatsuta*, to contact his scattered squadrons to give them a rendezvous near Matshushima Island at dawn, but later he used wireless to order the Seventh Squadron to search the battle area for damaged ships. As soon as it was light reports began to come in from various Japanese ships by wireless of four groups of surviving Russian ships all of which were brought to action and either sunk or captured during the forenoon.

In the Battle of Tsushima wireless telegraphy as used by the Japanese was an outstanding success and its employment must take a share of the credit for the resounding Japanese victory. On the other hand it is doubtful if in fact the lack of efficient Russian wireless contributed much to their defeat. Admiral Rojestvensky's policy of wireless silence was undoubtedly the correct one in the circumstances. He might have achieved something by jamming the very first enemy report but this would have needed a degree of skill and alertness of which his operators were scarcely capable. Naval wireless communication came of age in the Russo-Japanese War. Japanese strategy was often based upon it, and its efficiency in their hands contributed much to the defeat of the Russians. What we now know as radio warfare was surprisingly well developed especially by the Russians. Nevertheless the unrestricted use of wireless by the Japanese gave them much more information than the Russians obtained from listening.

Another seven shore stations had been established on the Atlantic coast of the U.S.A. immediately after the manoeuvres of 1903, and by the beginning of 1904 all the remaining

5. United States Naval Radio Stations on the East Coast 1904.

Mostly Slaby-Arco sets of 1¼ kw with a range
of about 75 miles.

Scale (Nautical Miles)
0   100   200   300   400   500

Cape
Elizabeth
Portsmouth Navy Yard
C. Ann
Boston Navy Yard
Newport   C. Cod
Montauk Point
New York
Navy Yard   Nantucket Light Vessel
Highlands of Navesink

C. Henlopen
Annapolis   ATLANTIC
Washington Navy Yard
Norfolk Navy Yard   Cape Henry   OCEAN
Beaufort
Cape Hatteras

Charleston

Pensacola   St.
Navy Yard   Augustine

Cape Canaveral
Jupiter
Inlet
GULF OF
MEXICO

Dry Tortugas
Key West

forty-five sets purchased from Slaby-Arco had been installed in
ships of the U.S. fleet. Three more sets were purchased from the
American Fessenden Company to fit out three more ships in
May 1904. By November 1904 there was a chain of seventeen
stations down the Atlantic coast (Map 5) from Cape Elizabeth,
Maine, to Key West in Florida, three stations on the Pacific
coast, four in the Caribbean area and two in the Philippines.
Throughout 1904–5 comparative trials of the various types of
sets continued. The few officers who knew about wireless were
very fully occupied not only with these trials but because the
U.S. Navy had been given the responsibility for commercial as

well as naval wireless seawards from the coast. As a result there was little progress in the use of wireless in naval warfare; captains and admirals did not seem particularly interested and the operators were left on their own to do much as they pleased.

Germany now had five naval wireless stations covering the North Sea coast and some seventy-five ships, that is practically their whole fleet other than torpedo craft, equipped with Telefunken sets (Note 9). They planned another four stations to cover the Baltic. The Italian Navy had nineteen government coastal stations, many of which were also available for commercial purposes. These and the ships of the Navy were equipped with Marconi apparatus. France lagged behind using the Ducretet-Rochefort system, which still used plain aerial and could not be tuned: they had five stations on the Channel and Atlantic coast and one in the Mediterranean, and plans for more in Corsica and North Africa. Norway, Sweden, the Netherlands and Austria-Hungary had all adopted the Telefunken system and had begun to set up shore networks and to equip their ships.

By 1905 the British had decided that wireless was to be standard equipment in all ships larger than destroyers. They had improved their sets and introduced the 'Standard Wireless Installation 1905' which embodied a separate transmitter and receiver for Tune A and for Tune B, but had some common parts. It was powered direct from the ship's mains instead of batteries and it was able to read Poldhu using the Marconi magnetic detector and headphones. The pure Marconi set as such was abolished and its parts embodied in 'service' installations.

There was now a chain of seven shore stations equipped with the new set from Felixstowe south about to Roches Point near Cork. Experiments were being made with a new wavelength, C Tune, and a range of 250 miles had already been obtained. Communication although not perfect was much improved and 'the probability of an Admiral receiving a cipher message when within 1,000 miles of Poldhu is distinctly good'. In war the Marconi high-power station at Cape Breton would also be available.

There is little doubt that from every point of view the Royal Navy at this time had the most efficient wireless communication system in the world. They had introduced three channels of communication, had standardized their equipment and by a blending together of specialized naval requirements and the genius of Marconi had produced the best material. To this was added the high technical competence of the officers and men of the torpedo branch and the backing of senior officers who saw the great possibilities of wireless communications. It is interesting that in this innovation the Royal Navy was ahead of other countries. With other new devices such as the submarine and aircraft the reverse was the case. The reason is clear. Submarines and aircraft, if anything, threatened to weaken sea power as applied with a battlefleet strategy whereas wireless telegraphy aided it.

By the middle of 1905 therefore most of the principal navies of the world had adopted wireless of one kind or another. It was fitted in nearly all battleships and cruisers, and there were chains of low-power wireless stations round the coasts. Wireless was useful for two main functions: first, in a fleet for reporting the enemy as by the Japanese at Tsushima and for giving major tactical directions (it was not as yet sufficiently rapid or reliable to use for manoeuvring); second, when in range, that is within about a hundred miles of a wireless station, to pass messages from ships to the shore and vice versa, connecting the former, so to speak, with the telegraph network. The British had a third use which was to broadcast messages to ships at sea within 1,000 miles of Poldhu.

The main problem of the day was interference and congestion of the ether (Note 10). Most countries could still only transmit on one frequency and the Tunes A and B of the Royal Navy were also used by merchant ships equipped with Marconi apparatus. Other countries had plans to build high-power stations ashore and some were actually under construction. It was widely believed, however, that high-power stations would jam all transmissions within 100 miles. Most countries therefore were continuing to extend their low-power coastal chains. In spite of Marconi's transmissions across the Atlantic, wireless was no rival as yet to the cable network, and all long-range messages continued to go by this means. The future development of wireless telegraphy clearly depended on tuning, so that a number of wavelengths could be used simultaneously.

Wireless was clearly the major development in the period

covered by this chapter, but other uses for electricity did not stand still. The most important of these was the searchlight. By the turn of the century the range of the torpedo had doubled. It could now be used effectively at the same range at which the 24 in. searchlight of 25,000 candle-power could normally pick up a torpedo boat, that is at about 2,000 yards. It therefore became important to increase the range of searchlights. By 1903 the French had standardized on a 75 cm. (30 in.) light of 33,000 candle-power and in their new battleships of the 'République' class mounted six of them (Diagram 6), two at the mastheads and four low down below the upper deck shining through ports fore and aft in the ship's side where they were protected from splinters in action. The German and British Navies developed a 36 in. (90 cm.) searchlight of about 40,000 candle-power, increasing the range at which a torpedo boat could normally be seen to 3,000 yards. The Germans were ahead in this development and went over entirely to the large searchlight. The 'Braunschweig' class of battleships were completed in 1905 with four 36 in. searchlights and the 'Hamburg' class cruisers with two. In Great Britain trials with 36 in. searchlights which were electrically controlled were still being carried out in H.M.S. *Caesar* and *Good Hope*, but there were plans to fit two in the new battleships of the 'King Edward VII' class in addition to the usual 24 in. lights. The searchlights in these ships were grouped with 12 pdr and 3 pdr guns to give eight separate batteries to repel torpedo craft from whatever direction they approached.

As with wireless, it was in the Russo-Japanese War that the searchlight was first seriously used in action. In the Japanese torpedo attack of 8 February 1904 on the Russian fleet at anchor off Port Arthur, the Russians were taken completely by surprise as war had not been declared. Most of the ships had peacetime lighting and only the cruiser *Pallada* was using a searchlight. In spite of this and the two Russian destroyers on patrol, the eleven Japanese destroyers were not sighted and succeeded in torpedoing three ships. Throughout the siege of Port Arthur, searchlights were used by the fortress as well as by the guardship at the entrance and were normally kept on all night. The ships carried 24 in. searchlights while those mounted ashore were 36 in. After the sortie of the fleet on June 23 the tide prevented its re-entering Port Arthur. The

6. Searchlights 1904 - 1908

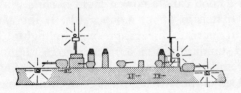

French Battleship
Republic 1905.
Six 30 inch (75cm) S.L.
(Four mounted in hull. One on
superstructure. One at masthead.)

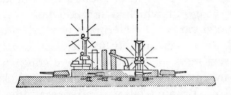

German Battleship
Braunschweig 1904.
Four 36 inch (90cm) S.L.
(Mounted on centreline.)

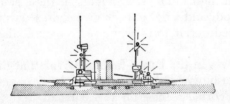

British Battleship
King Edward VII   1905.
Two 36 inch S.L.
Four 24 inch S.L.
(36 inch on each side of forebridge.
Two 24 inch aloft.
Two 24 inch on superstructure aft.)

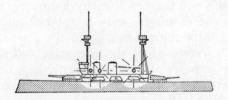

British Battleship
Lord Nelson 1908.
Six 36 inch S.L.
(Three each side of boat deck.)

ships had therefore to spend the night at anchor outside. Here they were able to defend themselves against a series of torpedo attacks in the light of the 36 in. searchlights mounted ashore, none of the Japanese torpedo craft succeeding in getting within range.

At the Battle of Tsushima, the Russian fleet, although four of its most modern battleships had been sunk by gunfire, was still in formation at sunset and doggedly making for Vladivostck under the command of Admiral Nebogatoff. At 1930, as already related, the Japanese main units stood away to leave the field free for the twenty-one destroyers and thirty-two torpedo boats to attack. Before it was dark many of these craft were seen ahead and the Russian fleet turned away and steered to the southward. The first attack was beaten off without loss by the Russian battlefleet using searchlights, but it then split into two divisions; one under Admiral Nebogotoff switched off its searchlights and escaped to the northwards (Note 11), the remaining ships, still on a south-westerly course, kept their searchlights on, sweeping for the Japanese torpedo craft. As a result they drew all the remaining attacks on to themselves. In a series of assaults, the Japanese torpedoed the battleships *Sissoi* and *Navarin* and the cruisers *Nakhimov* and *Monomakh*, thereby halving the remaining Russian strength. In the light of their searchlights, however, the Russians succeeded in sinking three torpedo craft and damaging many others.

The fact that when an attacking torpedo vessel was caught in the beam of a searchlight it was blinded and could see nothing was confirmed. On the other hand the gunners were given a perfect aiming point. The new lesson was that it was suicidal to 'search' all the time with searchlights which merely attracted the enemy's attack. It was clear that searchlights at night should normally be kept off and the beams only exposed during an actual attack to give an aiming point for the quick-firing guns. Searchlights could only be kept on all the time in future when mounted in forts ashore or in ships at anchor.

In the early years of the century, while there was an increase in the use of electricity in warships for auxiliary machinery, the British Navy stuck to hydraulic power for gun turrets. Electricity was increasingly used to hoist ammunition from the magazines to the secondary armament and on a larger scale for coal hoists, for hoisting boats and for ventilation fans. In the 'Formidable'

class it was used for the after capstan to avoid the long steam
pipes which would otherwise be necessary. There was, in consequence, a need for greater generating capacity and extra
dynamos were fitted in the 'Canopus' and 'Formidable' class
battleships and 'Cressy' class armoured cruisers as they came in
for refit.

The German Navy used electricity in much the same way.
The battleships of the 'Braunschweig' class had 1,100 electric
lights, seventeen fans and some twenty ammunition, coal and
boat hoists but the guns were hydraulically operated. They had
four dynamos with a total generating capacity of 363 kw. In
the Italian Navy electric steering was used in the new 'Vittorio
Emmanuele' class battleships.

Electricity was most widely employed, however, in the United
States Navy in which the new armoured cruisers of the 'Colo-
rado' class can be taken as an example. Not only were the guns
worked entirely by electricity but electric power was used for
all boat hoists, for closing watertight doors and driving fans,
pumps and air compressors. In all there were 147 electric
machines and the total power required was 780 kw. provided
by six dynamos. In general, in spite of a greater use of electricity,
it was still mainly a matter of choice. There were alternative
ways to do most things and electricity for these auxiliary
purposes still cannot be said to have had a great effect on sea
power.

In 1902 the British Admiralty had appointed a committee to
study electrical equipment in warships. The committee noted
that auxiliary machinery in British ships was powered by three
different types of engine – steam, hydraulic and electric. They
commented that it would obviously be an advantage to standardize on one system. They concluded that an all-embracing
electrical system had many advantages. Electric motors had
less wear and tear than reciprocating machinery; they involved
no hot steam pipes in living spaces and there would be no
danger from steam leaks. They also pointed out that it was
easier to run electric cables behind armour and easier to make
watertight joints at bulkheads than with pipes. Furthermore all
auxiliary machinery could be run by power supplied by another
ship or from the shore and this would be of great value if the
ship was damaged as well as during a refit. The only disadvantage was that electric motors would not run underwater

whereas some steam and hydraulic machinery could be made to do so.

The committee heard evidence that the British electrical systems for laying and training guns were inefficient; they noted, however, that these were superimposed on gun mountings designed to be hand operated. Officers who had seen the American system for guns believed it was more efficient and lighter than the British hydraulic system. They therefore recommended a great increase in electrics in H.M. ships including the working of the guns but said that a trial should first be made. They made also a number of general recommendations about electrical systems in ships: an increase in voltage from 100 volts, to which it had been advanced in 1900, to 200–230 volts; a ring-main distribution system and the introduction of steam turbo-generators.

Probably the most important auxiliary use of electricity in this period was the advances in naval gunnery that it made possible. In the early years of the century, battleships expected to fight at a range of about 2,000 yards. All was therefore concentrated on training the gunlayers to shoot straight and for the guns crews to develop a high rate of fire. Fire control was limited to the indication of the target by voice pipe, the passing of a few ranges and the order to open fire. The captain had then only to wave his cap and shout 'Let 'em have it, my lads' and all hell was let loose from 12 in., 9·2 in. and 6 in. guns. While the lighter calibres were expected to smash the enemy's upperworks and funnels to pieces, the heavy guns were to drill holes in his armour and get at his vitals. It was doubtful, however, whether the enemy would be so obliging as to allow a superior fleet to get into such a position and might try to avoid action. In this case it would be necessary to pursue, engaging at longer range the while. The guns themselves had been designed with high muzzle velocities to penetrate armour plate and if elevated sufficiently would carry ten times the range at which action was fought at the time. Attention therefore began to be concentrated on engaging at much longer ranges.

Experimental firings showed that spotting the fall of shot to correct range and deflection was essential and that this was best done by an officer stationed aloft in the foretop. If spotting was to be possible, the guns had to be fired together in salvoes with the same range and deflection on every gun. This could only be done by installing range and deflection transmitters with receivers at every gun and fire gongs to order the guns to fire. It was electricity which made this possible, and by 1905 the Royal Navy had designed a complete fire control system which included order instruments to pass such commands as 'Controlled' (Fire), 'Commence', 'Cease Fire' and 'Independent' (Fire). The design of the *Dreadnought* with an armament of 12 in. guns only was the direct result of the demand for long-range fire and with the new electrical fire control equipment raised the expected range of a battle from 2,000 to 10,000 yards. The Russo-Japanese War confirmed the need for long-range gunnery and for fire control if it was to be effective.

III

Developments Prior to the First World War

THE SUCCESS of the Marconi long-range wireless stations created a demand for similar facilities in other countries. With the lower frequencies on which they operated in order to obtain longer ranges, it was soon found that the difference in wavelength was sufficient for them to be worked at the same time as low-power stations without interference. The first country to order a high-power station was Italy and they gave the contract to Marconi in 1903. The station was built at Coltano near Pisa, and when opened in July 1904 had the most powerful transmitter in the world. It was able to communicate with Eritrea, a distance of 2,238 miles and was also, of course, available for broadcasting to ships of the Italian Navy wherever they might be in the Mediterranean.

During 1905 the U.S. Navy wished to cover the Caribbean area with shore wireless stations because of its increased strategic importance with the construction of the Panama Canal (Map 7). It could not be covered by a network of low-power stations in U.S. territory as they would be too far apart to communicate with each other. They decided therefore to instal four high-powered long-range stations at Key West in Florida, San Juan in Puerto Rico, Guantanamo in Cuba and in the Panama Canal zone itself. The contract was given to the American De Forest company who provided 35 kw. alternator driver spark transmitters with a range of about 1,000 miles. To complete the coverage a fifth station with a power of 10 kw. was installed at Pensacola. All these stations were completed successfully by early 1906 and were able to provide wireless communication

7. United States Naval High-power chain in the Caribbean 1906.

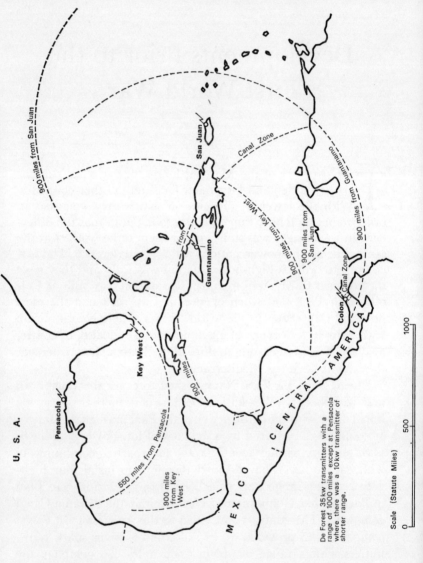

U. S. A.

Pensacola

Key West

San Juan

Guantanamo

Canal Zone

Colon

MEXICO

CENTRAL AMERICA

900 miles from San Juan

550 miles from Pensacola

900 miles from Key West

900 miles

900 miles from Key West

900 miles from San Juan

900 miles from San Juan

900 miles from Guantanamo

from

De Forest 35 kw transmitters with a range of 1000 miles except at Pensacola where there was a 10kw transmitter of shorter range.

Scale (Statute Miles)

0   500   1000

between the United States and the Panama Canal zone as well as coverage for ships in the Caribbean Sea.

Since 1903 the British Navy had been satisfied with their arrangement whereby the powerful Marconi shore station at Poldhu was used by them for a proportion of its time, but by 1906 they began to plan their own high-power stations. The original intention was to provide coverage for the North Sea, Channel and south-west approaches, using three stations with a range of 500 miles and these were to be put at Horsea Island in Portsmouth harbour, at Cleethorpes in Lincolnshire and at Fraserburgh in Scotland. This plan was, however, overtaken by the development of stations with a range of 1,000 miles. The need for a station at Fraserburgh then lapsed but a station at Gibraltar was substituted, so extending the coverage to the south, yet none of these stations was completed in this period. In Germany the Telefunken Company built a very large station at Nauen near Berlin and the Imperial Navy built another, with a range of 900 miles, at Norddeich near Emden to cover the North Sea. From 1905 onwards it was possible for the ships of the U.S., German and Italian Navies as well as the British to receive messages at a considerable distance from their coasts although they were not always able to reply.

Early in 1906 the Royal Navy carried out a number of competitive wireless exercises in their three main fleets. A great deal was learnt and there was a substantial improvement in wireless discipline when the annual manoeuvres took place in midsummer. These manoeuvres involved the Channel, Atlantic and Mediterranean fleets and thirty-three battleships, sixty-nine cruisers and some two hundred torpedo craft took part. All the battleships and cruisers were fitted with wireless and were able to use Tunes A and B and to read transmissions from Poldhu.

The manoeuvres were in two phases, the first being to investigate the problem of the defence of the Home ports and a surprise attack on the Channel fleet. From this phase came a complaint that telephone communication for harbour defence in the Portsmouth Command was inadequate, which later led to a demand for special wireless sets for this purpose. Wireless was, of course, used by the ships in this phase but not without criticism. One report said, 'It is remarked that the working of W/T was most inefficient, not because it didn't work but because of the enormous number of useless and obsolete messages transmitted which had to be received and decoded.' The second phase took place out in the Atlantic and its purpose was to test arrangements for the defence of trade against a '*guerre de course*'. The Red side which was to defend trade consisted of the Channel fleet based on Milford Haven and the Mediterranean fleet at Gibraltar. The Blue side, which was to attack trade, consisted of the Atlantic fleet based at Berehaven in Ireland. In this exercise all messages were in code and the Marconi station at Poldhu was used to broadcast messages to both sides four times a day, all ships being instructed to cease transmitting five minutes beforehand.

The Channel fleet under Sir Arthur Wilson threw out its cruisers to search for the commerce raiders and kept them under wireless control. The fleet itself remained concentrated and in touch with the wireless station in the Scilly Islands, using repeating ships when necessary. Independent cruisers were told that if they lost touch they were to close in until they regained it. The Channel fleet then with local modifications tuned all its wireless sets to a new Tune F of about 1,000 m. (300 kc/s) which it used for communication while it did its best to jam the 'enemy' on Tunes A and B. Tune F was successful for communication and was completely undetected by the 'enemy'. The attempt to jam was not so successful, one report saying: 'No serious interference was caused by intentional or unintentional jamming, though the enemy resorted to this for forty hours without ceasing.'

The actual course of the manoeuvres need not concern us except to note that a despatch from *The Times* correspondent was intercepted by the 'enemy' to their advantage. It is of interest however that the Channel fleet's strategy was based with success on the use of wireless. As a result of experience gained in the exercises it was recommended that the Navy should cease to use Tunes A and B so as to avoid interference by commercial traffic. On the technical side it was recommended that earphone reception should always be used in future and that the 'inker' and tape should be discarded altogether. Future sets should have alternators in their transmitters to give a more musical note and roof aerials should be used so that more and lower frequencies could be employed. On completion of the manoeuvres the Admiralty summoned representatives of the fleet to a conference and it was decided that destroyers should be fitted with wireless, that some ships should be given higher-powered sets and that a new branch of specialist telegraphists should be formed.

In 1906 an International Radio Telegraphic Conference was held in Berlin. It was concerned mostly with making all commercial stations in the world able to communicate with all ships, and with the procedure and arrangements for sending and receiving wireless telegrams. It made provisions also for the allocation of wavelengths which affected warships. It established two wavelengths for the public commercial service, which were 300 m. (1,000 kc/s) and 600 m. (500 kc/s); all public coastal stations were required to operate on one of these frequencies and 300 m. (1,000 kc/s) was established as the normal wave for all ships and on which they were required to be able to work. Ships were allowed to use other wavelengths provided they did not exceed 600 m. (500 kc/s). Small ships which could not have aerials large enough to transmit on 300 m. (1,000 kc/s) were permitted to use shorter wavelengths. Shore stations not used for public service were allowed to use any wavelength below 600 m. (500 kc/s) or above 1,600 m. (187·5 kc/s). The convention had to be ratified and did not come into effect until the middle of 1908.

The Royal Navy, however, made their plans in accordance with it and established six 'tunes' as they called them which they lettered from P to U (Note 1).

By the end of 1906 the British had decided to have two types of wireless set for the larger warships and they were designed and fitted during 1907. 'Service Installation Mark I' grew out of the 'Standard Installation 1905' and was of moderate power (1½ kw.) and able to transmit on five tunes from Q to U. It was powered from the ship's mains with a rotary converter, and the operator was installed in a silent cabinet using headphones and a receiver which incorporated the Marconi magnetic detector. The 'Standard Installation Mark II' was more powerful and grew out of the set produced for the experiments with Tune C in 1905. A set of this type had already been fitted in the revolutionary new battleship *Dreadnought* and nine other battleships and armoured cruiser flagships. The 'Service Installation Mark II' was of 14 kw. using an alternator and a spark transmitter which gave a less raucous note. It could transmit not only from Tunes Q to U but on two new lower-frequency tunes too (Note 2). The 'Service Installation Mark II' was in future to be supplied to all new battleships and battle cruisers and was to replace the Tune C Mark II as it was called which had been installed in the *Dreadnought* and the nine flagships. The bulk of the Royal Navy, some 110 vessels, however, were given 'Service Installation Mark I'.

In 1907 the *Vernon* experimental department, in accordance with the recommendations following the 1906 manoeuvres, designed a wireless set for destroyers. This set was only required to have a range of fifty miles and was therefore of low power. It transmitted on a new and shorter wavelength because it was only possible in these ships to use a short aerial. Trials were carried out in H.M.S. *Usk* and forty-three of the latest destroyers of the 'River' and 'Tribal' classes were fitted during the year (Note 3).

In 1907, too, the 'Instructions for the Conduct of W/T Signalling' were issued by the British Admiralty. They included an organization allocating the various wavelengths or tunes to various purposes. A fleet at sea in Home waters would keep in touch with the shore by listening to broadcast routines from Poldhu. Tunes were allocated for sending messages back to commercial or naval shore stations and another tune was reserved for the flagship to keep in touch with scouting cruisers or any other detached ships. A fleet at sea would manoeuvre and communicate between ships by visual signals and as each ship had only one wireless set a system of what were known as wireless guardships was instituted. In a fleet a separate guardship would be detailed to listen on each wave. Messages received by these guardships would be passed by them to the flagship by visual signal (Note 4).

Communication between the Admiralty and ships on foreign stations was still by cable but could be extended a bit to ships at sea by the low-power wireless stations at Gibraltar, Malta and Hong Kong. The use of wireless guardships in a fleet showed a need for a small low-power wireless set with which to pass signals to and from the flagship. Such a set was also required for use in harbour and obviously had possibilities for intercommunication in the fleet at sea and for manoeuvring. The design of a set of this type also was therefore put in hand in the *Vernon*.

During 1905–6 the U.S. Navy had continued its policy of purchasing wireless equipment from a number of companies so that their merits and deficiencies could be compared. In this period they bought fifty-seven sets from eight different companies and they were of twenty-three different types. All except four, which were from the German Telefunken Company, were of American manufacture (Note 5). Twenty-five of the new sets were installed ashore: these included the Caribbean stations already mentioned and completed the Atlantic and Pacific coastal chains. The Atlantic coastal chain of twenty-four stations could pass messages to the Caribbean network, but the Pacific coastal chain of ten stations was only connected to the east coast by the inland telegraph. Another five stations in the Philippines with others at Guam and Honolulu were connected to the U.S.A. by a new all-American transpacific cable laid in the early years of the century. Seventy-eight ships, that is all big ships, had wireless, but as with the shore stations there was a wide diversity of type and power (Note 6).

In the U.S. Navy the training of operators had fallen far behind the fitting of equipment. There had been few exercises at sea since 1903. Early in 1906 the Atlantic fleet carried out a very simple exercise on its way to the Caribbean. A scouting line of five cruisers was thrown out to try and find a floating dock which was being towed from the U.S.A. across the Atlantic. The results were varied and in his report the C.-in-C. Atlantic Fleet said that wireless could not be used with certainty between ships of a scouting line and the main body. In fact very long ranges were obtained by some ships, the greatest being 640 miles with a Shoemaker 1·25 kw. set in the *Maryland*. Some other ships could not get more than 120 miles. The wireless sets in the fleet were of four different makes: Slaby-Arco, Fessenden, De Forest and Shoemaker; and the difficulties were almost certainly due to a failure to tune to the same wavelength (Note 7). In a subsequent exercise in which jamming was tried, it had no more success than in the British exercises. Wireless telegraphy in the U.S. Navy gained some publicity however when, in 1906, U.S.S. *Chicago* happened to be at San Francisco during the appalling earthquake in April of that year, and her wireless provided the only communication with the outside world for two weeks.

During 1907 the American De Forest company developed a

radio-telephone set. The value of such a system for tactical communication in a fleet was obvious and the Navy Department purchased two sets and fitted them in the U.S.S. *Connecticut* and *Virginia* for trials. The trials were made somewhat hastily but the sets proved successful. This system was, however, far ahead of its time: the transmitter used the Poulsen arc and the receiver a mixture of crystals and thermionic valves, all of which were completely new inventions. Twenty-six more sets were ordered at once to equip a U.S. squadron which was to make a round-the-world flag-showing cruise. The sets were hastily constructed by the de Forest Company and installed in the squadron in under three months. The result was almost total failure. The sets were seldom used and were landed on return; the U.S. Navy dropped its interest in radio-telephones for some ten years. The principal reason for this was that the senior officers of the fleet were not in the least interested and preferred to manoeuvre by their well-tried visual methods. The sets also proved, understandably, to be very unreliable. The hasty manufacture and installation, the lack of maintenance instructions and spares and the squadron's absence from the U.S.A. all contributed to this. Matters were made worse because they operated on the same frequency as the ordinary wireless sets and so could not be used at the same time. A far-sighted plan by the Navy Department to introduce a tactical radio system in the U.S. fleet therefore came to nothing.

By 1908 radio was installed in all surface vessels of the U.S. Navy, including torpedo craft. There was still no standardization of equipment and there was a large number of different types fitted both ashore and afloat. The transmitters were all still spark sets which blanked out practically the whole known radio spectrum. There was still only one frequency used by both ships and shore stations which was approximately 400 m. (750 kc/s). Nevertheless this material was ahead of the organization. Senior officers still showed little interest in wireless and there had consequently been no serious development of radio for strategical or tactical purposes. It was simply used as an extension of the inland telegraph system. Radio discipline was practically non-existent. Operators made no effort to limit power when sending messages over short distances and interference was frequent. Ships often simply shut down their radios at sea so as to avoid receiving undesirable orders. Moreover there was a great deal of 'operator conversation' and the sending of unauthorized private messages.

A point has now been reached where it is necessary to make another digression into technical matters. Up to 1906 the only kind of transmitter had been the spark. It had greater power when driven by an alternator with a transformer than by batteries with an induction coil but it still had many disadvantages. It was very inefficient as the waves were not transmitted continuously but in a series of bursts following each other at the sparking rate (Diagram 3). The sparking rate could not be substantially increased because of ionization and so there was a considerable proportion of the time when no transmission was being made (Note 8). It was also very difficult to tune the transmission to a single frequency and so the spark still blanketed a large proportion of the usable radio spectrum. At the same time the noise picked up in the headphones, although improved by the use of alternators, was still difficult to distinguish from atmospherics which consequently interfered badly with reception. Many scientists in the radio field set about trying to solve these problems. It was obvious to all that the aim was to transmit continuous rather than damped waves (Diagram 3, fig. 4), and in the next few years, five different inventions improved transmitters (Note 9).

The first of these was Fessenden's Rotary Spark Gap invented in America. In this he used a toothed wheel rotating between electrodes. A spark occurred each time a tooth passed an electrode and was quickly cut off again. This imparted a shock to the aerial circuit which then continued to oscillate at its natural frequency and this reduced the damping. At the same time the sparking rate was increased making the transmissions nearer to continuous waves, and emitting a whistling note which stood out from a background of atmospherics (Diagram 3, fig. 2). Another system was the quenched spark gap developed mainly by the Telefunken Company in Germany. In this the sparking rate was increased by decreasing the length of the spark and increasing its breadth by various means. The oscillating circuit was 'quenched' immediately it reached its maximum but as for the rotary spark the aerial circuit was allowed to continue oscillating at its natural frequency. Immediately it ceased to oscillate it received another impulse from the oscillating circuit, the condenser of which had been charged in the meantime. This effect also approached a continuous wave (Note 10). Marconi with his rotating disc discharger or timed spark gap did better still. With a staggered toothed wheel a still faster sparking rate was obtained and the transmissions overlapped giving a musical note (Diagram 3, fig. 3). It could, however, only be used for very long waves, was bulky and needed careful adjustment.

The first real continuous wave transmitter was the Poulsen arc which was developed by the Telefunken Company. This was based on the discovery in 1900 that an electric arc could be made to 'sing' (Note 11). At first, however, it proved of somewhat limited range. Finally Alexanderson in the U.S.A. produced a very high-frequency alternator which was able to generate an alternating current on wireless frequencies which could be transmitted as continuous waves. In 1906 it could already transmit on 80 kc/s. The fact that all these transmitters were only suitable for low frequencies did not matter. Low frequency was what, at the time, was needed for long-range communication. They made it possible to divide the radio spectrum up into a larger number of different channels, solved the problem of mutual interference and vastly increased the amount of traffic that could be put 'on the air'.

In the same period a considerable advance was made in receivers with the discovery of the crystal detector. This was much more sensitive and less prone to interference by atmospherics than earlier systems but it was at first less robust than Marconi's magnetic detector which continued in use, often as a standby, for many years. True continuous waves such as those produced by the arc transmitter and the high-frequency alternator could not be picked up by any of the early receivers at all. This was because they had no sparking rate and it was the frequency of the sparking rate which was in the audible range. The first receiver to detect continuous waves was the Poulsen 'tikker' (Diagram 3, fig. 5) which literally chopped up the incoming signal into an audible frequency so that it could be heard. The second and far more successful method was the heterodyne receiver. In this a continuous wave was generated in the receiver which was slightly out of phase. When superimposed on the signal received, it had the effect of making it audible (Diagram 3, fig. 6). These transmitters and receivers were developed during the period 1906 to 1914 by various companies in Great Britain, Germany and the U.S.A. They did not all come on to the market at once; this and following chapters will say when and by whom they were used and will show the improvements in communication which resulted from their introduction.

In 1909 the new British shore wireless stations which had been building during 1907–8 were completed (Map 8). There were three high-power stations at Horsea Island, Cleethorpes and North Front, Gibraltar, and a fourth was planned at Rinella in Malta. These stations were designed jointly by *Vernon* and Marconi and had 100 kw. spark transmitters. The function of these stations was not only to communicate with each other but to replace Poldhu and distribute orders and information to H.M. ships in European waters (Note 12). Messages were sent to ships by routine broadcasts on long wave by Cleethorpes, North Front and later by Rinella. Horsea Island was used as an experimental station and to communicate at fixed times with Gibraltar and Malta. These stations therefore extended the area in which ships could formerly have received Poldhu, and brought the whole system completely under Admiralty owner-ship and control. At the same time they gave the Admiralty communication with Gibraltar and later with Malta, which was independent of the commercial cable system. The cable, however, remained the only link with the ships on more remote foreign stations. The high-power stations only distributed orders and information to ships and did not improve the distance from which ships could send their messages to the shore. For this purpose the Admiralty provided another five new medium-power stations at Ipswich, Aberdeen and Pembroke Dock in Great Britain and at Malta and Gibraltar abroad. They kept a constant listening watch with Type 1 wireless sets and so were able to answer ships at 500 miles. The ten low-power stations round the British Isles with a range of 100 miles were retained in addition for local communication. A wireless station was also established at the Admiralty in Whitehall which was used to communicate direct with Cleethorpes and the three medium-power stations at Aberdeen, Ipswich and Pembroke Dock (Note 13).

During 1909 the U.S. Navy decided to instal a very powerful transmitter which could send messages a distance of 3,000 miles.

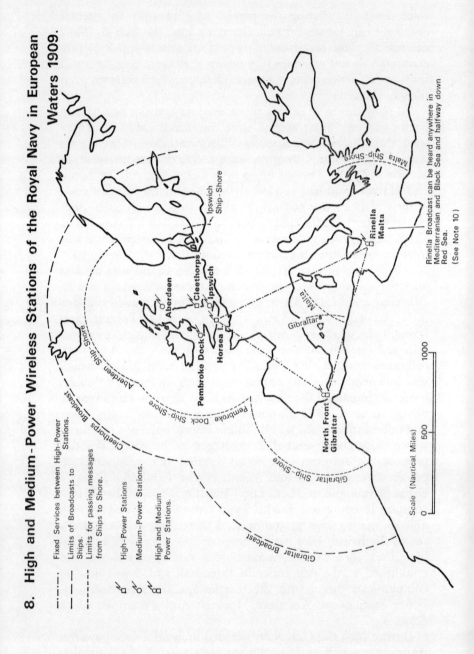

8. High and Medium-Power Wireless Stations of the Royal Navy in European Waters 1909.

—··—·· Fixed Services between High-Power Stations.
— — — Limits of Broadcasts to Ships.
- - - - - Limits for passing messages from Ships to Shore.

High-Power Stations
Medium-Power Stations.
High and Medium Power Stations.

Aberdeen
Cleethorps
Ipswich
Ipswich Ship-Shore
Pembroke Dock
Horsea I.
Aberdeen Ship-Shore
Cleethorps Broadcast
Pembroke Dock Ship-Shore
Gibraltar Ship-Shore
Gibraltar Broadcast
North Front Gibraltar
Gibraltar
Melia
Melia
Malta Ship-Shore
Rinella Malta

Rinella Broadcast can be heard anywhere in Mediterranean and Black Sea and halfway down Red Sea.
(See Note 10)

Scale (Nautical Miles)
0   500   1000

A contract for this set was awarded to the Fessenden Company who designed a 100 kw. rotary spark transmitter. The contract included two smaller 10 kw. sets to be installed in ships with which they were to be able to send messages at 1,000 miles. At the end of the year trials with the light cruisers *Salem* and *Birmingham*, in which these sets had been fitted, showed that they could only maintain touch at 600 miles and could not hear the shore station at more than 900 miles by day or 2,186 miles by night. The Fessenden equipment did not therefore meet its specification but it was accepted as it was undoubtedly the best on the market at the time. It was decided to build the new station at Arlington in Virginia near the Navy Department at Washington but it was not completed until the end of 1912. By this time the Federal Telegraph Company had developed an arc transmitter of 35 kw. and this was installed at Arlington as well. Trials carried out in 1913 showed a great improvement. In a voyage to Gibraltar, U.S.S. *Salem* received messages continuously to a range of 2,100 miles by day from both the rotary parks and arc transmitters. By night they were heard all the way to Gibraltar. The interest of these trials was that not only had a transmitter been produced which would enable ships to receive messages in the greater part of the North Atlantic but that the 35 kw. arc had proved as good as the 100 kw. rotary spark.

In September 1908 the U.S. Naval Radio Laboratory had been established to carry out experimental work. Reliance upon industry for wireless equipment had proved to have many disadvantages. The greatest of these was that the patent laws made it difficult for any one company to produce equipment which embodied all the latest ideas. The U.S. Navy then purchased the Poulsen arc patents from Denmark and began to experiment with this type of transmitter. They soon found that it was bulky and had a range of only forty miles and so they put it aside for four years. A new IP 76 crystal receiver was accepted from industry and proved so successful that it replaced nearly all the old receivers (of the Slaby-Arco, de Forest, Shoemaker, Massie and Stone types), thus becoming the first move in the U.S. Navy towards the standardization of equipment.

In the five years immediately before the First World War, the wireless experimental section of H.M.S. *Vernon* was kept very busy. In addition to the two main types of sets for ships, they had already produced a destroyer set and an auxiliary set for large ships (Note 14). These were followed by the high-power set for shore stations, a harbour defence set and a portable set. They did not confine themselves to sets for surface ships and shore stations and also turned their attention to aircraft and submarines. In 1909 a requirement had arisen for a wireless set to fit in 'Naval Airship No. 1' building for the Royal Navy. The principal function of this airship was to be reconnaissance and a wireless set able to transmit a distance of 300 miles was essential. The set designed had a 3 kw. transmitter and was of the quenched spark type but weighed some 500 lb. The airship, the *Mayfly*, as she was nicknamed, was a long time building and proved a failure as she was far too heavy. She was finally wrecked getting her out of her shed in 1911 and the wireless set was never tried.

Attention was then switched to wireless sets for seaplanes and early in 1912, with an aerial stretched across the wings, a transmitting range of eight to ten miles was obtained on 257·5 m. (116·5 kc/s). Nothing at all, however, could be received in a seaplane in flight because of the noise and interference of the engine. Later in the year a French Rouzet set was purchased, which weighed only 70 lb. and had a synchronous rotating spark gap with a power of ¼ kw. With this set thirty miles was obtained using a trailing aerial and four more sets were ordered, but reception was still impossible with the engine running. A more powerful Rouzet set (1 kw.) was used for airships. By 1914 *Vernon* had designed a new aircraft set of ⅔ kw., using an alternator and a synchronous spark transmitter, and reception up to a range of thirty miles had been achieved with it. Similar results were obtained in the U.S. Navy, and at first they too were unable to receive anything in flight. By 1912 they were receiving at fifteen miles but little further progress was made until 1915.

Apart from an unsuccessful attempt in 1903, no interest in fitting wireless in British submarines was shown until 1910. In that year, the Devonport flotilla began to experiment on their own and the submarine B3 was able to receive messages from a torpedo gunboat at a range of thirty-five miles. Later in the year B4 tried a transmitter and D1 received a message from a ship in Torbay as she was entering the Needles Channel. A submission was then made to the Admiralty that submarines should have wireless and in April 1911 they ordered the *Defiance* to design a submarine set able to send and receive messages at thirty miles. The set was designed therefore with a power of only ½ kw. and because of the limited size of aerial, a wavelength of 200 m. (1,500 kc/s). The transmitter was a simple alternator driven spark set while the receiver used the magnetic detector and both were put in a small silent cabinet inside the submarine. Submarines were progressively fitted with this No. 10 set, as it was called, and by 1913 all the modern submarines of the 'C', 'D' and 'E' classes had them.

The fundamental research in H.M.S. *Vernon* was concentrated on developing the quenched spark. This was something in which Marconi was not interested, so he could not be called upon to assist. The quenched spark was expected to allow a smaller, lighter and more efficient set for the same power than an ordinary spark transmitter. By 1911 a quenched spark set was nearing completion and was sent to sea for trials in the following year. It was found to have a marginally longer range but to be inferior to the existing sets in the fleet as its transmission was too broad and it interfered with adjacent wavelengths. The decision was therefore made in 1913 to abandon the quenched spark and interest shifted to the Poulsen arc as developed in the U.S.A. Two 24 kw. and two 14 kw. sets were purchased from the Universal Radio Syndicate and successful trials were carried out in H.M.S. *Vindictive* in the Mediterranean, the larger sets giving a range of 900 miles by day. The Poulsen arc allowed longer wavelengths to be used, tuning and shifting wavelengths was easier, it needed less power for the same range and the set was also smaller and lighter. A 100 kw. Poulsen arc transmitter was purchased for Horsea Island in 1913 – one of the reasons for the return of the Poulsen arc to favour was the improvement in a receiver for it. The Poulsen 'tikker' was not a great success but the development of the heterodyne receiver (Note 15) realized the full potential of this system of continuous wave transmissions.

In the same period technical progress continued in the U.S. Navy. The Naval Radio Laboratory had already decided after the trials of the Arlington station that the future lay in the arc transmitter used with a heterodyne receiver. By 1914, however, most of their transmitters both ashore and afloat were either of the quenched spark type designed by Telefunken, Chaffer or Lowenstein or the rotary spark type designed by Fessenden.

The decision had, however, already been reached to change to the Poulsen arc and ten 30 kw. sets of this type had already been ordered for the ten new 'Dreadnought' battleships under construction. The German Navy was also equipped with the Telefunken quenched spark transmitter and large ships also had auxiliary wireless sets. Surprisingly the French Navy had now gone over to wireless almost entirely and visual signals were seldom used. The French made a very slow start in this field and as late as 1909 were signalling slowly en clair with practically no drill or procedure and using plain aerial, considerable power and coarsely tuned receivers on a single wavelength.

With the gradual concentration of the British battlefleet in Home waters in the years before the war, attention was focused on its internal communications. The auxiliary wireless set was tried out in the 1910 manoeuvres and was found to be of great value. It was of too short a range for cruisers and a new set was called for with a range of about twenty miles. In 1911 a 'group system' was brought into force for the internal use of wireless in the fleet. In this each squadron had a separate wavelength and at sea kept a guardship on the Admiral's Wave. When the Admiral wished to make a signal to the fleet, he sent it on the Admiral's Wave and it was acknowledged by the squadron guardships who then shifted to their squadron wavelengths and passed it to their squadrons, shifting back to the Admiral's Wave to report that they had done so. This was better than the Admiral receiving an acknowledgment from every ship in the fleet but was still ponderous and slow. For manoeuvring, visual signals were much quicker in spite of the efforts made to speed things up by fitting buzzer communication from the wireless offices to the bridges of ships. Radio-telephones were considered and in 1909 H.M.S. *Good Hope* had experimented with one of local design. They were not considered sufficiently reliable, however, and it was believed that the advantages were not as great as they would seem. Because of difficulties of accent and articulation, the fact that there was no record and that if the signal was written down it would be no faster than morse, all militated against its introduction.

In the British naval manoeuvres of 1911 one of the main objects was to test wireless communications. A large number of ships took part including five new 'Dreadnought' battleships and three battle cruisers. Red was composed of the Home Fleet and Blue of the Mediterranean and Atlantic Fleets; together the two Blue fleets were superior to Red but individually weaker. The exercise took the form of Red trying to engage one of the Blue fleets before they could concentrate: a problem which seems to have fascinated the naval strategists of the day. Communications were therefore of most importance to the Blue fleets in order to effect their concentration. Red decided in consequence to do their best to jam them. The Blue fleets communicated on T Tune and the *Dreadnought,* the Red flagship, talked to her cruisers on R Tune, with U Tune reserved to report the enemy battlefleets. The Red fleet decided to try and jam T Tune at three-quarters power continuously so as to prevent it being used even for very short signals; in the event the Blue fleet operators got used to the jamming note and by varying their own note slightly found they could read signals through it. The Red fleet subsequently believed they should have waited until Blue started a signal before trying to jam. Continuous jamming was not in any case believed to be practicable in war as insufficient would be known about the characteristics of the enemy wireless sets. It was also noted that it was never evident what effect jamming was having on the enemy. In fact jamming as a wireless counter-measure was to be little used in the future for with the introduction of a large number of wireless channels, with musical notes and aural reception it had lost its potency. Throughout these manoeuvres wireless worked perfectly and there was little interference. If anything there was found to be too much reporting when more than one cruiser was in contact, but even so the Red fleet found that R Tune was sufficient and there was no need for the special U Tune to report the enemy battlefleet. There is little doubt that the Royal Navy held its lead in wireless telegraphy at this period and its organization and training, if not its equipment, were ahead of other nations.

Whereas the Royal Navy since 1907 had been employing eight or more frequencies, the Germans four and the Japanese and Italians three, the U.S. Navy was still a long way behind in the use of wireless in the fleet. The American equipment, while excellent, worked up to 1911 on only one frequency. In that year came the issue by the Navy Department of the first U.S. Naval Frequency plan in which the radio spectrum* was

* From 300 m. (1,000 kc/s) to 8,000 m. (37·5 kc/s).

divided into twenty-six different channels. The allocation of most of these was left to the fleet commanders, with only the calling frequencies being established (Note 16).

The ships of the U.S. Navy were not at this time able to calibrate their sets without expert help from the shore and they were unable to make use of the large number of channels laid down. During 1912, however, a Fleet Radio Officer was appointed to the Atlantic Fleet. He soon instilled a circuit discipline and refused to accept excuses of atmospherics for failure to receive messages. Practice in using wireless during gunnery firings was also obtained and a start was made to use it for tactical purposes. Next year a new Commander-in-Chief arrived and he manoeuvred the fleet for a whole day by wireless with success; visual signals were only used as a secondary system. Shortly afterwards the Atlantic Fleet of sixteen battleships on its way from Hampton Roads to Annapolis was caught in a squall and visibility fell to a few yards. The fleet then had no alternative but to be manoeuvred by wireless. The success with which this was done through intricate channels inspired confidence among senior officers and thereafter both wireless and visual signals were used to manoeuvre the fleet as a standard procedure. In 1912, too, a superintendent of the Naval Radio Service was appointed to take charge of all the shore stations and he was able to insist on a similar improvement to that obtained in the fleet. By 1913 therefore the organization and training of U.S. Naval Radio communications had been fully organized and was well on the way to justify the excellent material supplied to the fleet. Next year at Vera Cruz during the trouble with Mexico the U.S. Navy had its wireless communications tested under action conditions. Direct communication with the high-power station at Arlington, Virginia, or with the station at Key West in Florida was not found to be possible. The light cruiser *Birmingham* had to be stationed at sea in the Gulf of Mexico to relay signals from U.S.S. *Wyoming*, the flagship at Vera Cruz, to Key West.

As early as 1907 Marconi had inaugurated a transatlantic wireless telegram service from his station at Clifden near Galway in Ireland to Glace Bay in Nova Scotia. In 1910, when on a voyage to South America in a liner, he received Clifden on 6,000 m. (50 kc/s) at 4,000 miles by day and 6,775 miles by night. Such ranges clearly made intercontinental wireless communication possible and plans were laid to realize it in a number of countries. In 1911 the Italian station at Coltano was increased in power to 500 kw. and could then talk direct to the Marconi station at Glace Bay. In March 1912 the British Government signed a contract to build an Imperial Wireless Chain. The scheme was much delayed in Parliament and by the so-called 'Marconi scandal' (Note 17) so that at the outbreak of war only the stations in the United Kingdom, Egypt and India had been begun.

In August of the same year in the U.S.A. a high-power Pacific chain was approved. There were to be six stations, one in the Panama Canal zone, another on the Californian coast and others in the Hawaiian Islands, Samoa, Guam and the Philippine Islands.

Probably the most advanced long-range wireless network was that developed by the Germans. With the cable system of the world largely owned by Great Britain and with the only German cables from the fatherland passing through the English Channel, it was obvious that communication with the German colonies and their warships on foreign stations would be severed in war. It was therefore of paramount importance to them to develop a long-range wireless system. The hub of this network was the long-range Telefunken station at Nauen, near Berlin. This was able to communicate with another high-power station at Kamina in Togoland, nearly 3,000 miles away, which in its turn could talk to stations at Windhoek in German South-West Africa, Dar-es-Salaam in German East Africa and Duala in the Cameroons. From Kamina messages could also be sent to South America using the German-owned cables from Monrovia to Pernambuco. Naurn could also communicate with a commercial Telefunken station at Sayville, Long Island, U.S.A. There was however no direct wireless communication with the German possessions in the Pacific and the Far East, which therefore had to rely on the international cable system for communication with Germany itself, but there was a wireless station at Tsingtan and others at Yap and Augaur in the Caroline Islands, Nauru, south of the Marshall Islands, Apia, in the Samoan Group, and at Rabaul, in the Bismarcks.

The development of wireless was the outstanding influence of the electron on sea power in the first fourteen years of the twentieth century. Yet it was not the only one by any means and space will now be taken to follow the effect of the others.

In the Royal Navy some of the recommendations of the 1902 Committee on Electrical Equipment were put into effect. The voltage in ships was raised to 220, turbo-generators were introduced and ring main systems were installed both in battleships of the 'Lord Nelson' class and in armoured cruisers of the 'Defence' class completed in 1907–8. Although the use of electricity steadily increased, the recommendation that all auxiliary machinery should be electric was not implemented. Another attempt, however, was made to work the guns by electricity in the battle cruiser *Invincible*, launched in 1907. In spite of its success in foreign navies the experiment was a failure and electricity was judged to be inferior to hydraulic power. The British did not find it so reliable, the training and elevating of the guns was not so smooth and it took longer to trace and remedy defects. It was therefore replaced by hydraulic power when the ship refitted immediately before war broke out in 1914. Nevertheless electrical power supplies even in British ships steadily increased; for instance the battleship *Ajax*, launched in 1912, had three 200 kw. generators two of which were driven by turbo and one by a reciprocating steam engine; in the German battleship *Kaiser*, launched in 1911, the power was greater and she had four 220 kw. turbo generators as well as two generators of 175 kw. driven by diesel engines. In the U.S. Navy the total power was similar, the battleship *Arkansas*, completed in 1912, had four turbo generators of 300 kw.

For the propulsion of submarines when submerged the storage battery was improved so that its capacity for the same weight was greater. The result was that it was now possible for a vessel to remain submerged for the whole of daylight hours. When this capability was joined with long surface endurance using diesel engines and the reliability conferred by twin screws, it meant that the submarine was able to act offensively off the enemy coasts and was no longer confined to a defensive role in its own waters. This was done without increasing the size of the battery relative to the size of the submarine, indeed the opposite was the case and the battery size was substantially decreased. The British 'D' class, which were the first submarines capable of offensive work, had batteries weighing eighty-seven tons for a submerged displacement of 620 tons. Their predecessors, the

'C' class had batteries of sixty-six tons for a displacement of 320 tons submerged. Weight and space was thereby released for fuel, armament or other characteristics.

We left the searchlight in the last chapter at a point where the Germans had adopted the 36 in. light for their new battleships and cruisers and the British were also experimenting with this type. The lessons of the Russo-Japanese War had been absorbed by most navies and it was clear that searchlights would, in future, be needed to aim the guns of the secondary armament at enemy torpedo craft attacking at night and not to search or sweep for them. The allocation of searchlights to antitorpedo batteries had already become a fairly general practice in most navies. The range of the torpedo, however, continued to increase and it became important to extend the range of searchlights to keep step. The British in consequence went over to 36 in. searchlights in the 'Lord Nelson' class battleships (Diagram 6) and 'Defence' class armoured cruisers completed in 1907–8. Six of these lights were mounted along the boat deck in both these classes. The 'Dreadnought' had eight 36 in. searchlights mounted in a similar way (Diagram 9). The smaller 24 in. and 20 in. searchlights were retained for mounting at the mastheads, for signalling and for use in light cruisers and destroyers. The 'Dreadnought' also had three 24 in. searchlights, one of which was at the foremast head. Searchlights mounted aloft, however, were gradually removed to make room for the large control tops needed for long-range gunnery.

The protection of searchlights during day action and from the blast of the ship's own guns was clearly important and a disadvantage of the 36 in. searchlight was that it was too large to be unshipped and stowed behind armour when not in use. To a certain extent searchlights could be shielded from the blast of the main armament guns by putting them as far away from the guns as possible but this would not protect them from the enemy's fire. The French continued to mount searchlights low down in the hull of the ship, shining through ports in the ship's side. The 'Démocratie' class battleships completed in 1907–8 still had four 30 in. searchlights mounted in this way. Their arcs of training were somewhat restricted but as they were to be used with guns mounted with similar arcs this did not matter. To give additional all round coverage 24 in. searchlights were mounted at the foremast head and just abaft the main mast.

9. Searchlights 1906 - 14.

British Battleship
Dreadnought 1906.
Eight 36 inch S.L.
Three 24 inch S.L.
(36 inch mounted four a side at boat
deck level.
24 inch at foremasthead and on bridge.)

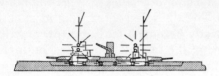

German Battleship
Nassau 1909.
Eight 43·3 inch (110 cm) S.L.
(Mounted in two groups high up
on superstructure.)

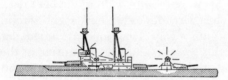

British Battleship
St. Vincent 1909.
Eight Twin 24 inch S.L.
(Mounted four each side at
boat deck level.)

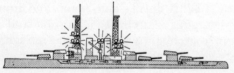

United States Battleship
Arkansas 1912.
Sixteen 36 inch S.L.
(Groups of six on each lattice mast
and four on derrick posts amidships.)

British Battleship
Bellerophon (Searchlights modified
                              1914.)
Ten 36 inch S.L.
(Grouped high up on superstructure
in the German manner.)

In 1909–10 with the invention of the heater system, the range of torpedoes was again doubled and it became necessary to increase searchlight ranges still more. The Germans produced a 110 cm. (43·3 in.) type which could illuminate a destroyer at 4,000 yards and they mounted eight of these grouped round the funnels and the bases of the masts in their dreadnoughts of the 'Nassau' and 'Ostfriesland' classes. The Germans also paid great attention to searchlight control and fitted iris shutters so that the lights could be kept burning behind them during night action, ready to be exposed at once when required. The British preferred a new type of searchlight in which 24 in. lights were mounted in pairs, the combined candle-power being roughly the same as the single German 43·3 in. searchlight. The 24 in. twin light could be manipulated to concentrate the beams for long range or to spread them to give greater horizontal coverage. The lights of the twin mounting could also to a certain extent be used independently. Another advantage considered important at the time was that the lights could be dismounted and stowed below by day. The new dreadnoughts of the 'St Vincent' class had eight pairs of 24 in. searchlights and this became the standard British arrangement for some years. The U.S. Navy adopted a searchlight system somewhat on the German plan. Instead of using 43·3 in. lights, however, they mounted a larger number of 36 in. searchlights. The dreadnoughts of the 'Utah', 'Arkansas' and 'New York' classes all had sixteen 36 in. searchlights, six in two tiers on each lattice mast and four on top of the derrick posts between the funnels. The U.S. Navy had also adopted the iris shutter whereas the French now had a venetian blind variety. French dreadnoughts of the 'Courbet' class had eight 36 in. searchlights arranged on lifts so that they could be lowered behind armour during day actions.

In 1912 the British began to revise their ideas. Manoeuvres had shown that a row of searchlights at boat deck level tended to give away a ship's inclination. They were in any case not altogether satisfied with the twin 24 in. and in the same year comparative trials showed that a new 36 in. searchlight designed jointly by H.M.S. *Vernon* and Portsmouth Dockyard was slightly superior. They therefore decided to fit them in future, starting with the new 'Queen Elizabeth' class battleships. At the same time the development of the torpedo, especially the use of the

21 in. type instead of 18 in., increased its range still more. They suspected that the German and American grouping of searchlights gave them the very necessary extra range by concentrating the beams. Experiments were therefore carried out in the battleship *Bellerophon* with a similar arrangement, and other ships were modified as they came in for refit. In the long term they decided to develop larger searchlights of 42 in. and 48 in. diameters.

Progress in long-range gunnery continued during this period and it was dependent, to a considerable extent, on electrical apparatus. It was very soon clear that it was going to be very difficult in the heat and smoke of action for the gunlayers at the guns to distinguish the target at long range. It was also going to be difficult to get all guns to fire at the same target. The solution was to have a 'master' or 'director' sight in the foretop, clear of smoke, and to devise a system so that the guns could follow its movements. Experiments with director firing were made during 1911 with a system using mechanical cables in H.M.S. *Bellerophon* and *Neptune* but were a failure. Success was achieved with an electrical system in H.M.S. *Thunderer* in 1912 and it was decided to fit the whole 'Dreadnought' battle-fleet. In this the gunlayers and trainers at the guns followed pointers in the turrets which aligned them with the director sight in the fighting top. The guns were all fired together by electricity by the director layer with a single trigger. Director firing made long-range gunnery possible under the expected action conditions. At the same time, electricity made it possible to centralize control in a 'transmitting station' below decks where deflection would be calculated, the mean of the ranges from a number of range finders found and rate of change of range determined. These improvements increased the effective range of gunnery from 10,000 yards to about 15,000 yards. Yet by 1914 only about half the British battlefleet had director firing, although all had centralized control with transmitting stations.

In addition to the very substantial advances in wireless telegraphy, there is no doubt that electricity had improved the efficiency of warships by 1914. It was used for a large number of purposes and it would now be difficult for ships to function at all without it.

IV

The Great War 1914–1915

THE GERMAN COMMUNICATION network achieved a major success even before the outbreak of war. It was able not only to pass the warning telegram to all their warships on foreign stations but to instruct their whole merchant fleet to seek shelter in neutral ports. As a result few German merchant ships fell into the hands of the Royal Navy. The British wireless system in European waters was equally successful in passing the warning telegram, but further afield it was less efficient. On the west coast of Mexico, for example, the sloops *Shearwater* and *Algerine* were only contacted through the courtesy of the U.S. Navy. They were in fact in some peril as the German cruiser *Leipzig* was in the vicinity and she knew that war had broken out. She had obtained the information through the German wireless station at Sayville on Long Island which was also able to warn the *Karlsrühe* and the *Dresden* in the West Indies. The French had trouble too: the Commander-in-Chief in the Pacific in his flagship, the *Montcalm*, was out of touch in the Tahiti area and there were fears that he might be brought to action by the German Squadron under Admiral von Spee.

The British decided without delay to destroy the world-wide German communication network. It was already in their war plans to cut the German cables passing through the Channel and this was done, in co-operation with the G.P.O., on 5 August 1914 (Note 1). The German-owned cables which ran from Monrovia in West Africa to South America were not cut as both terminals were in neutral countries. On the outbreak of war a sub-committee of the Committee of Imperial Defence was set up under Admiral Sir Henry Jackson (Note 2), to study an attack on the German overseas possessions. It concluded that attacks should not be made simply for territorial conquest but should be directed at German communications and coaling stations. The aim was to assist in the general command of the sea, especially in the destruction of the German warships on foreign stations. On August 8 H.M.S. *Astraea*, of the Cape Station, destroyed the wireless station at Dar-es-Salaam by gunfire and four days later H.M.S. *Minotaur*, the flagship of the China Station, dealt with the wireless station at Yap in the Caroline Islands in the same way. Simultaneously on August 24 troops of the Gold Coast Regiment landed in Togoland and in co-operation with columns from Nigeria and North Dahomey captured and destroyed the high-power wireless station at Kamina. In the Pacific a New Zealand expeditionary force occupied Samoa with its wireless station at the end of August; in the middle of September the Australian cruiser *Melbourne* destroyed the wireless station at Nauru and Australian troops landed from the *Sydney*, advanced inland and blew up the station on Rabaul. The *Sydney* then went on to Augaur and this wireless station also was put out of action. Finally a combined British and French expedition landed in the Cameroons and on September 27 the Duala wireless station was destroyed. This left only the stations at Tsingtau in China and at Windhoek in German South-West Africa but these were not of much use to the Germans as they were completely isolated and had no other station with which to communicate. The Tsingtau station was finally eliminated when the Japanese took the fortress on November 7, but Windhoek did not fall into Allied hands until 12 May 1915 as the expedition from South Africa which was directed upon it was delayed by a rebellion.

The German wireless network was therefore of little value to the German raiders. The United States Government imposed a rigid censorship on radio signals and the Telefunken station at Sayville could not be used after the first few days of war. Some communication was possible by wireless from Nauen with German merchant ships in Spanish ports and also by cable through neutral countries. As early as August 7 however Admiral de Robeck prevailed upon the Spanish authorities at Vigo to dismantle the wireless of German ships in port and two days later H.M.S. *Highflyer* at Lisbon reported that the Portuguese had already put the wireless equipment of twenty-six more German merchant ships out of action, but it was not until late October that a private wireless set used by the German

Consul in the Canary Islands was suppressed by the Spanish authorities. In general the German raiders were now on their own, and one of the reasons that Admiral von Spee headed across the Pacific was to try to regain touch with Germany by cable from a South American port.

If, during the hunt for German raiders, their communications scarcely existed, the British communications were far from perfect. It will be recalled that outside Home waters and the Mediterranean the British depended upon cables and a few low-power wireless stations at naval bases. The Germans made an attempt to attack the cable system: the *Nürnberg* cut the transpacific cable at Fanning Island on September 7 and the *Emden* was in the process of severing the cables at Cocos Island when she was caught by H.M.A.S. *Sydney*; communications were not unduly affected (Note 3), the cable system was in fact maintained intact throughout the war. One new cable was laid in 1914 from Peterhead to the Kola Inlet to improve communications with Russia and the existing cable system was kept in working order by forty-seven cable ships, thirty-seven of which were British (Note 4). Nevertheless cable communication could only contact ships in harbour and the control of ships at sea in general had to be maintained by direct wireless messages from ship to ship.

The use of wireless for communication proved of very great value on many occasions. In the very early days of the war, Admiral Cradock in the West Indies very nearly trapped the *Karlsrühe* through co-ordinating the movements of his flagship, the *Suffolk*, with the cruisers *Berwick* and *Bristol* by direct wireless signals. The first indication that the *Emden* was in the Indian Ocean was sent out by wireless. It was broadcast by the S.S. *City of Rangoon* after she had spoken to an Italian ship which had been stopped by the raider, so saving many ships from capture. Wireless probably scored its most notable success in the early part of the war when the *Emden* arrived at Cocos Island. Her presence was reported by the wireless station and the signal was picked up by H.M.S. *Minotaur* escorting an Australian troop convoy from which H.M.A.S. *Sydney* was detached to destroy the raider.

The opposite, however, was often the case and the absence of efficient wireless proved a severe disadvantage. The communications of the ships operating off the coasts of South

America against Admiral von Spee were particularly bad; normally they were by cable through the ambassadors and consuls in the area and took at least two days to get through and sometimes longer (Note 5). The wireless station at Port Stanley in the Falklands was only of low power and atmospherics in the area caused serious interference. Fortunately the neutral radio station at Montevideo was allowed by the Uruguayan Government to pass messages in cipher. Nevertheless it was the sending of H.M.S. *Glasgow* into Coronel to use the telegraph which gave away her presence to the Germans, resulting in the defeat of the British Squadron at Coronel. News of the Battle of Coronel took no less than three days to reach the Admiralty. When Admiral Sturdee was sent out, efforts were made to improve matters. H.M.S. *Defence* was ordered to transfer her experimental arc transmitter to the *Invincible*, and the *Vindictive*, fitted with another arc transmitter, was sent to the vicinity of Ascension Island to try to establish communication with Admiral Sturdee but without success.

On occasion linking ships had to be used to extend wireless communication. When Admiral Jerram was away in the *Minotaur* destroying the wireless station at Yap, H.M.S. *Triumph* blockading Tsingtau could only get in touch with him to tell him of the imminent declaration of war by Japan on Germany by extending the *Yarmouth* and the French cruiser *Dupleix* towards him to relay the message. Ships with the powerful Mark I set could, however, communicate at great distances. Admiral Patey, commanding the Australian Station, wished to get in touch with Admiral Jerram in the China Station in early August 1914. His flagship H.M.A.S. *Australia* off New Guinea was heard calling by H.M.S. *Minotaur* which was north of the Philippines at the time, some 2,500 miles away. In early December H.M.S. *Berwick* in the West Indies communicated with H.M.A.S. *Australia* off the Galapagos Islands in the Pacific.

In general, when within range, communication between ships proved remarkably reliable. The spark transmitters which still sent their messages over a comparatively wide band of frequencies coupled with the use of broadly tuned receivers was mainly responsible, but the system had one great disadvantage. The enemy were often able to pick up the messages, too, and much information was obtained from the wireless signals of the opposing side. Precautions against the interception of

H.M.S. *Ajax*, circa 1885
Three 24-in. searchlights, two forward and one aft, can be clearly seen.

H.M.S. *Terrible*, circa 1903
Completed in 1898 this was the first ship in the Royal Navy to have an extensive electrical system for power as well as lighting. 24-in. searchlights can be seen in the tops and on the wings of the bridges. The gaff to carry the wireless aerial, which was vertical, can be seen extending upwards from the main topmast. Just before the gaff the masthead semaphore is still mounted.

H.M.S. *Neptune* in 1911
Wireless aerials for the type 1 set can be seen slung between the masts and then down to the quarterdeck. Twin 24-in. searchlights can be seen on the platform at the base of the main tripod.

(Photos: Imperial War Museum)

PLATE I

H.M.S. *Arethusa* in 1942
Fitted with air warning radar type 279.

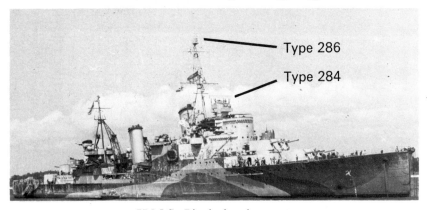

H.M.S. *Birmingham* in 1942
Fitted with gunnery control radar type 284 and combined warning radar
type 286.

German destroyer *Z.39*
Fitted with Seetakt radar.
(Photos: Imperial War Museum)

PLATE II

messages by the enemy were not general in the early days, and signals were normally sent by the direct method from ship to ship.

There are numerous examples of the interception of enemy wireless; for instance, H.M.S. *Gloucester* on patrol south of the Straits of Messina on 5 August 1914 reported that the strength of the German wireless signals indicated that the *Goeben* must be at Messina. This was true; she was there coaling at the time. H.M.S. *Berwick* in the West Indies heard the *Karlsrühe* calling the liner *Kronprinz Wilhelm* which was known to have left New York just before the outbreak of war. As a result the *Karlsrühe* was interrupted when arming the liner as a commerce raider. Later on the *Karlsrühe* heard British cruisers closing in on her and took evasive action (Note 6). On yet another occasion the *Karlsrühe*, off the coast of South America, deduced from intercepts that a number of British ships were searching for her. The *Glasgow, Monmouth, Otranto, Macedonia* and *Cornwall* were all in the vicinity at the time. She therefore refused to answer the merchant raider *Kronprinz Wilhelm* which was calling her, and cleared the area. On September 14, on the other side of the world, the *Emden* in the Bay of Bengal also realized from intercepted signals that her presence had been detected and decided to leave the area and make for a new hunting ground. Admiral Cradock, before the Battle of Coronel, could clearly hear the wireless of the German Squadron but wrongly believed that the *Leipzig* was detached and that he could cut her off. Although at this time ships could often hear the enemy, they could not gain very much information; they had no idea of the direction of the enemy signal, only its strength and whether it was approaching or receding. Often very false impressions were received; for instance, the *Nürnberg* in the central Pacific reported at the end of August that she could hear H.M.A.S. *Australia* and other British warships very close when in fact they were off Samoa, 2,000 miles away. A British wireless station in Newfoundland just before the outbreak of war reported it could hear the *Dresden* and *Karlsrühe* in the vicinity when they were, in fact, in the West Indies.

It would be quite wrong, however, to suggest that no one was conscious of radio warfare at all. One of the reasons for the success of the *Emden* as a commerce raider was that she kept rigid wireless silence and listened for British wireless signals.

The ships hunting her often did the same. H.M.S. *Hampshire* off the Andaman Islands was keeping silence but was embarrassed by civil wireless stations in India calling her en clair to give her the latest news of the *Emden*. She had to put in to Port Blair to send a cable to request them to desist. The *Emden* herself received no information of the approach of the Australian troop convoy with its powerful escort because it was keeping wireless silence (Note 7). Admiral Sturdee in his approach to the Falkland Islands also kept rigid wireless silence and Admiral von Spee consequently received no warning of his presence.

Jamming was attempted on occasion by both sides but, as forecast during manoeuvres, did not prove very successful. At the very beginning of the war, H.M.S. *Berwick* was ordered to jam the *Karlsrühe*'s signals off Havana without success. On August 5 when H.M.S. *Gloucester* was shadowing the *Goeben* after leaving Messina, the *Goeben* tried again without success, to jam the *Gloucester*'s signals.

On the outbreak of war the British wireless network in Home waters was much the same as had been established in 1909. There were one or two more low-power stations round the coast and 'Destroyer' stations had been established at the main destroyer bases. Horsea Island had been given an arc transmitter of 100 kw. purchased from America. It had a range of 2,500 miles and was able to communicate with H.M.S. *Europa*, fitted with an experimental 14 kw. arc set, as far away as the Levant. The main change in 1915 in Home waters was the establishment of sixteen new 'Auxiliary' wireless stations round the coast, from Fair Isle and St Kilda in the north to Newhaven and the Scilly Islands in the south, as well as in Ireland. These stations were to communicate with the vast armada of yachts, trawlers and drifters which comprised the Auxiliary patrol and the minesweeping service. The Auxiliary patrol had been brought into being as the main anti-submarine measure. The theory was that the ubiquity of these patrols would prevent submarines coming to the surface in British coastal waters and so would force them to seawards to charge their batteries. It was important of course for the patrols to be able to report U-boats so that hunting forces could be set on their trail. In the early stages few of the trawlers and drifters had wireless and so they had to be grouped with yachts which were fitted with it, but the *Vernon* began to design a special set which did not need a trained operator and which could transmit one of three standard signals simply by turning a handle. Another anti-submarine measure was the introduction of small non-rigid airships or 'blimps' and Lord Fisher stated that a wireless set was their most important requirement.

The British Naval Wireless Instructions of 1915 list twenty-eight different frequencies in use from 109 m. (2,743 kc/s) to 4,260 m. (70 kc/s). The shorter waves were used by auxiliary wireless sets and by destroyers, submarines and small ships, while the long waves were employed by the powerful shore stations. It was now possible with the new transmitters to divide the original band of frequencies allocated for ships by the 1906 International Conference into twelve instead of five different wireless channels.

Important though the improvement and extension of wireless communications in Home waters proved to be, it was of small consequence compared with a completely new development. Before the outbreak of war, no government department in Great Britain had contemplated trying to decipher secret enemy messages even if war should break out. Even after war broke out the formation of such an organization came about almost by chance. The use of radio by merchant ships had been severely restricted and so the civilian Marconi stations ashore had little to do. The Admiralty wireless station at Stockton had a passive role too and was used to ensure that merchant ships complied with the rules. Before long these stations began to pick up strange enciphered messages which they sensibly passed to the Admiralty. The Director of Naval Intelligence, Rear-Admiral Oliver, had these messages on his desk and was trying to make up his mind what to do about them when he chanced to meet Sir Alfred Ewing who was the Director of Naval Education. Sir Alfred had made a lifelong study of cryptography as a hobby and asked to be allowed to study the messages. Without much investigation he established that they were German signals sent from the high-power station at Nauen and that they were enciphered groups from a secret code book.

At the time there was a very great need to obtain information of the movement of the German High Seas fleet. The whole of

British naval strategy depended upon the Grand fleet being able to bring the German High Seas fleet to action if it came out for any purpose, but there was at the time virtually no sure way to detect it leaving harbour. Any idea of a close blockade of the Bight by the Grand fleet had been given up well before the war as it was rightly believed to be too dangerous in an age of torpedoes, mines and submarines. Our own 'overseas' submarines, although able to patrol off the enemy bases, had not at this time wireless transmitters powerful enough to reach the British shore stations from the Bight and the use of carrier pigeons could not be considered a reliable substitute. The wireless sets of the British seaplanes were of shorter range still, and the machines themselves, with their unreliable engines, were loath to go far out to sea; in any case they could not reach the Bight from their bases on the east coast. In the early stages, therefore, the Grand fleet had to keep at sea and make sweeps with its cruisers to the southwards. This strategy had of course severe limitations: the High Seas fleet might put to sea just as the Grand fleet had returned to its bases to coal, and in any case the wear and tear on the fleet and the men who manned it was severe. Finally the loss of five cruisers in the North Sea to U-boats during 1914 made even the policy of periodic sweeps dangerous. It was obviously of exceptional importance if the enemy wireless could be exploited in any way to fill this appalling gap in our intelligence system.

Sir Alfred Ewing was therefore asked by Admiral Oliver if he would form a department to see if German ciphers could be broken, and he at once gathered together a nucleus from masters from the R.N. Colleges at Osborne and Dartmouth, the cadets from which had been mobilized. Shortly afterwards two amateur radio enthusiasts approached Admiral Oliver and said that, given certain equipment, they would be able to receive German radio traffic on frequencies of about 400 m. which were those used by the German ships in the Heligoland Bight and by the U-boats. A station was at once set up for them at Hunstanton in Norfolk, yielding a great increase in the number of messages received. The German communications on this frequency band were extremely important. At the outbreak of the war the Germans believed that the British would at once attack them in the Heligoland Bight. They therefore devised a defence system under Admiral Hipper who commanded the scouting forces;

this consisted of patrols which in the early stages consisted of wireless-fitted trawlers, U-boats and destroyers with cruisers ready to put to sea in support. The whole of this system depended on wireless to co-ordinate its operations and report the enemy; wireless on the 400 m. band was freely used. At first little could be gleaned from the messages but a start was made to build up experience of radio traffic and to organize this new division of the Naval Intelligence Department which later became famous as Room 40, where it was accommodated in the Admiralty.

Fortunately luck was on the British side. A code book taken from a German merchant ship in the Antipodes was sent home and was found to be the same as that used by German auxiliary vessels and minesweepers and also by the Zeppelins. A far more important capture soon followed. Early in September 1914 the German cruiser *Magdeburg* was wrecked off Odensholm in the Baltic and the body of a German warrant officer was washed ashore clutching a copy of the naval code book; this fell into the hands of the Russians who sent it to the Admiralty. It did not mean that the German ciphers could be read at once. The groups from this code book were reciphered and it took some weeks to unravel how and to find the key. While this was being done, wireless intelligence had its first success (Note 8). On October 17 the Germans sent four old destroyers to mine the northern entrance to the Downs. Room 40 detected that the movement was imminent, and although it was believed to be an attempt to raid the Allied naval forces on the Belgian coast, the cruiser *Undaunted* and four modern destroyers succeeded in intercepting and sinking all four of the German ships.

Two weeks later the High Seas fleet made its first move but it was not detected. The German battle cruisers, supported by two squadrons of battleships, bombarded Yarmouth and Gorleston and were not sighted until they ran into patrol vessels off the Norfolk coast. Admiral Beatty's battle cruisers were in harbour at Cromarty at the time and the rest of the Grand fleet was in Lough Swilly in Ireland. The German ships were therefore able to make the raid virtually unopposed, and this was a striking illustration of the total inadequacy of any type of reconnaissance at the time.

Before the High Seas fleet made another move, Room 40 had unravelled the way in which the *Magdeburg* code book was reciphered. It was not a very complicated system and fortunately at this stage the Germans only changed it every three months. On December 14 Room 40 deciphered messages which told them that the German battle cruisers would leave the Jade river early the next day and return late the following evening. The messages gave no indication of their purpose or destination. The Admiralty, not without scepticism, acted on this information. They decided in consultation with Admiral Jellicoe not to send the whole Grand fleet, which was much in need of rest and maintenance, to sea but to use Admiral Beatty's battle cruisers and the Second Battle Squadron accompanied by a proper complement of cruisers and destroyers. An intercepting position was chosen in the Dogger Bank region where the ships would have a chance to cut off the enemy's retreat if he raided the coast. This position was perfect, and when on the morning of December 16 the German battle cruisers were reported to be bombarding Scarborough and Hartlepool, superior British forces were at sea between them and their base. Unfortunately bad weather, a falling visibility and some lack of co-ordination of the searching forces led to the escape of the German Squadron. Nevertheless the new method of obtaining intelligence had worked. Knowledge of a German fleet movement had been obtained in plenty of time to deploy intercepting forces and it was only bad luck that had prevented their destruction. There were, however, some aspects of the operation which called for sober thought. In fact unknown to the British the whole High Seas fleet had been at sea in support of the operation. Its presence was not suspected until midday when it broke wireless silence and gave its position which was deciphered by Room 40. Roughly one-third of the Grand fleet had therefore been manoeuvring in close proximity to the whole High Seas fleet and the Germans subsequently believed that they had missed the greatest opportunity presented to them during the entire war. The British in detaching one battle squadron had taken the precaution of using the one which consisted of their fastest and most modern ships, but the situation had been one of great danger.

Although in the operations brought about by the German bombardment of Scarborough and Hartlepool, the great importance of wireless intelligence was shown, it was realized that to be able to read the enemy's signals by no means provided a complete answer. Most operation orders are issued in writing and are never sent by wireless; it is therefore only from the consequential signals, such as amendments, warnings to detached forces and such signals as those to minesweepers to sweep passages clear by a certain time and others to open the boom defences that a picture can be built up. Despite the short-comings the new intelligence system gained in stature and more staff were recruited, mainly from the universities who were able to provide men of really first-class intellect. The number of listening stations was expanded and constant watch on a greater number of frequencies was maintained. It should be mentioned that most of those who knew of the existence of the new intelligence system thought it all too good to be true and did not believe it could last. The Germans would change their books, they said, and that would be the end of the matter. By the end of 1914, however, another German code book had fallen into Room 40's hands when a fishing boat trawled up a chest from one of the destroyers sunk by the *Undaunted* off the Dutch coast in October.

The Grand fleet from the beginning was conscious of what it could give away by a too liberal use of wireless. A knowledge of the information that the British radio intelligence was obtain-ing from the Germans greatly increased the precautions. If it could be avoided the Grand fleet did not use wireless at all when south of Kinnaird Head. The fleet was manoeuvred by visual signals by day but at night anything brighter than small shaded lights was obviously too dangerous. Wireless silence therefore might have to be broken in emergency at night or in fog or low visibility, but every effort was made to operate the fleet so that there were few alterations of course, speed or formation at night. If essential the expected movements would be signalled before dark and carried out without signal at the time ordered. At this time visual signalling in the fleet was considerably faster than wireless. Using flags and repeating cruisers, manoeuvring signals could be executed in two to three minutes which was a remarkable achievement in so large a fleet. Wireless, in spite of buzzer circuits from wireless offices to the bridge, generally took from ten minutes to a quarter of an hour. Although wireless silence was normally in force at sea the intention was that immediately contact was made with the enemy wireless would be used freely to report. When the fleets were actually in sight of each other, full use would be made of it for manoeuvring or any other necessary purpose.

In the middle of January 1915 the Germans at very short notice decided to send their battle cruisers with supporting ships to reconnoitre the Dogger Bank. The operation order was therefore sent to Admiral Hipper, commanding the scouting forces, by wireless on the morning of January 23. The signal not only gave the times of sailing and return but the forces to be used and their object; this message was deciphered by Room 40. The Admiralty just had time to order Admiral Beatty and his battle cruisers and the Harwich force to an intercepting position. They also took the precaution of ordering the Grand fleet to sea in support, although it could not get there in time. The rival forces therefore met early on the morning of January 24 and the Battle of the Dogger Bank was fought. That the victory was not more complete was disappointing and no fault of wireless intelligence. The interception was in fact planned so that the British ships would be between the Germans and their base. That this did not happen was because Admiral Hipper was behind schedule and so the forces met head on, and when the Germans turned for home it became a stern chase.

If there had been doubters before the Battle of the Dogger Bank, there were few afterwards, and wireless intelligence came of age. From the beginning it had been obvious that the secret that we could decode the enemy messages was vital; security from the first was excellent and very few people knew that enemy wireless signals were even being read. Soon after the Battle of the Dogger Bank, however, what had been long feared happened. The Germans changed their cipher key. Fortunately they did not also change the code book and in twenty-four hours, Room 40, working with its whole staff, managed to break the new cipher and all was well again. It does not seem that at this time the Germans even suspected that their messages were being read. They have been accused of being complacent but it must be remembered that they did not know of the loss of the three signal books and did not realize that many of their low-power signals could even be received in England. The very rapid establishment of an organization to decipher signals undoubtedly took them by surprise.

· · · · ·

It was obvious that in the hunt for the raiders during 1914 the British communications outside European waters had left much to be desired. At the end of December 1914 plans were made to erect two higher-powered stations at Jamaica and Bermuda and they were completed by May 1915 (Map 10). These stations were given the Type 1 ship set, a spark transmitter of 14 kw., which had a range of 800 miles and the stations were some-times just able to talk to each other. Their communication with the Admiralty, however, was still by cable, and their main purpose was to communicate with ships on the America and West Indies Station. By January 1915 the Admiralty had decided to extend this system to cover the main trade-routes of the world. To do this they requested the Marconi Company to design and manufacture a standard set which guaranteed 1,000 miles. Marconi produced a 30 kw. synchronous spark gap set and a total of eleven stations were erected. For mid-Atlantic they were at Demerara, in British Guiana, and Bathurst, in Gambia, and on the Cape Station, at Port Nolloth and Durban. The Indian Ocean was covered by stations at Aden, Ceylon, Mauritius and the Seychelles, while in the Far East stations were erected at Hong Kong and Singapore. Finally a gap in the North Atlantic was closed by a station at St John's, Newfound-land. These stations were, as those at Bermuda and Jamaica, for communication with ships; few could talk to each other and their contact with the Admiralty was maintained by cable. Standard stations in British territory could not cover the South Atlantic and so Marconi was requested to instal more powerful stations at Ascension Island and in the Falklands. These were 150 kw. synchronous spark gap sets with a guaranteed range of 1,800 nautical miles. All of these stations except the Falkland Islands were completed and most of them were in operation by June 1915, providing the Royal Navy with a means of keeping in touch with its ships wherever they might be on the main trade-routes. Communications were still further improved by the completion of the high-power Imperial Wireless scheme station at Abu Zaabal in Egypt, and by the installation of high-power stations at Perth and Sydney by the Australian Government and at Bluff Harbour and Awanui in New Zealand.

A second serious deficiency in the British wireless organization was the lack of communication with their submarines on offen-sive patrol in the Heligoland Bight. As pointed out earlier in

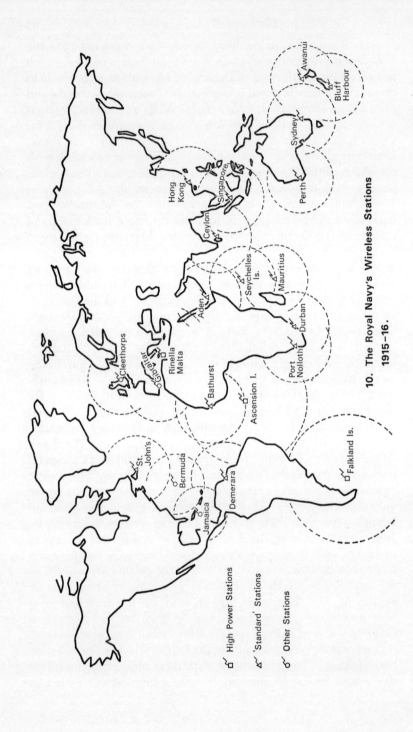

Awanui
Bluff Harbour
Sydney
Perth
Hong Kong
Singapore
Ceylon
Seychelles Is.
Mauritius
Aden
Durban
Cleethorps
Gibraltar
Rinella Malta
Port Nolloth
Bathurst
Ascension I.
St. John's
Bermuda
Jamaica
Demerara
Falkland Is.

◻ High Power Stations
◁ 'Standard' Stations
○ Other Stations

10. The Royal Navy's Wireless Stations
1915–16.

this chapter, their transmitters of only 1 kw. could not be heard by stations in England. Carrier pigeons were occasionally used but were not really of sufficient range or reliability. A submarine on patrol in the Heligoland Bight was therefore virtually out of touch altogether. When submerged by day she could neither receive nor send wireless signals. On the surface at night she could read a wireless broadcast from Ipswich wireless station but that was all. If a submarine sighted the High Seas fleet she could fire torpedoes but would be unable to report the fact before she returned to harbour.

It is true that a great deal of intelligence was amassed by offensive submarine patrols and indeed the operation leading to the Battle of the Heligoland Bight was planned on such information, but submarines were virtually useless as outposts for reconnaissance for the Grand fleet. When they were sent out in response to some movement made by the High Seas fleet, Commodore Keyes often accompanied them in a destroyer from which he could at least try to redispose them if what he could glean from listening on his wireless showed this to be necessary (Note 9). It seems odd that the naval staff and indeed the Commodore (Submarines) did not press for a longer-range wireless set for submarines before the war. The original Type 10 with its range of thirty miles was obviously only of use for submarines disposed defensively off the British coasts. Two other sets were designed, a Type 11 which was of no greater performance but was more compact, and a Type S of only ½ kw. which was for the very old submarines too small to take Types 10 or 11. The design of a new set was put in hand in H.M.S. *Vernon* during 1915 to remedy matters and was to be a 3 kw. arc set with large hinged masts to carry a roof aerial. This set was not ready to fit in submarines during 1915, so they remained virtually incommunicado on patrol.

The wireless sets of the German U-boats were little better, and there was a serious shortage of wireless operators. When *U24* sank H.M.S. *Formidable* off Start Point on New Year's Day in 1915, she was only able to report the fact by relaying her signal to Germany through another U-boat. Next month when *U27* communicated with the depot ship *Arkona* 140 miles away in the Ems it was considered a record. It does not seem that there were any arrangements for U-boats even to receive messages when out of range of their own transmitters. When it was wished to amend the conditions for the attack on trade when the War Zone was declared on the 4 February 1915, it was not found possible to contact *U30* which had already sailed for the waters west of the British Isles.

In February naval wireless intelligence added another club to its bag. The Marconi Company had developed a system of wireless direction finding just before the war. The principle was not new and was well known. It was a modification of the Bellini-Tosi system but used a new sensitive valve amplifier which meant it could pick up very faint signals totally inaudible to a crystal receiver. The system had been used by the British Army in France from the beginning of the war and was now offered to the Navy. Rear-Admiral Hall, the new Director of Naval Intelligence, at once made up for lost time and in a matter of months five stations from the Shetlands to Kent were set up to cover the North Sea and by cross bearings establish the position of any ship which used its wireless (Map 11).

In March 1915 Room 40 was responsible for the destruction of the German cruiser *Dresden* which had eluded her pursuers for some months since she escaped from the Battle of the Falklands. The radio station at Montevideo, as already noticed, was prepared to pass cipher messages and to give this facility to both sides. A message to the *Dresden* was intercepted giving a rendezvous with a collier 200 miles south of Mas Afuera. The message was sent home and decrypted and H.M.S. *Kent* kept the rendezvous. She sighted the *Dresden* but was unable to bring her to action because of her superior speed. Shortly afterwards an agent in Chile obtained a copy of a telegram giving another rendezvous with a collier at Juan Fernandez. Room 40 decrypted this message too and the *Dresden* was caught this time and sunk by the *Kent* and the *Glasgow*.

After the Dogger Bank, Admiral von Ingenohl was replaced in command of the High Seas fleet by Admiral von Pohl. The policy of the new Commander-in-Chief was to try to entice the Grand fleet to action with the High Seas fleet in the waters of the Heligoland Bight where he would have the advantage of his own minefields, U-boats and superior torpedo flotillas coupled with the proximity of his bases to succour damaged ships. Admiral von Pohl's first sortie as Commander-in-Chief was on 29 March 1915. Some of his battle cruisers were still

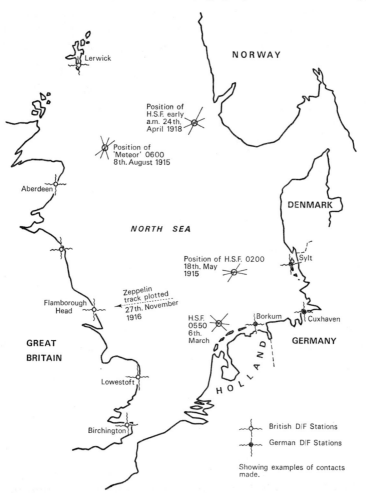

11. Direction-Finding Stations in the North Sea 1914-18.

under repair after the Dogger Bank but he had with him his three battle squadrons. For the first time the Zeppelins were used in close company with the fleet as scouts. The High Seas fleet sailed during the forenoon and proceeded to the north-westward carrying out tactical exercises during the afternoon. By teatime von Pohl had turned for home and he passed Nordeney at 2100 on his way to anchor in the Jade. The British radio intelligence had told them that the German scouting forces and some destroyers would put to sea on March 29 but they had no advance warning that the whole High Seas fleet was coming out. When they realized in the morning of the 29th that something more serious was afoot, probably from the chattering of the Zeppelins, they ordered the Grand fleet, the Harwich force and some submarines to sea. The Grand fleet did not sail until 1730 by which time von Pohl had turned homewards. When the Admiralty realized this they recalled the Grand fleet. The British were, of course, disappointed that no contact had been made and were inclined to believe that von Pohl had turned back as soon as he realized that the Grand fleet had put to sea. The Admiralty took Admiral Jellicoe to task for using wireless too much. Admiral Jellicoe replied that some wireless signalling had had to take place to call off the operation as this had to be done in the middle of the night before the fleet had concentrated. In any case he had had to break silence to acknowledge the Admiralty's recall. He pointed out that he had had to leave his bases in daylight and that this was undesirable as he was likely to be attacked or at any rate sighted by U-boats. There is no indication, however, that the Germans even realized that the Grand fleet had put to sea and in any case they never intended to go beyond the outer waters of the Heligoland Bight.

Admiral von Pohl made his next trip to sea three weeks later (Map 12). This time he had a more substantial aim which was to support a minelaying operation by the cruisers *Stralsund* and *Strassburg* off the Swarte Bank in the middle of the North Sea. Preliminary U-boat and Zeppelin reconnaissances were made and the minelayers sailed during the forenoon of April 17. The wireless signals inseparable from such an operation were intercepted by the British: four submarines were ordered into the Bight and the Grand fleet was to be ready to sail as soon as it was dark. In fact the Grand fleet put to sea an hour before the High Seas fleet and both steamed steadily out into the North Sea. The German minelaying operation was successfully completed by 0500 in the morning and shortly afterwards the High Seas fleet turned back towards its bases and was at anchor by 1700 on April 18. The British listening stations detected its return shortly afterwards and the Grand fleet was released to carry out exercises to the northwards.

Three days later von Pohl was out again. The usual indica-

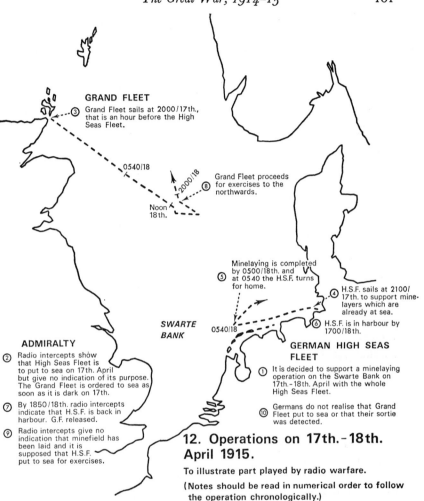

GRAND FLEET

③ Grand Fleet sails at 2000/17th., that is an hour before the High Seas Fleet.

0540/18

2000/18

⑧ Grand Fleet proceeds for exercises to the northwards.

Noon 18th.

⑤ Minelaying is completed by 0500/18th. and at 0540 the H.S.F. turns for home.

④ H.S.F. sails at 2100/ 17th. to support mine-layers which are already at sea.

⑥ H.S.F. is in harbour by 1700/18th.

SWARTE BANK

0540/18

GERMAN HIGH SEAS FLEET

① It is decided to support a minelaying operation on the Swarte Bank on 17th.-18th. April with the whole High Seas Fleet.

ADMIRALTY

② Radio intercepts show that High Seas Fleet is to put to sea on 17th. April but give no indication of its purpose. The Grand Fleet is ordered to sea as soon as it is dark on 17th.

⑦ By 1850/18th. radio intercepts indicate that H.S.F. is back in harbour. G.F. released.

⑨ Radio intercepts give no indication that minefield has been laid and it is supposed that H.S.F. put to sea for exercises.

⑩ Germans do not realise that Grand Fleet put to sea or that their sortie was detected.

12. Operations on 17th.-18th. April 1915.

To illustrate part played by radio warfare.

(Notes should be read in numerical order to follow the operation chronologically.)

tions of activity, including the signals for preliminary reconnaissances, anti-submarine sweeps and minesweeping, were intercepted by the British. Four submarines sailed from Harwich at once and the Grand fleet put to sea as soon as it was dark on April 21. The High Seas fleet sailed a few hours afterwards and steered to the north-westwards with no better purpose than to demonstrate that it was not blockaded in the Bight and was able to sortie if it wished. Zeppelins joined the fleet as soon as it was light, but after sinking a Grimsby trawler, it turned for

home only 130 miles from Heligoland. The British submarines
got into the Bight too late and the Grand fleet was recalled
shortly afterwards. The British were again certain that von Pohl
had turned back to avoid action with the Grand fleet. In fact
he did not know for some days that it had even put to sea.
Investigation showed that no wireless signals had been made
by the fleet and that the Germans could not have been warned
in this way. It was then believed that one of the Zeppelins must
have seen the Grand fleet, but suspicion finally fell on neutral
fishing boats which the fleet had passed in daylight. Von Pohl
did in fact learn of the Grand fleet's position from this source
but it was not the reason he turned back as this intelligence
did not reach him until April 27.

The Germans had for long also suspected that neutral trawlers fishing in the North Sea were responsible for betraying the
High Seas fleet's positions to the British and consequently made
efforts to keep these vessels out of the Heligoland Bight altogether. The German Navy certainly believed that British
forces were at sea much more than they were and so were not
surprised when they met them. As they kept rigid wireless
silence at sea they did not understand how radio intelligence
could give the British any information. These facts, coupled
with the belief that most of their local signals in the Bight could
not be picked up in England and that in any case they thought
their ciphers unbreakable, contributed to a situation in which
British radio intelligence was able to continue to glean priceless
information.

On May 17, in the middle of the crisis caused by the resigna-
tion of Lord Fisher as First Sea Lord and the replacement of
Winston Churchill as First Lord of the Admiralty, Room 40
detected that the High Seas fleet was again on the move (Map
13). The intercepted signal revealed that the whole High Seas
fleet was involved and there were indications that it 'intended
to attack by day' so that something more serious than the recent
sorties seemed to be in train. In fact Admiral von Pohl was
covering the laying of a large minefield on the Dogger Bank by
the four cruisers of the Fourth Scouting Group and he left the
Jade at 1930 on May 17. The Grand fleet and the Harwich
force were ordered to put to sea as soon as it was dark and all
the local patrols on the east coast were recalled. The latter
signal was intercepted by the Germans and decoded, and from

this they might well have realized that Room 40 was intercepting their traffic. In fact, they reasoned that the British would strengthen their patrols rather than recall them if they believed the High Seas fleet was at sea and so they attributed this signal to some other cause. In consequence they proceeded with their operation as planned.

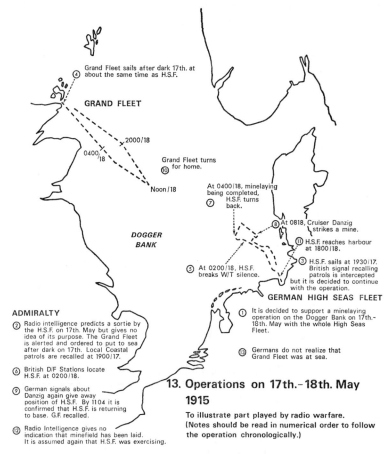

Grand Fleet sails after dark 17th. at about the same time as H.S.F. ④

GRAND FLEET

2000/18

0400/18

Noon/18

Grand Fleet turns for home. ⑩

At 0400/18, minelaying being completed, H.S.F. turns back. ⑦

⑧ At 0818, Cruiser Danzig strikes a mine.

⑪ H.S.F. reaches harbour at 1800/18.

DOGGER BANK

⑤ At 0200/18, H.S.F. breaks W/T silence.

③ H.S.F. sails at 1930/17. British signal recalling patrols is intercepted but it is decided to continue with the operation.

GERMAN HIGH SEAS FLEET

ADMIRALTY

② Radio intelligence predicts a sortie by the H.S.F. on 17th. May but gives no idea of its purpose. The Grand Fleet is alerted and ordered to put to sea after dark on 17th. Local Coastal patrols are recalled at 1900/17.

⑥ British D/F Stations locate H.S.F. at 0200/18.

⑨ German signals about Danzig again give away position of H.S.F. By 1104 it is confirmed that H.S.F. is returning to base. G.F. recalled.

⑫ Radio Intelligence gives no indication that minefield has been laid. It is assumed again that H.S.F. was exercising.

① It is decided to support a minelaying operation on the Dogger Bank on 17th.-18th. May with the whole High Seas Fleet.

⑬ Germans do not realize that Grand Fleet was at sea.

13. Operations on 17th.-18th. May 1915

To illustrate part played by radio warfare.
(Notes should be read in numerical order to follow the operation chronologically.)

At 0200 on the morning of May 18, the new British D/F stations made their first important contribution and placed the German flagship 126 miles north-west of Heligoland. Hopes of a fleet action ran high. Two hours later, however, as the minelaying operation had been completed and the weather was too bad for Zeppelin reconnaissance, von Pohl turned for home.

This movement was detected by British radio intelligence and reported by 0700, and just over an hour later the German cruiser *Danzig* struck a mine off the island of Sylt. The resulting wireless messages were intercepted and the position of the High Seas fleet left no doubt that it was on its way home. The British then assumed that the sortie was simply an exercise and radio intelligence gave no warning of the laying of the minefield. The Grand fleet was informed of this at 1100 and it then returned to its bases.

The signal recalling the Grand fleet was made by a new method. Up to now it had not been considered sufficiently reliable just to broadcast important messages to the C.-in-C. These signals therefore had to be acknowledged and this was liable to compromise the fleet's position. The new 'I method' involved the signal being addressed to some ship or station equi-distant from the transmitting station which would read and acknowledge the signal. The flagship would also read the message but would remain silent. It could then be certain that the signal had gone out correctly and it could be assumed with a greater degree of certainty than a broadcast that the flagship would also receive it correctly.

On May 29, the Admiralty again began to receive all the preliminary signals which presaged a sortie by the High Seas fleet. They sent two submarines into the Bight and ordered the Grand fleet to sail as soon as it was dark and concentrate in the middle of the North Sea. The German Battle Squadrons sailed shortly afterwards and the two fleets steamed steadily towards each other during the night. In the morning the High Seas fleet was sighted by the British submarine *E6*, which fired at the *Moltke* but missed her. The British submarine wireless sets were still not powerful enough to reach the coastal wireless stations and so this important intelligence did not reach the British until *E6* returned to harbour. The purpose of this sortie of the High Seas fleet was to cover the exit of the disguised minelayer *Meteor*, but Admiral von Pohl turned back before noon and left her to her own devices. Room 40 soon reported that the High Seas fleet was returning to its bases and the Grand fleet followed suit early in the afternoon. The British knew nothing of the *Meteor* and she passed to the eastwards of the Grand fleet and up the Norwegian coast to lay a minefield in the White Sea.

The *Meteor* returned safely to Germany on her own, but other sources of intelligence revealed that she had visited north Russia. On August 6 she sailed again and this time British radio intelligence gave warning. The intercepted signals gave the time of sailing but not her destination and Admiral Jellicoe, believing that she was again bound for the White Sea, sent a force of light cruisers and destroyers to intercept her off the Norwegian coast. The *Meteor* was in fact bound for the Scottish coast to lay a large minefield off Cromarty. This she successfully accomplished early on August 8, sinking the armed boarding steamer *Ramsey* which she met on the way. The British soon realized what had happened as a number of the mines were found adrift by patrols. They obtained the full facts shortly afterwards because the *Meteor* broke wireless silence to report laying her mines and sinking the *Ramsey*. The message was intercepted and decoded by Room 40 and her position obtained by the D/F stations. Measures were at once put in train to intercept her, and four squadrons of light cruisers converged on her and sank her off Horns Reef.

Admiral von Pohl made two more sorties during his period in command in September and October. The first was to cover a minelaying operation by the cruisers *Stralsund* and *Regensburg*, and the second to make a reconnaissance towards the Skagerrak. Both were detected by wireless intelligence in plenty of time but both were assessed as exercises, and the Grand fleet simply came to short notice but did not put to sea. In the sortie of October 24, *E6* again sighted the High Seas fleet and this time missed the cruiser *Rostock*. This was the seventh time that the German main fleet put to sea after the Battle of the Dogger Bank during 1915. Warning of every single sortie was given by radio intelligence, and in five of the seven operations the Grand fleet put to sea to try and force an action. In spite of this the Germans do not seem to have had an inkling of the amount of information the British were obtaining from their radio signals. On the other hand the knowledge of the information they were getting made the British very careful about using their own wireless and made them very security conscious.

The Germans were in fact already trying to listen to British signals and claimed that they could tell when the Grand fleet was at sea. They had built two D/F stations during 1915, but these were employed solely to help the Zeppelins navigate and find their way back to base. The British could hardly believe their luck, and it is true that but for radio intelligence they would not have been able to take precautions against any of the movements of the High Seas fleet and would probably only have known definitely about two of them.

The great value of the information was that it actually gave warning of impending movements in time for counter-measures to be taken, yet the exact intentions of the enemy were seldom broadcast by wireless for Room 40 to decipher. It is perhaps understandable that the Germans did not connect the movements of the Grand fleet with lack of their own radio security because it put to sea a number of times between March and October for exercises or other purposes. During the summer the Grand fleet made a special sortie when it was not synchronized with a movement of the High Seas fleet in the hope that it would be detected by the Germans.

That radio intelligence did not lead to greater success in battle was due more to the German strategy than anything else. Admiral von Pohl had claimed that his general aim in all these sorties was to entice the Grand fleet into the Heligoland Bight where he could engage it on advantageous terms. If this was really his strategy it would be essential that his departure should be advertised to the British so that they could fall into his trap. This he took no steps to do except to rely on British submarines to report him. One is forced to the conclusion that this was not his strategy at all for he never ventured more than 130 miles from Heligoland and never stayed at sea long enough for the Grand fleet to reach him from its bases even when it sailed a few hours before he did. His sorties were almost certainly for training, to keep up morale and to stifle criticisms in Germany that the fleet was doing nothing. In fact wireless intelligence supplied the final link in the overall British naval strategy. It enabled the Grand fleet to conserve its energy in the knowledge that it would be warned if the High Seas fleet came out for any serious purpose, and this could not be done by any other form of reconnaissance available at the time.

Radio intelligence also proved of great value against the Zeppelins whose raids began in March 1915 and continued during the summer. The Zeppelins used wireless freely and always reported as soon as they were airborne. Conscious that codes sent in Zeppelins on raids might fall into British hands, the Zeppelins had strict orders to land all codes except one called HVB before leaving on bombing missions. They were required to confirm by wireless on taking off that 'only HVB (was) on board'. This signal was invariably intercepted by the British listening stations and was a positive indication that the Zeppelin was on a raiding mission and not just making a reconnaissance flight in the North Sea. The position of Zeppelins was also pinpointed by the D/F chain without difficulty. In fact the British often knew more about the Zeppelins and their positions than the Zeppelins themselves.

During the first eighteen months of the war the spark transmitter and crystal receiver had proved perfectly satisfactory in Home waters. Longer ranges were however needed on the oceans and the main occupation of the wireless experimental section of H.M.S. *Vernon* was to develop the Poulsen arc. The arc could also be used with advantage to obtain better results with smaller sets. In addition to the submarine set already mentioned, 3 kw. arc sets were being designed for destroyers and as a secondary set in large ships. A more powerful 25 kw. arc transmitter for shore stations and as the primary transmitter for large ships was also being produced.

The *Vernon* was also experimenting with the thermionic valve. This valve was not new, but difficulties of manufacture, especially in obtaining a reasonable life, robustness and consistency of performance had prevented its introduction into service on a large scale (Note 10). Some of these difficulties had now been overcome and it began to be used in a number of ways. It was, first, a detector instead of a crystal for receiving spark transmissions; second, it was used as a generator in a heterodyne receiver; third, it could be used as an amplifier to make any receiver more sensitive and lastly it could be used as an oscillator in a transmitter in place of an arc. *Vernon* developed the second use and produced a much improved heterodyne receiver for the arc transmitters during this period. The third use had been developed by Marconi and was already proving as we have seen of great value for the interception of weak enemy signals. Its use as a transmitter had not got very far as it was limited by the very low power of valves of the period. The fitting of the vast number of wireless sets in auxiliary vessels, aircraft and shore stations required by the war was more than *Vernon* could compete with. Marconi was therefore called in to help to a considerable extent with design; for instance, for the new standard shore stations. The type number of transmitters and receivers were now listed separately instead of always being grouped together and some ships had more receivers than transmitters. There were thirty-five different types of transmitters listed as in use in the Royal Navy and twenty-eight receivers by the end of 1915.

In October 1914 the Admiralty decided to purchase some sets of Fessenden Underwater Sound Telegraphy from the U.S.A. This apparatus had originally been developed as an aid to navigation and safety at sea. It consisted of an oscillator mounted under water on each bow capable of transmitting a very loud audible signal. Ranges of over thirty miles had been obtained on trials. At close ranges no special receiver was required as the signal could be heard clearly through a ship's hull. The hope was that this apparatus could be used for signalling in a fleet, and the *Iron Duke*, Admiral Jellicoe's flagship, was fitted as well as seven other battleships and battle cruisers. The greatest need for underwater sound signalling was obviously in submarines and it was decided to fit all the 'H' class, then being built for the Royal Navy in Canada and the U.S.A. Plans were also made to fit the new fleet submarines of the 'J' and 'K' classes and the patrol submarines of the 'G' class which were under construction. The Fessenden gear was hardly used in the Grand fleet as the Commander-in-Chief was afraid it would give away his position to U-boats. It was found in any case that it was practically useless for passing a signal down a column of ships in line ahead. In submarines however a range of forty-five miles was obtained on one occasion and it was decided in November 1915 to fit all of them. It was decided to persevere in the Grand fleet, too, and one battleship was to try out a system with four oscillators to give better all-round coverage. Better results also, it was thought, could be achieved by stationary repeating cruisers on the beam of the battleship squadrons to get over the problem of trying to signal astern. In 1915 the Fessenden gear became the responsibility of the wireless department but did not find much favour except in submarines.

In summing up the effect of the electron on sea power in the period covered by this chapter, it was wireless and to a certain extent cables which dominated the scene. There were no night actions of any consequence to test the searchlights and advances in electrics generally were confined to some lessons in damage control. In Home waters there is no doubt that the most important new factor was not an extension or improvement of wireless but the advent of radio intelligence, which made possible the Grand fleet strategy of a distant blockade, with its savings on wear and tear of men and machinery and its relative safety.

V

1916 and the Battle of Jutland

ADMIRAL VON POHL died early in 1916 and on January 18 was succeeded as Commander-in-Chief of the High Seas fleet by Admiral Scheer. Scheer was an advocate of a more offensive use of the fleet and a period of increased activity began. Instead of trying to lure the Grand fleet into the Heligoland Bight, his strategy was to make sorties farther out into the North Sea, working in close co-operation with U-boats and Zeppelins, hoping to cut off and destroy an isolated part of the Grand fleet.

His first operation on March 5–6 was synchronized with a Zeppelin raid on the United Kingdom and his hope was to destroy the anti-Zeppelin patrols and any ships which put to sea to support them. He sailed after dark on March 5 and proceeded towards the Hoofden, as the Germans called the southern part of the North Sea between East Anglia and Holland. The British do not seem to have had any warning of this sortie and did not even detect that the High Seas fleet had put to sea. Their first intelligence came at 0530 in the morning when Admiral Scheer broke wireless silence. The British D/F stations at once plotted the position as twenty miles north of Terschelling. It took Room 40 two hours to decipher the signal but when they did it revealed that the whole High Seas fleet was at sea, steering south-west. The British patrols were at once recalled and the Grand fleet and Harwich force ordered to sea. The Germans in their turn intercepted the signal recalling the patrols and Admiral Scheer decided to advance no farther. Subsequently he made a long signal disposing all his forces and including orders to return to harbour. This was intercepted and decoded and the position of the Germans plotted by 1315. The

Grand fleet which had only just got to sea then carried on with exercises and returned to its bases next morning.

The March 6 operation is of interest in that although no contact was made by any of the forces involved, both sides knew something of what the other was doing by wireless intelligence. The Germans had come a long way since the summer of 1915 and had set up a special intercepting wireless station at Neumünster north of Hamburg, and it was here that they had their equivalent of Room 40. So far they had not been able to decipher important British messages but seem to have been able to read signals such as those to auxiliary patrol vessels which were in a simple code. It is probable that it was this organization which warned the High Seas fleet of what it could give away by bad radio security and which was responsible for the failure of the British to obtain prior warning of the High Seas fleet putting to sea on March 5. On February 27 Neumünster had partly read some signals which seemed to refer to the German raider *Greif*. This ship had put to sea through the Skagerrak on February 28. British wireless intelligence detected that a disguised vessel was coming out and forces were on the alert (Note 1). Three light cruisers and destroyers were sent across to patrol the Norwegian coast and when the *Greif* broke wireless silence off Egersund her position was at once plotted by the British D/F stations; she was intercepted and sunk by the northern patrol. Neumünster was not able to unravel the whole story and the British then made one of their periodical changes of cipher key and they got no more information for nearly a month. What is surprising is that they did not suspect why the *Greif* had been caught.

Before Admiral Scheer had time to plan another move, the British took the initiative. They mounted an operation with the seaplane carrier *Vindex* to bomb the Zeppelin sheds at Tondern. The *Vindex* was escorted by the Harwich force with Admiral Beatty's battle cruisers in support. The British kept strict wireless silence and so Neumünster was unable to obtain any warning of their approach. The seaplane attacks failed, however, and two British destroyers collided just as German seaplanes located them. The German battle cruisers then put to sea and with a rising gale the British were in an unenviable position. The Admiralty knew by their wireless intelligence of the German movement and ordered the crew of one of the destroyers, which was badly damaged, to be taken off and the force to retire without delay. In the end this was done but two British light cruisers collided during a night action with German destroyers. Both the Grand fleet and the High Seas fleet put to sea in the end to support their forces but with the worsening weather no contacts were made. Neumünster was however able to report the position of the British damaged destroyer and later of Admiral Beatty's battle cruisers from intercepted signals, but they took so long to decipher these messages that they were received by Admiral Scheer too late to be of use.

In April the High Seas fleet put to sea for the first time on wireless intelligence. Early in the morning of April 21, the British Second Battle Cruiser Squadron left Rosyth for a sweep in the Skagerrak and signals revealing this movement were intercepted by Neumünster. It took ten hours to decipher them but Admiral Scheer at once decided to attempt to intercept this isolated force with the whole High Seas fleet. British radio intelligence, in its turn, detected the impending German movement: the Skagerrak sweep was cancelled and the Grand fleet sailed at 2200 as soon as it was dark. During the night both fleets acting entirely on radio intelligence steamed towards each other: the Grand fleet to a rendezvous in the middle of the North Sea and the High Seas fleet towards Horns Reef. Before midnight the German light cruiser *Graudenz* struck a mine and at dawn, as weather was unsuitable for Zeppelin reconnaissance, Admiral Scheer decided to return to base. His retirement was soon known to the British through their listening stations: the Grand fleet returned to Scapa and the battle cruisers resumed their sweep of the Skagerrak.

In the spring of 1916 Room 40 began to decrypt messages intercepted between Berlin and Washington (Note 2) indicating that a Sinn Fein rising in Dublin was imminent. It was also discovered that a small ship with arms and ammunition was being sent from Germany to Tralee and that Sir Roger Casement was to go to Ireland in the submarine *U19* (Note 3). Reinforcements for the patrols were sent to Queenstown, the *U19* was successfully tracked all the way from Germany, the gun-running ship *Aud* was eventually intercepted by H.M.S. *Bluebell* and Sir Roger Casement was arrested soon after landing. Nevertheless the rebellion in Dublin broke out on April 24.

At noon on the same day the High Seas fleet put to sea. Its

stipulated aim was, as before, to try and cut off an isolated portion of the Grand fleet and, to ensure that the British reacted, Lowestoft was to be bombarded. A bonus would also, it was hoped, be obtained by this operation by its support for the Easter Rising in Ireland and possibly by bombarding the British submarine base at Yarmouth as well. At noon the British listening stations heard the German fleet flagship take over wireless control and this was a sure sign that the High Seas fleet was putting to sea. At 1550 the Admiralty ordered the Grand fleet to come to two hours' notice for steam, but the Grand fleet was by no means ready and was still coaling after its sortie of a few days before. The Harwich force and the submarines however were alerted on the East Coast.

At about 1600 the German battle cruiser *Seydlitz* struck a mine off the Friesian Islands and the consequential wireless messages were intercepted by the British and the position fixed by the D/F stations. At 2030 the local patrols on the East Coast were recalled and the Grand fleet, having completed coaling at 1900, put to sea. There was an exceptionally strong southerly gale blowing: the destroyers could make no headway at all and even the heavy ships were unable to make more than fifteen knots. At 2014 the British intercepted a German signal which when decoded revealed that the German battle cruisers were fifty miles north-west of Borkum and steering south-westwards with the High Seas fleet following some fifty miles astern. The actual objective of the German fleet was not known but from its position and course some deductions were made and the Harwich force and two groups of submarines were positioned to intercept. The Germans had picked up the signal recalling the British patrols and realized that they had been detected. Admiral Scheer believed at the time that the *Seydlitz* had been torpedoed by a submarine and that she had also reported the position of the German battle cruisers. As he had other intelligence reports of British ships off Norway and in the mouth of the Scheldt, he reasoned that the Grand fleet was split and not in the vicinity. He therefore proceeded with the operation. Lowestoft was bombarded early next morning and after brushes with the Harwich force the German battle cruisers evaded the British submarines, rejoined the main High Seas fleet and returned to harbour. British radio intelligence had not been able to give as much warning of this sortie as usual but neverthe-

less revealed sufficient information for the German intentions to
be deduced well in advance.

The original German plan for the sortie which led to the
Battle of Jutland was for a bombardment of Sunderland. The
plan included the co-operation of U-boats and Zeppelins and
on May 17, ten U-boats sailed to take up their positions (Note
4). These U-boat sailings were detected by British radio intelligence but the exact position of the patrols and their aim was
not known; there was only evidence that at least eight U-boats
were in the northern part of the North Sea. Admiral Scheer's
plan was originally to be put into force on May 23 but the
weather was too bad for the Zeppelins. The sortie was postponed
from day to day for the same reason until May 28 when a decision could be deferred no longer. On May 30 the U-boats would
have to return, so Admiral Scheer decided to put his alternative
plan into effect which would not require Zeppelin co-operation.
This was for a sortie towards the Skagerrak by which it was
hoped to entice a portion of the Grand fleet into action with
the whole High Seas fleet as well as to inflict casualties on it by
drawing it over the U-boats.

At midnight on May 28, Admiral Scheer made the signal
ordering the operation to take place and for the fleet to be
prepared to sail. British radio intelligence began to realize that
something was afoot in the forenoon of May 29 but could get
no definite information. Next day at 1130 a signal to the U-
boats was intercepted, telling them that they might expect to
sight the High Seas fleet during the next two days. During the
day more evidence that a sortie was imminent was deduced
from eleven signals to outpost vessels, minesweepers, U-boats
and aircraft. At the same time the D/F stations reported that
the German flagship had left Wilhelmshaven and was now at
anchor in the Jade roads seven miles downstream (Note 5).
Just before 1700, an important operational signal was sent to
all units of the High Seas fleet. It was intercepted by the British
but could not be decrypted as the Germans had recently
changed their basic code book and with this signal the cipher
key also changed (Note 6). Nevertheless Room 40 made the
correct deduction from the signal and at 1740 Admiral Jellicoe
was warned by the Admiralty that the High Seas fleet was
about to put to sea. He was ordered to sail and concentrate
eastward of the 'Long Forties' (Note 7). Nothing was known of

the German plan, which had not been sent by wireless, but sixteen U-boats were now known to be co-operating and it was clearly an operation of some importance.

By 2230 May 30 the whole British Grand fleet was at sea. It had taken 163 signals to organize its departure from Scapa Flow, Cromarty and Rosyth but all except twenty-four of these were made by semaphore, morse lamp, flags, telephone or telegrams. Some of the twenty-four wireless messages that were made were through shore stations and others by the very low-power auxiliary wireless sets so that Neumünster did not notice anything unusual. As he was leaving at 2200 Admiral Jellicoe made a general signal to keep wireless silence except on sighting the enemy or to reply to the Admiral. The only exception was that wireless guards were allowed to use their auxiliary sets to pass messages to the flagship in case of necessity. The fleet manoeuvred by visual signals by day but the Commander-in-Chief and the admirals commanding the battle cruisers from Rosyth and the Second Battle Squadron from Cromarty all used auxiliary wireless to manoeuvre their formations during the night, and also passed their 'intentions' in this way to the ships under their command. The Commander-in-Chief broke silence between 2300 and 0400 to order the *Campania* to return to harbour, to report his position to the Admiralty and to ask them to give instructions to the Eleventh Submarine Flotilla, but from 0500 May 31, strict silence was maintained by the whole fleet. The Grand fleet wireless organization was that all large ships kept watch on the Admiral's wave with H.M.S. *Benbow* ready to relay any signals to the Commander-in-Chief if the *Iron Duke* failed to hear them. H.M.S. *Revenge* guarded the long commercial wave, H.M.S. *Superb* guarded the medium-power station wave, H.M.S. *Hercules* the long wave to listen to the high-power station at Cleethorpes, while H.M.S. *St Vincent* listened on German frequencies to intercept any wireless signals they made. The flotilla cruisers stood guard for their destroyers, who, having only one operator, waited until they were ordered to set watch on the destroyer wave. Great advances in manoeuvring the fleet by wireless had been made since the beginning of the war. Tactical wireless messages could now be passed as quickly and easily as visual signals. The time taken to get a message through had been reduced from a quarter of an hour to two or three minutes.

The German Scouting Forces under Admiral Hipper sailed
at 0100 May 31, that is some two hours after the Grand fleet,
and Admiral Scheer followed an hour or two later. They too
kept strict wireless silence and manoeuvred by visual signal.
British radio intelligence therefore received no positive evidence
that the High Seas fleet had left harbour. They knew, however,
that the German flagship's call sign had been transferred to the
shore station at Wilhelmshaven and that this indicated from
previous experience that the fleet had sailed. Room 40 were
therefore fairly confident that Admiral Scheer was at sea and
the Admiralty informed Admiral Jellicoe of this at 1230 but
added that directional wireless indicated that the German flagship was still at anchor in the Jade at 1110. The last part of this
message was misleading, indeed it was untrue, and was the
result of poor co-operation between Room 40 and the Operations Division in the Admiralty. The normal call sign of Admiral
Scheer's flagship was DK and the Operations Division asked
Room 40 'where DK was', meaning where was the German
flagship. As the call sign DK had been transferred to the shore,
Room 40 replied that DK was at Wilhelmshaven and the
signal went out accordingly.

The sailing of the Grand fleet was, on the other hand, partly
detected by the Germans. *U32* sighted elements of Admiral
Beatty's force eighty miles east of May Island early in the
morning and she surfaced and made a report by wireless. *U66*
sighted the Second Battle Squadron sixty miles east of Kinnaird
Head and also reported. *U63* off the Firth of Forth intercepted
some of the British wireless messages as the fleet left harbour and
Neumünster, after pondering all night on something they had
picked up, reported that they thought two battleships or battle
squadrons escorted by destroyers had left Scapa Flow. Admiral
Scheer had all these reports by 0700 in the morning but convinced himself that they were isolated routine movements and
failed to appreciate that the whole Grand fleet was at sea.

The two fleets steamed steadily towards each other throughout the day, manoeuvring by visual signal and keeping strict
wireless silence; hundreds of pairs of eyes scanned the horizons
and hundreds of pairs of ears listened on about a dozen different
radio channels altogether. From time to time information from
shore wireless stations came in. For instance at 1018 Neumünster
told Admiral Scheer that they had picked up a weather report

of a type generally used only when the Grand fleet was at sea (Note 8). Between 1100 and 1200, H.M.S. *St Vincent*, listening on the German frequencies, began to detect some of the traffic as the Zeppelins ascended from their bases. Then at 1420 the Grand fleet operators on the Admiral's wave heard the light cruiser *Galatea* break the silence and transmit the first enemy report on power when she sighted Admiral Hipper's advanced screen. During the next forty-five minutes she followed this up with seven other messages amplifying the situation and reporting the sighting of the German battle cruisers. Then the *Falmouth* and *Nottingham* joined in and at 1521 Admiral Beatty in the *Lion* reported his position, course and speed to the Commander-in-Chief. On the German side it was the light cruiser *Elbing* which broke the silence ten minutes after the *Galatea* and reported an enemy armoured cruiser in sight. The message was received not only by Admirals Hipper and Scheer and the High Seas fleet but also by the British D/F stations, who quickly fixed the position. The Admiralty passed it to Admiral Jellicoe, taking only thirty-nine minutes to do so. By this time, however, he had ample information from the sighting reports of Admiral Beatty's light cruisers.

In this early phase the Germans made rather more signals than the British, and during the next hour, by which time the rival battle cruisers were in sight of each other, various ships had made a total of fifteen more wireless signals. In one of these Admiral Hipper reported his position to Admiral Scheer and it was nearly an hour before Admiral Beatty thought fit to report this to Admiral Jellicoe. Surprisingly, considering that it was vital at this time to conceal the fact that the whole High Seas fleet was at sea, Admiral Scheer replied at 1448 giving his position, course and speed. This very important signal was heard by H.M.S. *St Vincent* in the Grand fleet but she could not decrypt it and it does not seem to have been picked up by the British listening stations ashore, or if it was it did not receive the attention of Room 40.

The battle cruisers opened fire on each other at 1545 and the run to the south began. During this part of the action both sides continued to manoeuvre by visual signals, and even action and fire distribution orders were conveyed by this means. At 1610 the *Lion*'s wireless room was hit and put out of action but by this time she had reported to the Commander-in-Chief that the

battle cruisers were in action. During the run to the south by
the battle cruisers the main High Seas fleet was also manoeuvred
by visual signals but Admiral Scheer found it necessary to make
a number of wireless messages as well. At 1709 he reported his
position, course and speed again for Admiral Hipper's benefit
and this time the signal was picked up by the British listening
stations. Room 40 had deciphered the message, and the position
of the High Seas fleet was sent to Admiral Jellicoe fifty-one
minutes after it had been made. Even this remarkable per-
formance was too late, as |twenty-two minutes earlier H.M.S.
Southampton had sighted the High Seas fleet and made an
'Urgent Priority' signal reporting its position.

The second phase of the battle, the run to the north, then
began. Admiral Jellicoe, in spite of the need to conceal his
position if a general action was to be brought about, also felt it
essential to make a number of wireless signals. During the run
to the south he had already broken silence to give Admiral
Beatty his position, course and speed and to order the Third
Battle Cruiser Squadron to press on and support Admiral
Beatty. As the report from the *Southampton* of sighting the High
Seas fleet came in, he sent another to the Tenth Cruiser Squadron to take up the eastern patrol line and (Note 9) at 1651 he
made 'Fleet Action Imminent' to the Admiralty. Admiral
Jellicoe got away with it.

If Neumünster or the German D/F stations received any of
these signals they had not time to analyse them and tell Admiral
Scheer. The loss of the *Lion*'s wireless at a time when the delicate
problem existed of getting the Grand fleet into the best position
to meet the High Seas fleet was bad enough. It was followed at
1700 by the destruction of both the main and auxiliary wireless
rooms in the *Barham*, flagship of the Fifth Battle Squadron,
which was the other main formation in action with the High
Seas fleet. The two principal commanders in the battle cruiser
fleet were therefore bereft of their rado communications at a
particularly important time. Admiral Beatty had passed a
report of sighting the High Seas fleet via the *Princess Royal*, but
this message was received in the *Iron Duke* in a somewhat
garbled state. It was left mainly to Commodore Goodenough
in the *Southampton* to report the position of the High Seas fleet
and he made four amplifying reports during the run to the
north. This was not enough to establish the relative position of

H.M.S. *Vanoc* in 1941
A destroyer fitted with the fixed type 286 radar (A.S.V.II adapted).

H.M.S. *Verity* in 1942
A destroyer fitted with improved type 286 radar with a rotating
aerial for combined air and surface warning.

H.M.S. *Alisma* in 1942
A corvette fitted with the type 271 radar for detecting U-boats on the surface.
(Photos: Imperial War Museum)

PLATE III

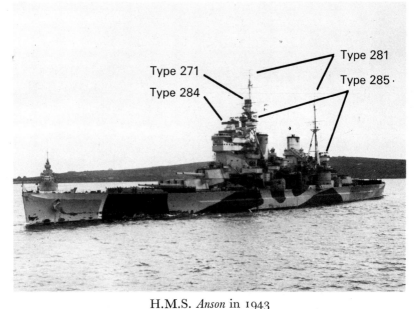

Type 281

Type 271

Type 285·

Type 284

H.M.S. *Anson* in 1943

A battleship fitted with type 281 for air warning, type 271 for surface warning, type 284 for surface gunnery control and type 285 for anti-aircraft gunnery control. 44-in. searchlights are still fitted and can be seen abreast the funnels.

Type 279

Type 285

Type 271

Type 285

H.M.S. *Curacoa* in 1943

This anti-aircraft cruiser is fitted with type 279 for air warning, type 271 for surface warning and type 285 for anti-aircraft gunnery control.

(Photos: Imperial War Museum)

PLATE IV

the two fleets as Admiral Jellicoe's wireless message to Admiral Beatty – 'Where is the enemy battlefleet?' – made at 1801 shows. A minute later, before any reply was received, Admiral Jellicoe made the decision to deploy to port and this signal, one of the most important of the whole war, was made by flags (Note 10).

As the two main fleets came into action the use of wireless became much less restricted, and both Commanders-in-Chief began to use it as well as flags for manoeuvring. On the British side the *Marlborough* reported being hit by a torpedo and that her speed had been reduced to seventeen knots. On the German side the *Frankfurt* reported the *Wiesbaden* disabled and a number of signals were made to try to arrange Admiral Hipper's transfer from the sinking *Lützow*. Admiral Beatty, in the *Lion*, was badly handicapped by having no wireless and was forced to use a searchlight to pass his signals, generally routed by the van of the battle fleet to the Commander-in-Chief. Admiral Hipper was in no better state, his flagship's wireless being also disabled, and he was trying to transfer to another ship by destroyer. All the German tactical signals, including the 'Kehrtwendung' or battle turn-aways, were now made by wireless and it is doubtful if such difficult manoeuvres in the smoke and heat of battle could have been executed in any other way. Throughout this phase, the *Southampton*'s wireless reports of the enemy battle fleet continued to come in regularly and were of exceptional value.

As night approached, Admiral Jellicoe made a number of wireless signals. At 2110 he made that the course of the fleet was south and seven minutes later ordered the battle fleet to form divisions in line ahead disposed abeam. At 2127 he told his destroyers to take station five miles astern of the battle fleet. Later he ordered the flotilla leader *Abdiel* to lay mines in the Horns Reef Channel and then finally he made his reference position. The signal to his destroyers at 2127 was intercepted and deciphered by Neumünster and passed to Admiral Scheer. This was a remarkable achievement as the British seldom broke wireless silence at sea and the German cryptographers had very little to work on. The British, in their turn, intercepted the signal from Neumünster to Admiral Scheer and deciphered it (Note 11). Admiral Scheer also made a number of signals to organize his fleet for the night. He ordered his destroyers to spread in a wide V formation and to attack the Grand fleet and

for the High Seas fleet to steer a course of SSE¼E at sixteen
knots for the entrance to the Horns Reef swept channel. At the
same time he gave the sequence of squadrons. All of these
signals were intercepted and deciphered by Room 40 but were
not passed out verbatim. They were paraphrased and summarized by the Operations Division.

Unfortunately the first of these signals sent to Admiral
Jellicoe at 2158 gave the rear ship of the High Seas fleet a
position which was obviously incorrect and this tended to
decrease further his confidence in radio intelligence. Another
signal at 2241 simply said: 'German Battle Fleet ordered home
at 2114. Battle Cruisers in rear. Course SSE¾E. Speed 16 knots.'
A later intercepted message was a request by Admiral Scheer
for air reconnaissance at Horns Reef but this, although decrypted by Room 40 and sent to the Operations Division, was
not passed to Admiral Jellicoe. Taken in conjunction with
reports from the *Nottingham* and *Birmingham* after an action
between the Second Light Cruiser Squadron and German
Fourth Scouting Group, Admiral Jellicoe did not get the
impression that the High Seas fleet was steering for the Horns
Reef swept channel. Between 2300 May 31 and 0125 June 1
Admiral Scheer sent another seven wireless messages, all of
which were decrypted by Room 40 and passed to the Operations Division. These signals, giving positions of the High Seas
fleet, courses and instructions for the German destroyers to
assemble at Horns Reef at 0400, left no room for doubt that
Admiral Scheer was retiring by the Horns Reef swept channel.
None of these signals was passed on to Admiral Jellicoe or even
summarized for him. The reason is obscure. It is possible that
the Operations Division thought they had, in their signal of
2241, told the Commander-in-Chief all he needed to know and
that further confirmation was not only unnecessary but risked
compromising the radio intelligence system (Note 12).

The moment is now opportune to leave communications for a
little in order to study the use of the searchlight in the battle.
Admiral Jellicoe had no intention of risking a night engagement
with the High Seas fleet. As night approached he therefore set a
southerly course in a cruising formation so as to be in a position
to renew the battle next day. Admiral Scheer also wished to
avoid action that night; indeed he wished to avoid action

altogether, and his sole aim was to reach his base without further fighting. Admiral Jellicoe's decision was undoubtedly the correct one. Chance in a night action could quite easily have meant that his losses would be so heavy as to forfeit altogether his superiority in 'Dreadnoughts' and so the command of the sea. Admiral Scheer on the other hand had much to gain. With the great superiority of the German Navy in night fighting it was quite possible for him to win a considerable victory. The Germans not only had better night-fighting equipment but their drill for using it was superior. All their 'Dreadnought' battleships and battle cruisers had at least eight of the powerful 43 in. searchlights whereas the British ships had 36 in. or twin 24 in. The German pre-'Dreadnoughts' and cruisers all had 36 in. searchlights against the 24 in. of most British light cruisers (Note 13).

In the control systems the Germans had a greater lead still. All their searchlights had iris shutters, they could be kept burning and ready behind their shutters at night action stations and the control of their searchlights was an integral part of the gunnery control system and was positive and accurate. The British had no shutters and so the arc of the searchlight had to be struck to use it, with the inevitable slight delay. The British had introduced a form of centralized searchlight control in some ships but it was not in the same class as that of their adversaries. The German night-action procedure was that when the enemy was sighted at night at over 1,650 yards, they turned away without firing. If at under 1,650 yards, the guns were loaded and trained on the bearing with range and deflection set, while the searchlights, following the lookout's binoculars automatically, were kept burning behind their shutters. The challenge would then be made and if the target proved hostile, the shutters would be opened, the enemy illuminated, and the first broadside fired instantly.

The British procedure started also with the sighting of an enemy and the making of a challenge. Searchlights would then be used but there would be flickering and spluttering while the arcs were struck and then the beam was seldom on the target and a sweep right and left had to be made to pick it up. Having found the target, the searchlight operators in the older ships would not find it easy to hold it if there was any motion on the ship. Having decided to engage, the fire control data would be passed and in due course the guns would open fire. There is little doubt that had the two battle fleets engaged at night at Jutland, the Germans would have invariably hit with their first salvo before the British had fired a shot. At the point-blank ranges at which the ships would have sighted each other the effect would have been devastating. In the event, the battle fleets did not meet and the night actions at Jutland took the form of fourteen brief encounters, mostly between British destroyers and German battleships.

Admiral Jellicoe stationed his destroyers astern of his battle fleet mainly so that he knew where they were and would not get involved in mistakes with his own ships; it was also so that he would have them under his control ready to resume the battle as soon as it was light. The High Seas fleet, however, passed astern of him during the night on a course for the Horns Reef swept channel into the Bight; in doing so it pushed its way through the British destroyer flotillas and it was in this area that all fourteen encounters took place. Four of the night actions involved cruisers and the first occurred as soon as it was dark. The German cruisers *Frankfurt* and *Pillau* of the Second Scouting Group sighted H.M.S. *Castor* leading the Eleventh Destroyer Flotilla and fired torpedoes which missed. Shortly afterwards the German cruisers *Hamburg* and *Elbing* also sighted the *Castor* and, after mutual challenging, switched on their searchlights and opened fire at a range of 2,000 yards. *Castor* replied, using her searchlights, and in a short but fierce battle both *Castor* and *Hamburg* were seriously damaged. Both sides then turned away and broke off the action.

The next encounter was between two opposing squadrons of light cruisers at much closer range. The British Second Light Cruiser Squadron consisting of the *Southampton, Dublin, Nottingham* and *Birmingham* met the German Fourth Scouting Group consisting of the *Stettin, München, Frauenlob, Stuttgart* and *Hamburg* on a converging course. Sighting was mutual and both sides challenged. The *Dublin* was the first to open fire, the range being already down to 800 yards, and she did so without using searchlights as her gunlayers could see the enemy without them. The whole German line then switched on their searchlights, illuminating the *Southampton* and *Dublin*, and returned the fire. On the British side only the *Southampton* used her searchlights, the other three ships using the enemy searchlights as an aiming mark. The action was very fierce but only lasted three-and-a-half minutes, during which the *Southampton* and *München* fired torpedoes. Both sides then turned away: the *Southampton* was seriously damaged in her upperworks, having thirty-five killed and forty-one wounded, mostly among her searchlight and starboard guns crews. She also had her wireless put out of action. The *Dublin* too was damaged and set on fire. The *Nottingham* and *Birmingham* were untouched and they were able to make good practice at the German ships, all except one of which were damaged and suffered casualties. The greatest success was that the *Southampton*'s torpedo hit the *Frauenlob* and she sank at once with the loss of all hands.

The next action involving a cruiser took place just after midnight. The British armoured cruiser *Black Prince* had become detached earlier in the action and was steaming at full speed to try and catch up the Grand fleet. She converged with the centre of the German battle line and was sighted by the battleship *Thüringen*. The *Thüringen* used her searchlights and 12 in. broadsides at 1,100 yards and, assisted by the *Ostfriesland* and *Nassau*, reduced the *Black Prince* to a raging inferno within a minute. The *Black Prince* never even had time to train her guns on the enemy and blew up with the loss of all hands. This was indeed a demonstration of German efficiency in night fighting.

Eight of the remaining ten encounters were between the German battleships, mostly those at the head of the German line, and British destroyers. All the destroyer attacks resulted from chance encounters rather than from deliberate attempts to find and attack the enemy battle fleet. All except the last three, during which dawn was breaking, were at very close range and all the attacking destroyers were seen by the German battleships and fired upon. Both sides were therefore surprised, and in this situation the German night-fighting technique with guns and searchlights proved more successful than the British torpedo control. Not a single German 'Dreadnought' was hit by a torpedo; the pre-'Dreadnought' battleship *Pommern* was indeed sunk but that was after it had begun to get light and the effect of searchlights was much diminished. Torpedoes which missed the German battle line sank the light cruiser *Rostock* and the destroyer *V4*, while the light cruiser *Elbing* was rammed and sunk by the battleship *Posen* while trying to cut through the line. The German gunfire sank the British destroyers *Tipperary, Fortune* and *Ardent* and seriously damaged the *Broke, Porpoise* and *Onslaught,* while the *Turbulent* was rammed and sunk by the *Westfalen* and the *Spitfire* seriously damaged in collision with the *Nassau.* At the same time the *Sparrowhawk* was rammed and sunk by the *Broke* and the *Contest* was also damaged in what became a triple collision for which the German searchlights and gunnery can be held partly responsible. The gunfire of the British destroyers during these attacks proved quite effective against the German searchlights, and the *Westfalen, Nassau* and *Rheinland* were all damaged in their funnels and upperworks.

Although Admiral Jellicoe, in his despatch, says that he placed his flotillas in the rear so that they would be able to attack the High Seas fleet if it tried to pass astern of him during the night, he gave them no instruction to this effect. The British destroyers were therefore in cruising rather than attacking formations. This fact must take some of the blame for their failure to do more damage, but the efficient German use of their searchlights, in addition to the damage by gunfire for which they were responsible, blinded and confused the destroyers and often caused their torpedoes to miss. Searchlights were an important factor, therefore, in the escape of the High Seas fleet.

Without British radio intelligence it is highly unlikely that the Battle of Jutland would have been fought at all. The German sortie would probably have taken place unchallenged and would have achieved nothing. After putting to sea, however, both sides misinterpreted the indications each received that the rival fleet was also out. The British mistake was entirely within the Admiralty as we have seen, but the Germans fed all the signals available to Admiral Scheer and he himself read them wrongly. One must, of course, take into account that British units, unlike the German, were at sea frequently, and none of the messages received reported more than a squadron. They therefore might well have been routine movements. In any case Admiral Scheer's plan depended on part of the Grand fleet being at sea so that he could cut it off and destroy it.

The interpretation of enemy reports was still in its infancy and there was plenty of evidence, if Admiral Scheer had wished to believe it, to indicate that the Grand fleet was out. Once the two fleets made contact, radio intelligence was not sufficiently rapid to be of any value. The information was generally too stale on receipt to be any use. Strategically, however, it could still have been of great value if it had been properly used. The British received and decrypted ample signals to show that Admiral Scheer was making for the Horns Reef swept channel during the night yet Admiral Jellicoe was either not informed or discarded the signals. Admiral Jellicoe's faith in radio intelligence was rudely shaken at the start when he was told that the German flagship was in the Jade when it had been at sea for nearly eight hours and was fast approaching (Note 14). It was unfortunate that the first decrypted signal during the night could be seen to be inaccurate as it put the High Seas fleet in a position where Admiral Jellicoe was quite certain it was not. It is of interest that this was no fault of the Admiralty. Room 40 decrypted the signal correctly and it was passed out to Admiral Jellicoe unaltered. The fault in position was made by the German cruiser *Regensburg*. It is therefore understandable that when later in the night radio intelligence seemed to conflict with enemy reports from his own ships, he believed the latter. The Operations Division in the Admiralty did not know of Admiral Jellicoe's doubts and so did not attempt to confirm the situation shown by radio intelligence although there was ample information with which to do so. It is, of course, also true that sailors ashore hate telling others at sea what to do. 'The man on the spot' was always believed to know best. Huge fleets, low visibility and the speed of modern actions had, however, made a great difference and the 'man on the spot' was often thickly surrounded by the 'fog of war' which intelligent help from the shore could do much to dispel. Room 40 made virtually no mistakes at all and their performance throughout the action was brilliant. The mistakes lay in the co-operation of Room 40 with the Operations Division. There were three causes, the first was the very proper need to safeguard this priceless source of intelligence and so to keep anyone not involved literally out of Room 40. Then there was the complementary feeling in the Operations Division that only sailors should have any say in the operation of the fleet. At the same time the Operations Division did not want to compromise radio intelligence by putting too much of it 'on the air'. This lack of co-operation was indeed the main cause of Admiral Jellicoe's failure to realize that the High Seas fleet was escaping by the Horns Reef Channel.

Having firmly fixed the blame for the failure of Admiral Jellicoe to appreciate that the enemy was passing astern, it must be admitted that it was, in fact, of academic importance. The only ways to stop the High Seas fleet entering the Horns Reef Channel would have been to seek a night action between the battle fleets or to risk a day action among the minefields. Admiral Jellicoe was determined not to hazard the Grand fleet in a night action because of the enemy's long-range torpedoes. With a knowledge of the enemy's superiority in night fighting, however, it is probable that his close-range gunnery directed by his vastly superior searchlight arrangements would have been equally devastating as was shown by the destruction of the *Black Prince*. What the likely result of entering the minefields would have been is shown by the damage to the *Ostfriesland* and later in the war to the *Goeben* and *Breslau* when they sortied from the Dardanelles (Note 15). The failure to use the priceless information provided by radio intelligence is therefore of most interest as an illustration of how too much secrecy and a lack of co-ordination between the cryptographers and the operational staff could bring it all to nought.

After the Battle of Jutland the communications of the Grand fleet came in for heavy criticism. Admiral Jellicoe had been severely handicapped by lack of information on three occasions. The first was around 1730 immediately before deployment when the two main fleets were about to meet. The second was around 1915, after the second German 'Kehrtwendung' when the two main fleets lost contact, and the third was during the night when the High Seas fleet passed astern and was involved in nearly a dozen skirmishes with British light forces in the process. In the first case, it must be remembered that the wireless rooms of the *Lion* and *Barham*, the two principal flagships in the battle cruiser fleet, had been destroyed in action. The two fleets were approaching each other with a combined speed of over forty knots and things were happening very quickly. Visibility was patchy and it was difficult to know who could see what. In the run to the north, eight enemy reports were, in fact, made by the *Southampton, Champion, Galatea* and *Princess Royal* and another five by the advance cruisers of the Grand fleet, but still Admiral Jellicoe had no clear picture and had to ask Admiral Beatty at 1801, 'Where is the enemy battle fleet?' In fact, Admiral Jellicoe made the deployment more from the sounds of gunfire and seeing the cruisers of his screen turn to port rather than from any enemy reports either by wireless or searchlight. The difficulty was not that the wireless signals failed to get through or were slow in doing so, but that the fault lay more in the tactical and navigational problem. An enemy report giving the position of the High Seas fleet from, say, the reckoning of the *Southampton* that had left Rosyth some nineteen hours earlier provided little idea of its position relative to the *Iron Duke* which had sailed from Scapa Flow at roughly the same time. Errors in navigation were enough to put the enemy on the wrong bow (Note 16).

In the second occasion when the Grand fleet lost contact with the High Seas fleet after the second 'Kehrtwendung', Admiral Beatty in the *Lion* and the faithful Commodore Goodenough in the *Southampton* passed six enemy reports in all, some of which were by searchlight, and again the trouble was not that they didn't get through. They did not send more as it had been one of the lessons of manoeuvres that it was a mistake to pass irrelevant or unnecessary signals, so clogging the wireless channels and probably delaying more important messages. It was, of course, extremely difficult in the patchy and uncertain conditions to know what the Commander-in-Chief could see and to guess what it was he wanted to know. At the same time the Grand fleet battle orders, although they stressed the need for light cruisers to report the enemy battle fleet before the main fleets made contact, said nothing about a continuing need for reconnaissance. The duties of light cruisers in action were, in fact, to attack the enemy light cruisers, to support our destroyers and to attack the enemy battle fleet with torpedoes. Finally the method in the flagship of displaying the reports that did come in was very primitive. It consisted of the 'Admirals Plot' manned by two staff officers who plotted the ship's position and any reports that came in by hand. It was therefore difficult for Admiral Jellicoe to get a good picture of the situation.

In the third occasion when the High Seas fleet passed astern during the night, no enemy reports were made after those reporting the two cruiser actions until the early morning. Many of the destroyers involved in five attacks on the German battleships were sunk or badly damaged and so could not make reports. Admiral Jellicoe had not organized any night searches to find and keep contact with the High Seas fleet and the Grand fleet battle orders did not list reconnaissance as a duty of destroyers. The wireless arrangements of destroyers were still somewhat primitive and none of the boats that survived thought it necessary to make reports. These actions were, moreover, seen from the Grand fleet and often from the *Iron Duke* herself. In the early morning attack by the Twelfth Flotilla in which the *Pommern* was sunk, Captain Stirling of the flotilla leader *Faulknor* reported enemy battleships in sight and later gave their course. These signals did not get through to the Commander-in-Chief and whether this was due to the *Faulknor*'s transmitter being defective or to enemy jamming is not known. It was, however, the only serious failure in wireless communication during the whole battle. Communicators can perhaps derive some slight comfort from the fact that even if it had got through, it would have been too late for Admiral Jellicoe to engage the High Seas fleet before it entered the swept channels and took shelter behind the minefields (Note 17).

To sum up the use of wireless in the Battle of Jutland it is safe to say that the huge 'Dreadnought' fleets of those days could not have been manoeuvred in the smoke and heat of battle or at night without it. The failures to report or in reporting the enemy were, except in one instance, not communication failures, but failures of a tactical or navigational nature. Communications were, in fact, extraordinarily reliable and would have been the envy of later officers of the high-frequency era in the Second World War. Admiral Jellicoe wrote in his despatch: 'The high state of efficiency of the W/T arrangements of the Fleet and the facility with which they were worked before, during, and after the action is a great testimony to the indefatigable work carried out by Commander Richard L. Nicholson (Note 18). His services have been invaluable throughout the war. A special word of praise is due to the wireless departments in all ships.' This commendation was well justified and in fact would have been appropriate if applied to the Germans as well.

The Battle of Jutland therefore did not lead to demands for technical changes in the wireless equipment of the fleet. Substantial improvements were, in any case, on the way. The main technical development of 1916 was the spread of Poulsen arc sets in the fleet. Probably the most important use of the arc was the fitting of the 3 kw. set in submarines. A similar set was being installed in destroyers and as a secondary in large ships. The shore stations were also being progressively fitted, the standard stations getting a 25 kw. set. The Poulsen arc was smaller and lighter than a spark set of the same power and had a considerably greater range. Longer wavelengths could be used and it was easier to tune, but as the arc transmitted continuous waves a special receiver was required. Before the arc could be used for area broadcasts, therefore, all ships had to be fitted with heterodyne receivers and this was being done.

In the thorough investigation of deficiencies in material and training that took place after the Battle of Jutland, great attention was paid to night fighting and the use of searchlights. During the autumn of 1916 a Grand fleet searchlight committee was appointed. They concluded that when searchlights were used at all they should be arranged so that they could be pointed accurately at the enemy as soon as he was sighted. The beams would then be exposed and fire opened at once. The use of searchlights to sweep and search for the enemy was believed to be a dangerous practice, and the only occasion when it would be justified would be when other searchlights were already on to engage the enemy. Trials with the large 48 in. and 42 in. searchlights were suspended on the outbreak of war because of the structural alterations which would have been necessary to mount them. Emphasis had been transferred to experiments with new Beck and Harrison systems to give a brighter light in the existing 36 in. and 24 in. searchlights (Note 19). At the same time experiments with various systems of remote control of searchlights were continued. Something much more radical than this was clearly required to meet the Grand fleet's requirements and the designs of completely new searchlights and control systems were put in hand at high priority. At the same time investigations into an alternative system of illumination by starshell were begun.

It is widely believed that the German fleet never came out again after Jutland but this is quite untrue. It made two more sorties in strength during 1916 alone. On the first of these, in August, Admiral Scheer intended to repeat his plan for the bombardment of Sunderland. In order to avoid a recurrence of Jutland where he was surprised and brought to action by the whole Grand fleet, he decided to use Zeppelins and U-boats for scouting in a closer-knit plan than before. At 0919 on August 18 the British intercepted a signal which when deciphered by Room 40 revealed that the High Seas fleet was to put to sea at 2100 that night. The Admiralty at once ordered the Grand fleet to a rendezvous in the middle of the North Sea and it got away by 1830, two and a half hours before the High Seas fleet. An important feature of Admiral Scheer's plan was a line of Zeppelins on reconnaissance between Peterhead and Norway to give warning if the Grand fleet came south. These Zeppelins left their bases in time to be on station if the Grand fleet reacted to the movement of the High Seas fleet if it was sighted by ordinary reconnaissance, for instance by British submarines. As it was warned by radio intelligence in advance of the movement of the High Seas fleet, however, the Grand fleet was able to pass the Zeppelin patrol line in darkness and before the Zeppelins were on station. The High Seas fleet was sighted by the British submarine *E23* at 0400 in the morning and she succeeded in torpedoing the battleship *Westfalen*. *E23* had the new 3 kw. arc transmitter, and for the first time submarine reconnaissance was able to get through a report that the High Seas fleet was at sea, which was a great advance; nevertheless she was not able to surface and make her report until 0916. By this time radio intelligence already knew what had happened and the information was in Admiral Jellicoe's hands nearly two hours before *E23*'s report was received. The spate of German wireless signals occasioned by the attack on the *Westfalen* was intercepted by the British and deciphered and the position ascertained by the direction-finding stations.

Whereas Admiral Scheer was well served by the U-boats and Zeppelins who reported the position of every major British force, Admiral Jellicoe had no air reconnaissance and complained that he was practically blind while his adversary shadowed him continuously. In fact Admiral Scheer could obtain no clear picture of the situation mainly because the interpretation of enemy reports from the air was in its infancy. Although Neumünster told him at midday that the Grand fleet was at sea he convinced himself that the reports he had received were of isolated units and that the Grand fleet, as it had not been seen by the northern Zeppelin patrol line, must be to the north of it. The operations during the day therefore very nearly led to a fleet action. Admiral Jellicoe, thanks to radio intelligence, was not as blind as he asserted. The Admiralty, from various intercepts, were able to send him the position of the High Seas fleet four times between noon and 1700. Neumünster also obtained some information for Admiral Scheer. They reported from deciphered signals the position of one of the British submarine patrol lines and of the light cruiser *Aurora*.

It is an indication of how far the British were ahead in radio warfare that they also received and deciphered these German messages, were able to deduce that one of their ciphers was compromised and the Admiralty ordered its use to be discontinued forthwith. The German sortie of August 19 is of great interest from many points of view, especially those of air reconnaissance and the operation of submarines with a fleet. Radio intelligence was, however, responsible for getting the Grand fleet to sea and countering the German move and was able to offset the great advantage to the Germans of their superior air reconnaissance by Zeppelins.

On 6 October 1916 the German submarine campaign against commerce was resumed and Admiral Scheer no longer had the U-boats to co-operate with the High Seas fleet. Not without misgivings he decided to try another sortie in the hope that he could achieve some results without them. At 1730 on October 18 he signalled his intentions for a sortie and the message was intercepted by the British and deciphered. The Grand fleet was brought to short notice but was not ordered to sail as it had been decided after August 19 to leave coastal defence south of Flamborough Head to submarines and light craft. The High Seas fleet sailed at midnight and by dawn was fifty-five miles north of Terschelling. At 0843 it was sighted by the British submarine *E38* who succeeded in torpedoing the light cruiser *München*. The consequent German signals were intercepted by the British and the position ascertained by the direction-finding stations. At 1700 Admiral Scheer ordered the High Seas fleet to return to harbour by the Horns Reef Channel. The signal was again intercepted and the fleet's position was again fixed by the direction-finding stations. Although the Grand fleet did not put to sea this was not for lack of information, and the local defences and submarines on the East Coast were fully alerted.

So ended the final sortie of the High Seas fleet during 1916. From now on the German submarine campaign became the dominant factor in the war.

The year 1916 saw cryptography really established as a permanent form of intelligence and not simply a temporary piece of luck which would only last as long as the enemy failed to realize it was being used. Radio intelligence had given warning of all the sorties of the German High Seas fleet during the year, all except one being before it sailed. It had become a specialized art and was able to succeed in spite of precautions taken by the Germans. There was a certain amount of luck when a code book was retrieved from the wreck of the Zeppelin *L32*, but success was generally due to the very high calibre of the cryptographers of Room 40. The Germans made many mistakes: for instance, when they changed the basic code book just before the Battle of Jutland they broadcast the fact. They also kept the old one in force at the same time and within a month the new one had become readable (Note 20). The cipher key, which had only been changed quarterly at the beginning of the war, was now changed about once a week, but they advertised a change by a period of silence and Room 40 normally had the answer by noon the following day.

The work of Room 40 very greatly increased during 1916, and already at the time of Jutland there were ninety cryptographers and some fourteen listening stations. The listening stations and the D/F stations were all connected by direct telephone to the Admiralty and the number of messages handled a day was well over a thousand. The Germans continued to use wireless because it was convenient, moreover they did not restrict it to essential messages and this can be contrasted with the British policy of the day. The 1916 Addendum to the Wireless Instructions said: 'It is a fundamental principle that wireless should not be used if the message can be passed by letter, landline, visual signal, etc.' The British continued their policy of great secrecy and did everything they could to make the Germans believe that their information came from other sources. No great secrecy was made of the D/F stations, but efforts were made to try to convince the Germans that spies were responsible for the information gained. The Germans were indeed constantly worried about traitors and there were many witch hunts, but they were undoubtedly too complacent about their cipher systems which they believed to be unbreakable. Too much secrecy, however, leads to problems as we have seen during the Battle of Jutland. A naval adviser, Captain Hope, had been attached to Room 40 since 1915 but there is no doubt that liaison with the Operations Division was still poor.

Radio intelligence was not only of use against the High Seas fleet. In April 1915 a German diplomatic code book had been obtained in Persia, and as there was a great deal of wireless traffic from Berlin to Madrid, to Vienna and to Bulgaria and Turkey, a special department was formed during the summer to decrypt it. Radio intelligence continued to be very useful about the Zeppelins too, and in August 1916 the light cruiser *Conquest* was positioned in the North Sea so that she was able to intercept and damage Zeppelin *L13* by gunfire, but increasingly from the autumn of 1916, radio intelligence was directed towards the campaign against the U-boats.

Radio intelligence was, in any case, no longer the only way to detect a sortie of the High Seas fleet. The fitting of British patrol submarines with the new 3 kw. arc transmitter meant that they could now report what they saw to the Admiralty. Up to now it had been accepted that submarines on patrol were likely to be out of touch. There were in fact three British submarines in the path of the German fleet during the Battle of Jutland. They had instructions, under a plan which had to be cancelled when the High Seas fleet put to sea, to lie on the bottom until June 21. The German fleet therefore passed over them without being attacked. It was in those days the habit of submarines to lie on the bottom after charging their batteries. The disadvantage of this practice was that they could not receive wireless signals. Later submarines were required to read wireless routines several times each night. After the Battle of Jutland submarine patrols became more permanent and the boats relieved each other on station, yet they could still only report when on the surface and might be kept down by the destroyers of the escort for some time. On the other hand a successful submarine attack was certain to cause the Germans to break wireless silence and then the D/F stations could get to work.

VI

The Last Phase of the Great War, 1917-18

THE MAIN SYSTEM of wireless communication for the Royal Navy did not alter very much during the last two years of the war. The arc transmitter was used more as heterodyne receivers were fitted throughout the fleet and the thermionic valve receivers came steadily into use to replace the crystal in standard receivers. Three valve transmitting sets of low power were also introduced, one for fire control between ships, one for communicating with aircraft and a third for use in fleet submarines. There was also a great expansion of wireless in the anti-submarine fleet of trawlers, in drifters and in motor launches for which a simple set was designed. Although reliable valves were now in production they were still of limited value in transmitters as the largest produced had a power of only 400 watts. Experiments were proceeding with a valve of 1,500 watts, but large valve transmitters to replace the spark and the arc were still a long way away. The most powerful and modern ship transmitter was now the Type 18 which was an arc set of 25 kw. This was only fitted in the latest ships and a more normal outfit for a battleship was the Type 1 (14 kw.) spark transmitter backed up by a Type 16 (3 kw.) arc. A Type 3 (1 kw.) spark auxiliary set complete with receiver was also carried as well as a Type 13 'after-action' simple spark with plain aerial for use if the main sets were destroyed in battle. In addition two crystal and one valve receivers were carried as well as a valve heterodyne set to receive arc transmission. At the other end of the scale a destroyer would normally carry a Type 15 (3 kw.) arc and a Type 4 (1 kw.) spark transmitter with one crystal receiver and one valve heterodyne receiver. The German development of wireless in their navy was broadly comparable with the British (Note 1).

In 1917 the British decided to dispense with the Fessenden system of sound telegraphy in ships of the fleet and only a few sets were kept for further experiments. Its future use was to be confined to submarines and their attendant vessels. Patrol submarines disliked signalling by this means in enemy waters as it was liable to give away their position to the enemy. It was still considered valuable when submarines were deployed on defensive patrol lines but the main use was for the fast submarines of the 'K' class which operated in flotillas with the Grand fleet. The flotilla leaders of the 'K' class were surface ships which kept touch with the rest of the fleet by wireless and used Fessenden to communicate with their submarines once they had submerged. In September 1917 a M. Langevin from France visited the signal school with his piezo-electric principle for supersonic underwater sound telegraphy. With this system it should be possible to signal without being heard by the enemy. Interest was shown but no system had been developed before the end of the war.

When the United States entered the war, on 6 April 1917, their radio equipment was of first-class quality and generally of longer range than that used by the rest of the Allies. The spark had been generally superseded by the arc and to a certain extent ashore by the Alexanderson alternator. In the organization of wireless communications the Americans were, however, a very long way behind the combatants. Radio communications in the U.S. Navy were still simply an extension of the shore telegraph service for conveying messages when required. The broadcast system of sending information to ships at sea was unknown and the direct method requiring an acknowledgement was still the normal one. In radio security they were further behind still and their communications were a gift to the simplest radio intelligence service.

The U.S. Navy battle squadron, under Admiral Rodman, which was sent to reinforce the Grand fleet was therefore refitted completely with British equipment and followed British procedure entirely. Most of the other U.S. naval forces sent to Europe were, however, intended to combat the U-boat and consisted of destroyers, submarine chasers and aircraft which did not need to work so closely with the British; in consequence these vessels kept their own apparatus. The U.S. Navy extensively fitted and used a voice radio, which had a valve transmitter and five frequencies, any one of which could be selected by pressing a button. With this set a far more efficient system of communication was introduced for convoys and hunting groups than had so far been used in the war. A second innovation produced by the U.S. Navy was the shipborne radio direction finder. They had experimented with such equipment in battleships and cruisers during the neutrality period and by the summer of 1917 had produced a set for destroyers. It proved of great value not only for obtaining a bearing when the U-boats transmitted but for checking relative positions in hunting groups and with convoys. American direction finding equipment was also set up ashore in France for use against the U-boats, and on the American coast for helping convoys to make a landfall in thick weather.

The U.S. Navy was also noted for its very powerful long-range shore stations. During the neutrality period, the U.S. Navy had practically completed their transpacific chain of high-power stations. With the opening of the Panama Canal they built a 100 kw. arc station at Darien which could communicate direct with Arlington, Virginia. The original plan for five stations to relay messages across the Pacific was cut down in 1915 to a 200 kw. arc station at San Diego, California, and two 350 kw. arc stations at Pearl Harbor and Cavite in the Philippines. The stations at Guam and Samoa, which were thereby by-passed, were given 30 kw. arcs for local communication. These stations were finally commissioned during 1917 and made the U.S. Navy independent of cable communication in the Pacific as well as the Atlantic. Communications across the Atlantic were also improved by taking over the German Telefunken station at Sayville and other civilian long-range stations.

During the last two years of the war, radio intelligence gained some notable information and continued to be of immense value to the Allies. German counter-measures also had their successes and radio warfare continued up to the end. Soon after the October sortie of the High Seas fleet in 1916 radio intelligence detected another German move. It was believed that it threatened the southern area and defensive precautions were taken. In fact it was a move of twenty-four destroyers of the High Seas fleet to Zeebrugge; by keeping close to the Dutch coast they evaded the Harwich force which was at sea, and arrived safely at their destination. When this German force raided the Dover barrage on the night of October 26–27 and the Downs on November 23, no prior warning whatever was received; also in the autumn of 1916 the Germans sent the raiders *Möwe*, *Seeadler* and *Wolf* out on to the trade-routes. The departure of these ships was made in great secrecy and radio intelligence failed to provide any useful information. In consequence they were not intercepted (Note 2). In November 1916, however, *U30* broke down on the way home. She met *U20* who escorted her but both U-boats ran aground in fog on the Danish coast. They reported their plight by wireless and the signals were also intercepted by Room 40. The British submarine *J1* on patrol in the vicinity was alerted and succeeded in torpedoing the German battleships *Grosser Kurfürst* and *Kronprinz* which had been sent out to cover the salvage vessels.

In January 1917 radio intelligence again revealed that a German destroyer flotilla was leaving for Zeebrugge. In consequence it was intercepted by the Harwich force, but after some night skirmishing managed to get through. In the late spring and summer of 1917 radio intelligence helped to destroy two Zeppelins scouting in the North Sea. The D/F stations were able to plot the positions of Zeppelins quite accurately and in April it was decided to try to destroy them whenever their patrols came within range of the new H12 flying-boats now stationed at East Coast bases. On May 14 an H12 flying-boat from Yarmouth destroyed *L22* off Terschelling and on June 5 another from Felixstowe shot down *L43* off Vleiland. After these two successes the Zeppelins adopted new tactics and were ordered to fly above the flying-boats' ceiling all the time. Thereafter no more were shot down, although flying high meant they were practically useless as scouts.

In October 1917 radio intelligence again gave indications of some German movement in the North Sea but could not find out what it was. Very large forces of cruisers and destroyers were sent out on patrol but failed to intercept the new and very fast German cruisers *Brummer* and *Bremse* which attacked a Norwegian convoy and sank nine merchant ships and their escort of two destroyers. The destroyers were not even able to get away an enemy report, and so the enemy returned to

Germany unscathed. In November, partly through radio intelligence but also on reports of British submarines, a superior British force succeeded in bringing the German Second Scouting Group to action in the Heligoland Bight. On this occasion the Germans were able to escape into the minefields and only a trawler was sunk. Then in December the Germans decided to make a two-pronged attack with destroyers on two convoys, the first off the East Coast of England and the second on its way to Norway. The first attack was misled by a British wireless signal intercepted and misinterpreted by the German destroyers, and they only sank two independent merchant ships. The second attack caught another Norwegian convoy and destroyed it with one of its escort of two destroyers, but not before one of them had made an enemy report to the Commander-in-Chief. Both groups of enemy destroyers escaped the ships sent to intercept them and returned to their bases. This disaster was mainly because radio intelligence obtained no warning of the sailing of the German ships at all. This was becoming frequent and in February 1918 German destroyers again raided the Dover barrage without any warning being received.

In April 1918 Admiral Scheer planned an operation with the whole High Seas fleet which had not put to sea in a single body except for exercises for nearly eighteen months. The two German successes against the Norwegian convoys had led to the British strengthening their escorts. They also provided covering forces as large as a division of battleships detached from the Grand fleet. Intelligence of this practice had reached Admiral Scheer through the reports of U-boats passing through the area and he determined to try and cut off and destroy not only the convoy but its covering force as well. Elaborate precautions were taken to defeat the British radio intelligence system and the fleet was concentrated as though for an exercise.

The High Seas fleet sailed on April 22 and set its course northward in dense fog, keeping rigid wireless silence. British radio intelligence obtained no information whatever of the movement. Admiral Scheer was forced by the dense fog to anchor for a time and succeeded in doing so without using wireless, a considerable achievement. When he got under way again, however, he was sighted by the British submarine *J6*. The orders to the captain of the submarine told him that British forces might operate in his area on minelaying missions and he was convinced that this was what was happening. He therefore made no enemy report at all and allowed the whole High Seas fleet to pass him on a northerly course. This was, of course, an amazing stroke of luck for Admiral Scheer, but the wheel of fortune took a turn. One of the propellers of the battle cruiser *Moltke* actually fell off, the turbines raced, the gearbox disintegrated and a large piece of metal flew through a condenser and flooded an engine room.

The *Moltke*, with the rest of Admiral Hipper's First Scouting Group was off the Norwegian coast at the time and her speed was reduced to six knots. Admiral Hipper, unwilling to cancel the operation, sent the *Moltke* back to join the main body of the High Seas fleet. He did not wish to break wireless silence and so despatched the destroyer *G103* to tell Admiral Scheer what had happened. The *Moltke* soon lost all power and came to a standstill; she then reported her predicament by wireless. The British D/F stations heard her at once and had her position fixed within minutes. The spate of German signals which followed showed clearly that the whole High Seas fleet was out and that it was off the south-west corner of Norway. Admiral Scheer now ordered the battleship *Oldenburg* to take the *Moltke* in tow and turned back for the Heligoland Bight. The Grand fleet at once put to sea but the High Seas fleet was able to pass ahead of it into the shelter of the minefields. There was just time to order the British submarine *E42* to an intercepting position and she succeeded in hitting the luckless *Moltke* with a torpedo and damaging her still more. Nevertheless the High Seas fleet escaped and this was the last time during the war that it put to sea.

The tight radio security the Germans adopted on this occasion had its dangers for them as not enough information about the operation was passed to the U-boats. On April 24 *U19*, returning from patrol, had sighted the German First Scouting Group and reported them as British cruisers. This might have given the whole operation away but in fact the British had already received the *Moltke*'s signal and knew the High Seas fleet was out.

As early as November 1917 the Germans had become suspicious about the extremely good British intelligence which had led to the action in the Heligoland Bight when their Second Scouting Group had been surprised by a superior force.

They were still inclined to blame careless talk in high places rather than their wireless security but nevertheless they took greater precautions. The success of these measures in the sortie of April 1918 had been complete. A radio intelligence system however good can always be rendered impotent by not using wireless at all and this is how they succeeded. The German radio intelligence service had always suffered from a dearth of material to work on but had also improved considerably. They were able to decipher portions of British messages and there is no doubt that when the High Seas fleet emerged for its final sortie, Admiral Scheer expected Neumünster to be able to tell him if the Grand fleet put to sea.

Neumünster, however, often gave incomplete or misleading information. In April 1918 they believed that considerable parts of the Grand fleet had been moved south to provide escorts in the anti-submarine campaign and that the Grand fleet crews had been depleted to man anti-submarine vessels. They had deduced this from something they had picked up telling them that the old Third Battle Squadron had been paid off. Their deduction was however wrong; the Third Battle Squadron consisted of pre-'Dreadnoughts' and was not part of the Grand fleet. Moreover, they were unable to obtain any indication of two facts of vital importance to the April 1918 sortie. One was the date and time of sailing of the Norwegian convoys and the other was the transfer of the Grand fleet base from Scapa Flow to Rosyth.

The decreased effectiveness of British radio intelligence against surface ships in the North Sea was, to a certain extent, offset by their submarines with their new wireless transmitters. The constant patrols at the exits of the swept channels out of the Heligoland Bight admittedly failed to sight the light forces which attacked the Norwegian convoys but they sighted the last three sorties of the High Seas fleet itself. That no enemy report was sent on the final occasion was no fault of the strategy or the communication system.

The failures to predict the sorties of surface ships in 1917 and 1918 were certainly not due to any falling off in the efficiency of the British radio intelligence system. It was now more efficient than it had ever been. It was at its peak and comprised some forty wireless stations manned by 800 men. The Germans towards the end changed their cipher keys daily but still Room

40 was able to cope. During the summer of 1917, in order to improve the liaison with operations, Room 40 was developed into a full intelligence centre. The main target was now no longer the High Seas fleet, and this, coupled with much less traffic to work on, probably contributed to the failure to detect the April 1918 sortie. Since the autumn of 1916 it was the German U-boat campaign which had claimed their prior attention.

By 1916 the German U-boats' wireless sets had been considerably improved. On the 25 April 1916 the recall of the U-boats attacking trade west of the British Isles had had to be broadcast by *U45*, sent out specially for this purpose. Next month *U20* set up a record by communicating with Germany at a distance of 770 miles. In the operations in the North Sea in which the U-boats co-operated with the High Seas fleet during the summer of 1916, they had no difficulty in communicating direct with Germany. The radio sets of U-boats of the medium size were of the quenched spark type but of only 1 kw. power. They were able to obtain considerable ranges, however, by the use of extensible aerial masts (Note 3). They could transmit on any of eight different wavelengths between 300 and 820 metres, using crystal receivers. When operations against commerce were resumed in the autumn of 1916, U-boats to the west of the British Isles were all able to talk direct to stations in Germany or Belgium and did so as a matter of routine. At the same time regular broadcasts were made to them from a station near Bruges and also from Nauen.

One of the main British counter-measures to the U-boats was to lay mine barriers in the Heligoland Bight, off the Flanders bases, and in defiles such as the Dover Straits and the Straits of Otranto. Later they laid the northern barrage right across from Scotland to Norway. The U-boat command were understandably anxious about the safety of boats going on patrol and so required them to signal that they had passed such dangers successfully. It was also essential that when they returned from patrol they should signal their time of arrival so that arrangements could be made to meet them with escorts and see that they entered by channels that had been swept and were clear of mines. In addition the U-boats were required to report when they left their operational areas and started on their voyages home. A U-boat therefore sent at least three wireless messages each patrol. In practice they sent very many more. It was often necessary to signal that they had laid a minefield, were short of fuel, had an engine breakdown or had run out of torpedoes or ammunition. Operational information which would be of value to other U-boats was also signalled. Areas of intense patrol activity, descriptions of Q-ships, suspected minefields and attacks on important ships were included. Often the U-boat command would order U-boats to report the situation in certain areas or to investigate traffic routes. Later when convoys were instituted, all U-boats would report sighting them and would signal among themselves in an effort to concentrate against them. The use of wireless to this extent obviously made for greatly increased operational efficiency and permitted U-boats to react to a changed situation quickly. On the other hand it gave a very great deal away. The Germans were, of course, aware of the danger of making these signals and by their standards confined them to essentials, but there is little doubt that in order to keep a tight control they used wireless more than was strictly necessary.

The British radio intelligence service had a number of ways of amassing its information. First of all it could tell how many U-boats were at sea and which ones they were by listening to their call signs. Then by using the network of direction-finding stations they could plot the position of every U-boat that made a signal. The direction-finding network had been extended to cover the western side of the British Isles with five stations in Ireland and others in Scotland, Wales and the West Country. In 1917 an Allied D/F network covered the Mediterranean too. There were twenty-one Italian stations, eleven French and eleven British in all. When to this information were added the distress messages of merchant ships attacked and the U-boat sighting reports of British patrols, the Admiralty, even if they had not been able to decipher any of the U-boats' messages, would be able to track practically every U-boat at sea. The knowledge of the U-boats' approximate positions and the number of them at sea provided one of the most important anti-submarine measures of the First World War. Ships could then be routed clear of U-boat concentrations and diverted at sea to avoid dangerous areas. Aircraft and anti-submarine vessels could be sent to hunt the U-boats or to escort ships which were threatened. One of the main reasons that the convoy system proved so successful was that it facilitated routing and diversions, shown to be necessary by radio intelligence.

In practice Room 40 could generally decipher the messages too. The U-boats used the fairly simple 'Playfair' cipher which Room 40 could usually read (Note 4). Room 40's luck held and signal books and ciphers were recovered from the wrecks of a number of U-boats in the last two years of the war. It was not only by reading the U-boats' messages that material for Room 40 was obtained. The broadcasts to submarines from Bruges and Nauen yielded plenty more. Nauen also put out propaganda stories of the U-boat campaign for the Press in neutral countries. Although carefully censored, these also filled in many gaps. In general, from these radio intelligence sources the Admiralty had a fairly complete picture not only of where all the U-boats were but what they were doing and where they were going. Other intelligence sources such as the interrogation of prisoners, the examination of salved U-boats and the work of spies in countries such as Belgium added their quota but played a small part compared to intelligence obtained from wireless.

Radio intelligence has been assessed as the most important single factor in the defeat of the U-boats in 1914–18, and as already shown the most important use of it was the general tracking of the U-boats and the routing of traffic clear of them. As an example of this tracking, in June 1917 *UC75*'s cruise was followed by the interception of four signals. She first reported in the eastern channel that she had successfully passed the Dover barrage and this established that she was at sea. Her next signal showed her approaching the coast of Ireland where, partly because her call sign showed her to be a minelayer, it was guessed that she intended to lay a field off Queenstown. The minefield was indeed laid and because of the advanced warning was promptly swept. She next reported from the Channel approaches that she was returning home and this was confirmed when she reported again after having negotiated the Dover barrage.

Sometimes radio intelligence led directly to the destruction of a U-boat. This happened many times and the degree to which wireless intercepts were responsible varied considerably. This can be illustrated by a number of examples. In April 1917 the minelayer *UC30* had been tracked as usual on her outward

journey through the Straits of Dover. Off the Scillies she
reported severe engine trouble and that she intended to head
for home by the north of Scotland. She was identified again
off the Fastnet and a week later west of the Hebrides which
showed she was only making three knots or so. Here she met
U50 who made a report of the meeting and described the plight
of *UC30* and this signal was intercepted by Room 40. Eventually
UC30 arrived in the North Sea, reported her time of arrival and
requested an escort. That same night British surface minelayers
laid a field across the swept channel she was about to use and
when *UC30* made another signal giving her position they
reinforced it with two more minefields. As a result *UC30* never
got home and almost certainly struck one of the mines which
had been laid to intercept her.

Sometimes the action taken was more direct. In May 1917
in the Mediterranean the French intercepted a signal which
located *U39* and another in which she arranged a rendezvous
with *UB50*. An aircraft was sent to the position and bombed
UB50, damaging her so that she could not dive. *UB50* had
therefore to enter Cartagena where she was interned. Such
interceptions did not always succeed: for instance, in September
1917 *U70* was damaged by a mine near the Goodwin Sands
but was able to surface and report by wireless. The signal was
received by both sides who both sent out aircraft and later
surface vessels to look for her. For two days the game of hide
and seek went on, many signals were made and at one time
Bruges warned *U70* that five British destroyers were looking
for her. They were indeed doing so, acting on *U70*'s own signals
and only missed her because *U70* gave her own position in-
accurately. Although bombed by British aircraft and depth
charged by surface vessels, *U70* was eventually towed into
Zeebrugge.

On occasion radio intelligence simply indicated the best
place to patrol. In November 1917 the route used by U-boats
north of the Sandettie shoal on their way in and out of the
Flanders bases was established by radio intelligence. On
November 1 *E52* which had been sent to patrol this route
torpedoed and sank *UC63*. The sinking of *UB71* by *ML413*
in April 1918 in the Straits of Gibraltar was also partly due to
radio intelligence. Intercepts had revealed that *UB71* had sailed
with two other U-boats from Germany for the Mediterranean

and the patrol, of which *ML413* was a part, was established especially to intercept them. In October 1918 *UB90* was tracked throughout her patrol by a number of signals which she had made. On her way back she reported her position and asked for an escort and the British were able to send the submarine *L12* to an intercepting position in which she torpedoed *UB90*.

It has already been shown how information from radio intelligence was of value in deciding where to lay minefields to catch the U-boats. In October 1917 signals to *U106* were deciphered giving her a new route home through the minefields as the one originally ordered was now dangerous. This signal was intercepted and the British submarine *E51* was sent straight out to mine the new route. In December signals to *U84* and *U96*, giving them their rendezvous to meet escorts on their way home, were intercepted and *E51* was again sent to mine the vicinity. As a result *U75* was sunk leaving for patrol, a success which the British learnt from yet another intercepted signal. In December 1917 and January 1918 new British minefields were laid at the end of one of the German searched channels. The German minesweeper *Doggerbank* was sunk after escorting *U71* to sea but the signal from other ships reporting the sinking gave the position wrongly. *UB22* escorted by the torpedo boat *S16* therefore left by the same route and both were mined, this incident being reported by another escort. All these signals were intercepted by the British who thereby knew the effect of their minelaying almost as soon as the Germans. Again in May 1918 intercepted signals addressed to *UC11* gave away the precise route of the swept channel into Zeebrugge which was promptly mined by the British.

Sometimes radio intercepts indicated technical defects in allied minefields or showed ways they could be improved. In November 1917 the laying of the Dover barrage with a new type of mine began and by the end of the year over 4,000 mines were in place. It was known that eighteen U-boats passed through the Straits in December alone and that they made the passage on the surface at night. As a result of this monitoring of wireless signals it was decided to illuminate the barrage and force the U-boats to dive into the mines. In June 1918 intercepted signals, after *U86* had been damaged by a mine in the northern barrage, showed that the antennae of the American mines were too long and so they were shortened.

On occasion, of course, the British heard of incidents of which they would have known nothing except for the decoding of enemy messages. In December 1917, for instance, they learnt that *U96* had rammed and sunk *UC69* off Cape Barfleur in the Channel.

Radio intelligence gave the British plenty of warning that the large U-cruisers of the *U151* class were going to operate in the area of the Azores and the Canary Islands. In October 1917 they tracked *U156* through the North Sea and out into the Atlantic. In November they intercepted signals between Germany and her Naval Attaché in Madrid arranging for *U156* and *U157* to meet a small schooner at Ferro Island in the Canaries to take on a cargo of a rare metal needed in Germany. The British submarine *E48* was sent to keep the rendezvous and succeeded in hitting *U156* with a torpedo but it failed to explode. Three months later signals were intercepted giving a rendezvous between *U153*, *U154* and *U62* south-west of Cape St Vincent. The British submarine *E35* had just returned to Gibraltar from patrol but was sent at full speed to the position. Here on May 11 she torpedoed and sank *U154*. On 22 April 1918 a signal intercepted from Nauen indicated that a U-boat was being sent to the American coast. Another intercepted signal showed that this was *U151* which had already sailed and was being tracked. The U.S. Navy were warned in time to take precautions. They were also told that it was vital that nothing should be done which would show the Germans that the Allies had advance information. *U151* was followed by a number of other U-boats to the American coast and the British were generally able to give the U.S. Navy advance warning.

Sometimes it was possible to use a greater degree of subterfuge. In the summer of 1917 the British were aware that the Germans could read their comparatively simple mine-clearance code. They also realized that minefields were being laid by German submarines to a regular schedule. In June 1917 *UC42* laid a field off Waterford and it was expected that it would, in the ordinary course, be renewed in August. It was therefore announced in the mine-clearance code that it had been swept but it was left intact. On August 4 *UC44* arrived and ran on one of *UC42*'s mines. *UC44* was subsequently salvaged and her signal books and radio sets were recovered.

On 21 October 1918 the Germans halted the war on

commerce and recalled all their U-boats. The High Seas fleet was at this time planning a final sortie under Admiral Hipper, its new Commander-in-Chief. The sortie was to take the form of a raid into the Thames estuary in the hope that small British units would put to sea and be destroyed in detail. The plan required the co-operation of every U-boat that could reach the area in time. Room 40 was in some disarray as the Germans had just introduced a new book of call signs and it was proving difficult to identify the U-boats, but the number of U-boats at sea and their whereabouts were worked out. From the tracking of the unidentified U-boats the plan began to be revealed to the British, showing a number of patrol lines off the bases of the Grand fleet. On October 29 the High Seas fleet was ordered to raise steam, but suddenly to Room 40's astonishment they relapsed into plain language and it was clear that a mutiny had taken place.

The Germans fully realized before the end of the war that the British intelligence system knew far more than it should have done. They made careful investigations and were still convinced that their ciphers were unbreakable and that this could not be the reason. They realized that wireless signals at sea gave away some information and tried to cut them down. They felt, however, that if they stopped all signals from U-boats they would lose control and the rate at which they sank ships would fall off drastically. The British continued with every effort to make the Germans believe that their excellent intelligence was due to traitors and spies and the Germans were inclined to believe them, some of them going as far as to suspect Admiral von Tirpitz himself.

Radio intelligence was certainly the most important electrical or electronic factor in the defeat of the U-boats but it was not the only one. At the outbreak of the war the only anti-submarine detecting devices were visual or physical. In other words the submarine itself, its periscope, bubbles or oil leaks had to be sighted or actual contact with the submarine hull had to be made in order to find it. The physical devices took the form of nets of various kinds, of contact mines and of weapons towed deep behind a ship which exploded when they touched the submarine. Before long the British considered trying to detect the presence of a submarine by its magnetism but very soon found that this would only be discernable at a very short range. They then tried to listen to the noises made by a submarine and find its position that way. This method showed some promise and microphones underwater were discovered to be capable of hearing a submarine's propellers at considerable distances.

The Royal Navy's systematic investigation of the detection of submarines by underwater sound dates from January 1915 when they began to make experiments in the Firth of Forth. In June they set up an experimental station at Hawkcraig and by the end of the year had developed a portable non-directional hydrophone which could hear a submarine at three miles when lowered over the side of a stopped and silent ship in calm weather. Two hundred of these hydrophones were ordered but they were only capable of telling that a submarine was in the area and had no way of pinpointing it so as to guide an attack by depth charges. A fixed shore hydrophone for harbour defence was also produced but probably most progress was made in designing hydrophones for submarines themselves. In March 1916 *B3* was fitted with a fixed plate hydrophone on each bow and she was able to obtain bearings of propeller noises within two degrees by pointing the bow of the submarine towards the target and comparing the strength of the noise in the two hydrophones. A similar system was tried out in a drifter but without much success as the hydrophones were too close to the surface.

On 6 July 1916 the motor-boat *Salmon* off Lowestoft thought she heard a U-boat on her hydrophone very loud and close. She dropped a depth charge and wreckage came up. At the time she was believed to have sunk *UC7* which was known to have been lost in this period; modern research, however, shows conclusively that *UC7* was mined off Zeebrugge. Nevertheless, the incident encouraged the development of hydrophones and by the end of the year a portable directional hydrophone had been designed and 800 of these were manufactured and distributed during the next five months. At this point there were no less than 2,500 non-directional hydrophones in service. It was intended to outfit large auxiliary patrol vessels with two portable hydrophones, one directional and one non-directional, as well as two plate hydrophones built into the bow. Small patrol vessels would simply have the portable versions and submarines only the plate hydrophones. Destroyers were too noisy to have any hydrophones at all. In January 1917 progress was sufficient for the Admiralty to form special hunting flotillas equipped with hydrophones. They stationed four of these flotillas consisting of six motor launches each in the English Channel during June and shortly afterwards another twelve flotillas of four trawlers each all round the British Isles.

When the U.S.A. declared war in April 1917 they had already set up an experimental station to develop the hydrophone and the Fessenden Company had soon produced a sensitive microphone (Note 5). They too discarded any idea of magnetic detection as of too short a range for practical purposes. In June the British and French pooled their ideas with the Americans although development continued separately in the various countries. The early directional hydrophones were also lowered over the side of the ship which still had to stop to use them. They were then rotated by hand to obtain the bearing of the noise, but a single hydrophone only indicated the direction of a submarine and gave little idea of range. To obtain a position two or more hydrophone-fitted vessels had to plot their bearings.

In practice there were many difficulties. Not only did the ship using the hydrophone have to stop but she also had to stop every machine on board that made a noise. Every ship in the vicinity had to stop too so as not to mask the sound of the submarine. The hydrophones could only get results in calm weather as even the lapping of waves against the ship's side was enough to interfere. The hydrophone flotillas had to be well practised on live submarine targets if they were to achieve results. They had also to have good communications and be well trained to triangulate the bearings, but despite these problems the hunting flotillas believed they detected submarines almost daily and often followed them for hours on end. Hunts were often spoilt by the noise of passing traffic, by deteriorating weather or by the submarines sitting on the bottom and remaining silent.

The hunting flotillas generally proceeded in line abreast about a mile apart, steaming at slow speed for ten minutes or so and then all stopping together to listen (Note 6). Even when strong hydrophone effect was heard it was not easy to attack. The attacking ship had to haul in her hydrophone and steam fast over the last known position of the submarine to drop her depth charges. The noise of her screws then drowned the noise of the submarine in all other hydrophones which could not therefore help to keep track of the U-boat as the attacking ship approached. With the directional hydrophone, therefore, patrol vessels could do more than just detect that a submarine was in the vicinity and by cross bearings obtain its rough position. It was seldom possible to pinpoint the submarine in less than a 400-yard circle and so no depth-charge attack had much chance of success. It was in any case very difficult to pursue a submarine as it took so long to haul in the hydrophone, get under way and then stop and get it out again. About the only claim that can be made for the early hydrophones is that by detecting the presence of U-boats in certain areas it was sometimes possible to deduce that they had laid mines.

To try and design a hydrophone which could be used with the ship under way a towed version was developed in both Great Britain and the U.S.A. Early experiments in the United Kingdom were sufficiently successful for the Admiralty to think that they had made a breakthrough. They began to plan a barrier right across the North Sea from Scotland to Norway using a large number of patrol vessels towing hydrophones. In the late autumn of 1917 this new 'fish' hydrophone, as it was called, came into service. It was a torpedo shaped vessel twelve feet long and eighteen inches in diameter which was weighted and towed deep behind a patrol vessel on a wire 130 feet long. Inside it was a rotating directional hydrophone controlled electrically from a silent cabinet on board the towing vessel. Nothing was audible with the towing vessel's engines running but when they were stopped a submarine could be heard at four miles and a bearing within five to ten degrees obtained. The advantage of the 'fish' hydrophone was that it could be used immediately the towing vessel's engines were stopped and before the ship slowed down, whereas with the portable directional hydrophone it took from five to eight minutes from the order to stop engines before the hydrophone could be lowered into the water. The 'fish' hydrophone certainly made it possible to pursue a submarine but it still could not be used to attack. In practice the towed hydrophone proved only marginally superior to the type which was lowered over the side. In the U.S.A. types of towed hydrophones were also used from small airships or blimps and a special hydrophone was designed for use from a seaplane after it had landed on the water. Special hydrophones were still used for harbour defence but a more effective device for this purpose proved to be a new magnetic method of detection in which short range did not matter so much. This was a large loop of wire laid on the bottom at the harbour entrance which proved able to detect the magnetic disturbance when a ship or submarine passed over it.

By October 1917 the British had twelve shore hydrophone stations in service with eleven more projected. There were 1,201 yachts, trawlers, drifters and motor launches fitted with hydrophones in the auxiliary patrol in the Royal Navy alone and the U.S. Navy had a substantial fleet of sub-chasers. The hydrophone flotillas were used to try and clear the way ahead of convoys as well as to follow up reports of sightings of U-boats and to hunt in areas where merchant ships had been sunk. They were also used in barrages such as the one across the St George's Channel or the Straits of Otranto. Yet results in general were very disappointing and a submarine was seldom detected. In December 1917 the admiral commanding at Milford Haven came to the conclusion that it would be better to use the hydrophone ships as escorts and that hydrophone patrols were of little value. The Admiralty, on the other hand, considered that even if they sank no U-boats, they harassed them and even this was helpful.

Of the thirty-five U-boats sunk by patrols during the war, the vast majority of successes were the result of sighting either the U-boat on the surface, its periscope, an oil slick or air bubbles. Hydrophones were used on a number of occasions when U-boats were sunk but cannot be said to have done more than assist. In April 1918 *ML413*, on patrol in the Straits of Gibraltar at night, was lying stopped and listening. She heard *UB71* approaching on the surface on her way from Germany to the Adriatic. Very shortly afterwards *UB71* came in sight and a collision was avoided by a few feet. The U-boat then dived and *ML413* dropped four depth charges which were close enough to sink *UB71*. The depth charges were, however, dropped not by hydrophone but by the line of the submarine's wake before diving. In July 1918 *UB107* was sighted off Scarborough by a motor-launch, who summoned trawlers and an armed yacht to hunt. Later the U-boat broke surface, was seen and heavily depth charged by three trawlers. Then the trawler *Calvia* heard the U-boat on its hydrophone and the armed yacht *Vanessa* dropped more depth charges. Later still, yet more depth charges were dropped on oil and air bubbles. Which of these attacks destroyed *UB107* is not known but it is just possible that it was the one which was directed by hydrophone.

In August 1918 *UC49* was damaged off Start Point by the explosion of one of her own mines and this attracted the destroyer *Opossum* and patrol vessels to the spot. Hydrophones were used but *UC49* countered them by sitting on the bottom for some hours. She was however pinned down and every time she tried to move she was heard and more depth charges were dropped. Finally she broke surface, dived again and was then sunk by depth charges dropped on the swirl.

In August 1918 the Folkestone end of the Dover barrage consisted of mines controlled from the shore. These were designed to be used in co-operation with a shore-controlled hydrophone. On the 12th *UC71*, returning from operations to the west, submerged and tried to pass the barrage close to Folkestone. She was heard on the hydrophone and a line of mines was fired. *UC71* was damaged but managed to get through to Zeebrugge. On the 24th *UB103* returning from the Bay of Biscay took the same course. She was also heard and a line of mines was again fired. This time the U-boat was destroyed. Right at the end of the war *UB116* was given orders to penetrate into Scapa Flow and attack the Grand fleet itself. She made the attempt on October 28 but was detected by the magnetic loops and also destroyed by the explosion of a line of controlled mines.

It was obvious that the hydrophone as designed in the First World War could never be a real answer to the submarine and by the end of the war little advance with the apparatus in service had been made either in Great Britain or America. The German submarine campaign was indeed defeated by the Allies but the contribution of the hydrophone cannot be classed as higher than a useful bonus.

Just before the armistice some experimental progress was made. It was obvious that a prime requirement was to produce a submarine detecting device that could be used by destroyers and convoy escorts, which could be used under way and with the help of which an attack could be made with depth charges. The U.S. Navy had introduced the C-tube soon after they entered the war; this was a rotating hydrophone sticking through a ship's bottom. When all was quiet with the ship stopped it worked, but by no means solved the problem. Right at the end of the war they mounted four sensitive Fessenden oscillators in the bow of a destroyer but it was found that she still had to stop to use them. Another important requirement for a depth charge attack was for some method of finding the range. The British tried a transmitting oscillator using M. Langevin's piezo-electric principle in the hope of getting an echo from the submarine and by timing it, thus obtaining the range. They had not got beyond the stage of lowering a single transmitting oscillator over the side before the end of the war. With the armistice, co-operation between Great Britain and the U.S.A. ceased and they followed their own separate experiments.

The new British ideas on searchlights had been developed in the year following the Battle of Jutland and this piece of equipment began to be fitted in the fleet in July 1917. The new system consisted of a more robust 36 in. searchlight than those designed in 1913, fitted with a Harrison type lamp and an iris shutter. A new way to mount the searchlight was introduced in which it was put on top of a special splinter-proof tower. Beneath the light in this tower were the manipulators who kept the searchlight on the target looking through slits. The target was indicated to them by an electrical indicator of the Evershed type controlled from the bridge. All ships of the Grand fleet were fitted with these searchlights by the end of the war, battleships and battle cruisers generally having eight 36 in. lights and cruisers two to four 36 in. lights. Destroyers had a single 24 in. searchlight as before except that it had a Harrison type lamp and iris shutter.

The importance of searchlights undoubtedly declined with the introduction of starshell. The British brought in starshells (Note 7) after the Battle of Jutland when they believed they were used by the Germans. They were fired from guns of the secondary or anti-aircraft armaments. Starshells had the great advantage that they did not give away the position of the ship using them. If badly aimed they would, of course, illuminate friendly ships and once fired could not be switched off like a searchlight. Whereas a searchlight could illuminate the enemy at once, a starshell took time to burst and then it might not be in the right place. The 1918 Gunnery and Torpedo Orders for the Grand fleet clearly envisage starshells and searchlights being used in combination to secure the best results.

Probably the greatest extension of the use of electric power in warships during the last two years of the war was in the U.S. Navy. The new 'California' class battleships laid down at the end of 1916 and beginning of 1917 had turbo-electric propulsion. There were two huge turbo-generators totalling 37,000 h.p. which drove four alternating current motors at 3,400 volts, one for each shaft. The advantage claimed was a flexibility in design which made better underwater protection possible. The shafts were much shorter than for steam turbines and the turbo-generators were in tandem on the midship line with the boilers outside them. All were in separate watertight compartments. It was claimed that the weight and space needed was the same as for steam turbines and that at cruising speeds, when only one turbo-generator was required, the system was more economical. There were additional advantages; for instance, the propellers did not race in a seaway. These ships were practically 'all-electric' in auxiliaries too. All the guns, ammunition hoists, capstans, pumps and steering gear were electric, power being supplied by four 300 kw. auxiliary turbo-generators. The U.S Navy kindly supplied the British Admiralty with full particulars. They were received with interest but the principle was not followed in the Royal Navy.

   Although the British were not interested in electric propulsion, their new ships made ample use of electric power. The post-Jutland design battle cruiser, H.M.S. *Hood*, had eight 200 kw. generators, four of which were driven by reciprocating engines, two by turbines and two by diesel engines. She had 3,300 internal electric lights (Note 8), while eighty-nine large auxiliaries such as pumps, winches and lifts and thirty-six small, from a saw bench to a mincer in the galley, were electrically driven. There were also 210 ventilating fans and sixty-three other alternators and generators for various purposes. The German 'Baden' class battleships completed in 1917 had more power still with four 400 kw. turbo-generators and two 300 kw. diesel generators.

·   ·   ·   ·   ·   ·

In this last chapter dealing with the First World War, the time has come to summarize the effect of the electron on sea power during the struggle. Clearly the main influence during the First World War was in the sphere of communications, and other influences had a comparatively minor role. The telegraph cable was of exceptional value to the Allies. It proved astonishingly invulnerable in the hands of those who commanded the sea but useless to those who didn't. It had the great advantage that messages could not, with only rare exceptions, be intercepted by the enemy. Communication was therefore immune to crypto- or traffic-analysis and gave nothing away. Wireless telegraphy had the great advantage over the cable, on the other hand, that it could contact ships at sea and could broadcast messages simultaneously to a large number of stations. It could also send messages across hostile territory which was of particular service to the Germans.

Wireless was of very great value for the control of naval forces at sea and, taking all factors into account, it proved of more value to the Allies than to the Germans. Wireless, however, had the very great disadvantage that it could be intercepted by the enemy and subjected to analysis and even the breaking of codes. The fears of the early years that it would be easily jammed or counterfeited did not materialize. Without doubt it provided a better source of intelligence than had ever been available before.

The effect of the electron on seapower was generally to make conventional methods of waging war more effective. In other words it did not produce a new dimension in maritime warfare as did the submarine but it greatly increased, for instance, the effectiveness of a battle fleet. It is also clear that it aided the stronger fleet, the anti-submarine campaign and the raider hunters more than the weaker fleet, the U-boats or the raiders themselves. For Great Britain its effect was the opposite to that of the two other great innovations of the twentieth century. The electron helped those who commanded the sea, whereas the submarine and aircraft were of more assistance to the weaker power.

VII

Between the Wars, 1919-39

AT THE END of the First World War long-distance communication by wireless depended, as it had from the beginning, on long waves and high power. In this the U.S.A. now held the lead. From their 350 kw. arc transmitters in the Pacific chain they had gone on to a new 500 kw. transmitter at Annapolis and a 1,000 kw. station building in France for the U.S. Navy (Note 1). All these transmitters were arcs which, although they transmitted continuous waves, were by no means perfect. They emitted harmonics and it was difficult to keep their frequency steady with the result that they transmitted a broader wave than was desirable (Note 2). The high-frequency alternator on the other hand transmitted only one narrow frequency; it was ideal for large shore stations which operated on a fixed wavelength but was not suitable for use in ships (Note 3).

In 1919 Marconi suggested to the British Government that the pre-war Imperial Wireless scheme should be revived, but he proposed that it should be revived in a completely different form. Instead of a chain of stations relaying messages from one to another, he recommended low-frequency stations in Great Britain, South Africa, India, Australia and Canada, sufficiently powerful to communicate directly with each other. He was encouraged to suggest this, as the year before his 200 kw. timed spark transmitter at Caernarvon had been received in Australia on 14,000 m. (21·4 kc/s). In 1921 a new 100 kw. valve transmitter at the same station had also reached Australia. Valves were still of very limited power and the 100 kw. of this station was obtained by connecting fifty-four of them in parallel (Note 4). The Imperial Wireless Chain was delayed by arguments about whether it should be operated by governments or private enterprise. Finally a compromise was arrived at. The G.P.O. in Great Britain began to build a large 500 kw. valve transmitter at Rugby, and Marconi obtained contracts to build the stations in Australia and South Africa.

While the new Imperial Wireless Chain was building, doubts began to be felt about the very principles of its design. The increase in the use of wireless in general, especially for broadcasting, made more channels of communication imperative. About the only way to do this was to extend the radio spectrum upwards into the higher frequencies. The higher frequencies had always been of limited use as their range did not seem to extend much beyond the horizon and so they could only be used for short distances. In the post-war period there were large numbers of amateur radio enthusiasts, and to keep them happy and at the same time prevent them interfering with serious users they were allocated the higher frequencies on which they were allowed to transmit on low power.

In the early twenties these amateurs noticed that their transmissions on high frequencies not only extended to the horizon but often reappeared at considerable distances beyond. The same effect was noticed by the Marconi Company when experimenting with high-frequency short-range radio links. In 1921 amateurs in Great Britain and the U.S.A. sent messages across the Atlantic with a transmitter of only 1 kw. on a wavelength of 230 m. (1,300 kc/s). Two years later amateurs were using high frequency and communicating freely across the American continent and throughout Europe. These discoveries stimulated research by the large radio companies, notably by Marconi. In 1923 Marconi in a voyage in his yacht *Elletra* from Falmouth to the Cape Verde Islands received 1 kw. transmissions from Poldhu on 97 m. (3,092 kc/s) at 1,250 miles by day and 2,230 by night. The next year a 17 kw. transmission from Poldhu on 92 m. was heard in Australia. World-wide ranges were therefore possible on the higher frequencies with quite moderate power, but the problem was that reception was intermittent and there appeared to be substantial 'skip distances' in which nothing could be heard at all.

Nevertheless by 1924 Marconi felt he knew enough about high-frequency wireless to be sure that a reliable long-range system was possible. He therefore recommended that the low-frequency high-power concept for an Imperial Wireless scheme should be scrapped and a high-frequency system substituted. Canada, South Africa and Australia followed this suggestion but the construction of Rugby by the G.P.O. was continued partly because it was nearly completed and partly because the Royal Navy had an interest in it for broadcasting to their ships all over the world. High frequency with its skip distances was clearly unsuited for this purpose. The British Government, however, signed a contract with Marconi for a high-frequency station for communication with Canada. By 1926 direct and reliable high-frequency communication was established between Great Britain and Canada, Australia, India and South Africa. The Marconi Company was mainly responsible for this system

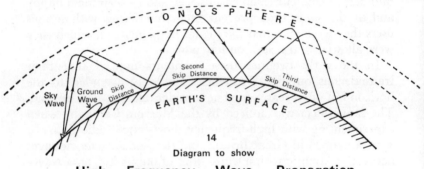

14
Diagram to show

High   Frequency   Wave   Propagation

and the stations had fixed directional aerials which concentrated the transmissions in the right direction. The frequencies, generally different at night, that were found to be best were used and so for these fixed services skip distances did not matter. The advantages of this system were that much cheaper and smaller transmitters could be used with very much smaller aerial systems. The extension of the radio frequency upwards also, of course, brought into use a large number of extra channels and so greatly increased the amount of traffic that could be put on the air. For the first time, therefore, wireless really rivalled the cable system for world-wide communications. From 1927 onwards few new long-wave stations were built for point-to-point services throughout the world.

By this time the behaviour and theory of high-frequency waves were well established (Diagram 14). In a high-frequency transmission two components result: the first of these is the ground wave which has a comparatively short range not much beyond the horizon; it was this wave which was received in the early days of radio. The second component is the sky wave which is refracted in the ionosphere enveloping the earth and returns to the surface and can be received again. This is the explanation of the blank space or skip distance in which it cannot be heard. The wave is then reflected by the earth up to the ionosphere again where it is yet again refracted earthwards and so on right round the globe. The length of the skip distance varies with the frequency and the height of the ionosphere, which changes from night to day. Reception at long distances is more a question of being in the position where the wave returns to earth than of transmitter power.

After the armistice the Royal Navy was reasonably satisfied with its wartime wireless organization and equipment and no great need for change seemed necessary. Economy of course meant the closing of many stations but, in general, communications continued as before. Material could, however, obviously be improved by the introduction of valve transmitters to replace the spark and the arc. The design of a new 10 kw. valve set (Type 36) was put in hand for large ships and was sent to sea for trials in H.M.S. *Antrim* in 1921; valve transmitters for destroyers and submarines (Types 37 and 38) were also designed in 1922 with ranges of 500 to 600 miles. The only other developments of this period were a low-frequency ship-borne direction-finding gear and a radio-controlled target ship. The latter was H.M.S. *Agamemnon* which came into service in the middle of 1921. Her steering gear and the fuel pumps for the boilers were radio controlled from another vessel. A clockwork device was used to stop the ship after a certain time had elapsed if the radio control failed.

Up to 1925 there was little fundamental research except to study the problem of atmospherics. In 1926 the Royal Navy began to be interested in the higher frequencies: a trial was carried out that year on three bands of frequencies, between Horsea Island wireless station and H.M.S. *Yarmouth* during a voyage to Hong Kong. Progress with high frequency in an age of economy was not particularly rapid, and as late as 1928 Rinella wireless station received a new low-frequency high-power transmitter.

By 1929 indeed Cleethorpes wireless station was able to communicate direct with Singapore, Ceylon and Halifax on high frequency (8,630 kc/s) and Horsea Island with Hong Kong (8,570 kc/s). Communication by Cleethorpes to and from Gibraltar and Malta remained on low frequency (90·2 kc/s). The Admiralty now had for the first time direct wireless communication with its foreign stations which was independent of the cable system. Broadcasts to ships were still on low frequency, that for home waters being on 88·2 kc/s sent out from Ipswich wireless station. Communication by ships with the shore also continued to be on low frequency and in home waters was on 107 kc/s. In addition a high-frequency ship-to-shore system was in use but was still largely experimental. Horsea Island kept constant watch on 8,570 kc/s for any ships in home waters or the America and West Indies, South African, New Zealand or Australian stations, which wished to pass messages direct. The number of shore wireless stations maintained by the Admiralty had by 1929 been drastically reduced. There were local wireless stations at all naval bases but there were now only Horsea, Cleethorpes and Ipswich with Pembroke in reserve in the United Kingdom. Abroad there was in general one large wireless station for each foreign naval station. The huge direction-finding network of the war was reduced to one station at the Lizard.

There was one interesting development which was discovered almost by chance. It was found that the new G.P.O. station at Rugby transmitting on 15 kc/s could be received by a totally submerged submarine without raising an aerial above the surface. This meant that submarines on patrol in war could receive messages submerged by day as well as on the surface at night. A special insulated loop aerial was designed and fitted for this purpose and special routines for submarines were instituted when required. An attempt to extend this form of communication to facilitate the operation of submarines with the fleet was, however, not a success. Signals transmitted by H.M.S. *Barham* on trials in 1930 with the submarine *Oberon* on 63·16 and 111 kc/s were unreadable.

Experiments with high frequency continued during the early thirties on frequencies as high as 20,900 kc/s and ships were fitted with the requisite transmitters and receivers. In 1930 a high-power high-frequency transmitter was being designed for

Horsea Island to provide world-wide communication. High frequency had an additional advantage in wartime in that it was found to be more secure, because it was much harder to obtain accurate bearings by direction-finding equipment especially on the 'sky wave.' For communication by ships with the shore, however, although it gave on occasion very long ranges, it was far less certain than low frequency.

The U.S. Navy had ended the war in a rather different position from the British. Apart from the battle squadron which had been attached to the Grand fleet and had used British equipment and organization, they had had no war experience with their main fleet. Their contribution had been almost entirely in air and surface anti-submarine forces. With the ending of hostilities and the onset of economy both organization and training deteriorated. Nevertheless in 1920 the U.S.S. *Ohio* was commissioned as a radio experimental ship (Note 5) and the shore radio stations were reorganized on a substantial scale. It must be remembered, however, that the U.S. Navy was also responsible for all seaward government and commercial wireless traffic which brought in revenue of about 1 million dollars a year. In the reorganization which was to meet commercial as well as naval purposes, there were no less than eleven high-power stations, thirteen medium-power and seventy-two low-power stations as well as fifty-four direction-finding stations.

Matters came to a head after the 1923 manoeuvres in the Canal Zone which brought to light many shortcomings in material, maintenance and training. There was no shortage of theory and one side kept strict radio silence and attempted to mislead the 'enemy' by using two submarines to make dummy messages. The other side allowed practically unlimited use of radio and pandemonium resulted. Enemy reports took hours rather than minutes to get through but with the curious advantage that they never even heard the opposing submarine's attempts to mislead them and so were not misled! After the manoeuvres the recently appointed Commander-in-Chief U.S. fleet made a full statement of what he considered was required to remedy matters and what was needed for the future communications of the fleet. His proposals were that battleships should have a high-power low-frequency arc transmitter backed up by a lower powered low-frequency valve transmitter (75 to

550 kc/s) and two other valve transmitters were to cover the higher frequency range (1,500 to 4,000 kc/s), one of which was to be able to use voice. There were to be eight receivers in all, one low frequency to receive broadcasts from the shore, three medium frequency for strategic fleet use and four high frequency for tactical purposes.

The Navy Department took interim measures to try to improve the situation and converted a number of spark sets to use valves. They also improved broadcasts to the fleet and produced a tentative modernization plan. The new Naval Research Laboratory which had just been established and which had taken over radio development was by now interested in high frequency. Early in 1925 the opportunity presented by a cruise of the fleet to Australia was taken to do trials. U.S.S. *Seattle* was given a high-frequency experimental transmitter working on 5,700 kc/s and she succeeded when in Melbourne in exchanging messages direct with Washington, a distance of nearly 10,000 miles. The Navy Department without delay decided to equip all its high- and medium-power shore stations with high-frequency transmitters able to work up to 18,000 kc/s. For calling the twenty-eight shore stations on high frequency, four frequencies were available for each station, one from each of the 4 mc., 8 mc., 12 mc. and 16 mc. bands; the frequency which best fitted the skip distance was used. The need to retain some high-power very low-frequency transmitters to communicate with submarines was also provided for.

At the same time the Navy Department amended their modernization plan for the fleet to include the high frequencies and produced a new frequency plan extending from 15 kc/s to 19,000 kc/s (Note 6). Finally in 1926 they produced a firm modernization plan. This was to take account of aircraft, long-range gunnery and the increase in the size of the fleet. Technically all the arc and spark transmitters and all receivers were to be replaced by sets using valves. Sets were to be of navy design, standardized and able to cover the high-frequency band up to 20,000 kc/s. All naval wireless equipment was subsequently designed at the Naval Research Laboratory, partly to meet specialized needs but also because industry was too busy selling private radio receivers for entertainment. Components were, however, still purchased from industry.

The modernization was to be gradual and paid for out of

annual budgets as ships came in for refit. In 1927 the fitting of high-frequency transmitters in some ships was slowed down and they kept their old low-frequency transmitters for a bit longer. This was caused by doubts about the efficiency of high frequency. By 1928, however, all spark and arc transmitters had gone (Note 7). In 1929 the 1926 plan was revised to take account of a demand for more radio channels and the consequent need for more equipment. It emphasized the use of high frequencies and so new and improved radio sets, all using valves, were embodied in the plan. In 1930 alone 327 new type sets were installed in the fleet and the modernization continued during 1931 and 1932. Most of this equipment was still in use at the beginning of the Second World War.

At the end of the war the British had closed down Room 40 and, as already related, had paid off the vast majority of their listening and direction-finding stations. Everyone involved was sworn to secrecy and the policy was to try to conceal the incredible advantage that had been obtained from radio intelligence. Even the official history of the war had to be very reticent on the subject and in consequence was the poorer for it. Indeed, some facts such as the sailing of the Grand fleet before the High Seas fleet for the Battle of Jutland did not really make sense. The hope, of course, was that in a future war, radio intelligence especially cryptography could be used again. Sir Alfred Ewing, then Vice-Chancellor of Edinburgh University, was nearly arrested when he referred to the work of Room 40 in a speech in 1932. The Admiralty also refused to allow Admiral Hall to publish the parts of his memoirs which dealt with cryptography.

The British Foreign Office had acquired a taste for the activities of Room 40 during the war when they had been supplied with extremely important information. They therefore set up an equivalent organization to Room 40 with the intention of using it in peacetime and some of its personnel were re-employed. In 1922 Lord Curzon, the Foreign Secretary, had this organization established as the sole Government cryptographic establishment with the duty of serving not only the Foreign Office but the services and other government departments as well (Note 8). The Foreign Offices of other countries followed the British lead, including the United States, which established the famous Black Chamber (Note 9), and the Weimar Republic in Germany. More significant to our subject was the immediate growth of foreign naval cryptographic departments. The United States and French Navies already had cryptographic sections during the war, and although these were cut down they remained in being. The German Navy made a careful study of their part in the war and the activities of Room 40 became obvious to them. They set up a small department known as B-Dienst during the twenties and the Japanese Navy did the same in 1925. The British efforts to conceal their success with cryptography were therefore a failure. Gradually incidents began to leak out, especially in France and America, and a close study of the war obviously left some unexplained gaps to which the breaking of codes and ciphers provided the only explanation.

Efforts were, however, made in Great Britain to render their ciphers unbreakable. Instead of transposition or substitution systems (Note 10) a reciphering table was introduced. This was a book of completely random four-figure groups of numbers which were subtracted from the groups taken from the Code Book. The place in the reciphering table at which to begin was indicated by a secret group at the beginning of the message. To start the message one line lower in the reciphering table meant that the whole message would come out completely different. It could therefore be sent in as many different forms as there were lines in the reciphering table. With such a system the cryptographer could only begin to get results when the same part of the reciphering table is used continuously. Naval general call signs were also introduced in which the ship making the message used any one of a large number of them. This concealed what ship was making the signal and its identity could only be revealed by deciphering the message.

After the armistice the Royal Navy continued its experiments with M. Langevin's piezo-electric oscillator for submarine detection. It became known as the asdic after the initial letters of the Allied Submarine Detection Investigation Committee set up in 1917. In 1921 an oscillator was sent to sea in H.M.S. *Antrim* and was able to obtain echoes from a submarine at over 2,000 yards. The speed of the ship during these trials was, however, only just over two knots. It was believed that the range at which an approaching submarine would normally be detected would be 1,200 to 1,400 yards. Asdics was originally to have been simply a ranging device to use in conjunction with hydrophones, but it soon came to be recognized as a detection device in its own right which was superior to any hydrophone. By using a stiffened canvas cylinder to enclose the oscillator and reduce turbulence it was found that it was quite possible to use asdics with the ship moving at slow speed. The submarine could be found initially by sweeping with the beam in azimuth until an echo was obtained. At the same time the asdic oscillator itself was found to be a good hydrophone as well. Probably its most important asset was that it would detect a silent submarine and even one resting on the bottom.

At this point it is necessary to explain roughly how an asdic set works. The oscillator which was built up of a sandwich of quartz crystals and steel plates was about 18 in. in diameter and 6 in. thick, and protruded through the bottom of the ship where it could be rotated in azimuth. To transmit, an alternating current was applied to the oscillator causing it to vibrate and emit a very loud supersonic note in the direction in which it was pointing. This note was controlled by the operator using a transmitting key to give a short 'ping' which travelled to the target at the speed of sound in water. It was then reflected by the steel hull of the submarine and returned to the oscillator where it was picked up and then amplified and made audible in the operator's headphones using a valve heterodyne receiver. The range was obtained by measuring the time between the transmission and the return of the echo. The operation of the set was, however, complicated by many factors. Echoes were also received from the bottom and from fish, tide rips and ship's wakes. With practice, however, these could be discounted by the quality of the echo, the extent of target and by the 'doppler' effect generally obtained from a moving submarine (Note 11). In addition there was trouble with what was known as 'quenching' in rough weather. The asdic operators therefore needed a great deal of training to become proficient. In the early twenties a school for operators was set up at Portland and a number of patrol vessels, among which were *P40*, *P59*, *Cachalot* and *PC74*, were fitted with asdics to give practice at sea.

By 1924 much progress had been made, the most important development being a thin steel streamlined dome round the

oscillator which allowed it to be operated at fourteen knots
without any falling off in efficiency. The A/S Flotilla at Portland
now included four 'R' class destroyers fitted with asdics, while
H.M.S. *Campbell* and eight 'V' and 'W' destroyers of the Sixth
Destroyer Flotilla in the Atlantic fleet had the new Type 114
asdic set. Careful analysis of dummy depth charge attacks on
target submarines indicated that twenty-six per cent of them
would have been successful and another nineteen per cent
partly so. Out of seventy-two practice attacks on the fleet by
submarines, fifty-eight were detected by the asdic-fitted
destroyers although the picture was confused by some sixty-five
false echoes which to be safe also had to be attacked. In 1925
the Second Destroyer Flotilla attached to the Mediterranean
fleet was fitted with a new Type 115 asdic set which had a wide
angle transmission for use when searching for submarines as
well as the narrow beam for attacking. The wide angle sweep
was very soon found to be inferior to the narrow beam even for
sweeping and was discarded. Some trouble was now being
experienced with the asdic domes which were not proving to be
strong enough. The domes were fixed and so had to stand the
destroyer's full speed, but experiments with duralumin domes
were encouraging and subsequently proved satisfactory. Step-
by-step sweeping, 'non-sub' and lost contact drill and other
asdic procedures were all by now well established. More
problems were however being encountered, especially in the
Mediterranean, with temperature layers which bent and
distorted the asdic beams.

In the immediate post-war period, British submarines had
two plate hydrophones, one on each bow, and a revolving
directional hydrophone on top of the bow. They were also fitted
with the Fessenden sound signalling gear. In 1923 H.M.
Submarine *H32* was fitted with an experimental asdic set
Type 113 but on top instead of underneath the hull. Subsequently a number of 'L' class submarines were given a similar
installation. Submarines had been quite successful during the
war in sinking U-boats, and the original intention was that they
would be able to gain contact with another submerged submarine by the active use of asdics and so fire torpedoes. The use
of asdics to ping when submerged, however, was likely to give
away the position of the submarine and so was unpopular.
Happily the oscillator was found to be a far better hydrophone

than either the plates or the rotating directional set and so it was normally used just to listen.

By 1926 there were seven submarines with asdics which was used passively for a number of purposes; one of these was to make torpedo attacks from depth on surface vessels without using a periscope. It was also valuable in helping with attacks when the periscope was employed and could be used, of course, for signalling. Active transmitting was still expected to be of use for attacking other submerged submarines and studies were also being made at the time of its use for keeping station while submerged for attacks on fleets by groups of submarines. The new submarine *Oberon* was given a specially designed Type 116 asdic set which could be used either from underneath or on top of the hull by an ingenious system of reflecting plates. On trials it was found to be too heavy and complicated and the later *Odin* class were given a Type 118 which was underneath and very similar to a destroyer set.

In 1926 it was decided to try an asdic set in the new cruiser *Cornwall*, but it did not prove a very great success. A special set for fitting in trawlers in war was tried out in H.M.S. *Blackwater*. Few other ships were fitted with asdics for the next three years which were a period of consolidation rather than expansion. Oscillators and domes were improved, training intensified and many tactical trials carried out. The 'pounce' attack was developed in which a destroyer approached slowly and at 400 yards shortly before contact was lost (Note 12), speed was increased for the depth-charge attack. This resulted in forty per cent of attacks being successful. A five depth-charge pattern was now standardized and the requisite racks and throwers fitted in destroyers which had asdics. In 1927 hydrophone experiments were finally abandoned and asdic remained the sole anti-submarine detecting device in the Royal Navy.

The only other country to develop an active acoustic submarine detection system between the wars was the U.S.A. At the end of the war in 1919, as already related, the exchange of information with Great Britain ceased. By that time the British were conducting experiments with asdics and the Americans knew exactly what they were doing. The U.S. Navy fully realized the potential of the British system but considered the quartz oscillator a 'rather crude device'. Experiments were, however, continued by an Underwater Sound Group of the Naval

Research Laboratory with the aim of developing a supersonic echo-ranging system, but progress was slow compared with the British and it was not until 1927 that the U.S. had experimental sets ready for sea. Sonar sets as they called them were installed in several vessels during the year but gave only very short ranges and then only with the ship steaming at three to four knots. Interest then seems to have shifted to the acoustic problems of submarines. By 1929 the JK sonar had been produced for them which was a passive supersonic directional hydrophone using a sonar transducer. It proved far better than the old SC hydrophone. In the next two years they also produced the QB echo-ranging set for submarines.

In the period between the wars the Royal Navy, in spite of the fact that starshell had become the primary method of illumination at night, expended a considerable effort in improving their searchlights. The number of searchlights carried was less, capital ships generally having only four 36 in. lights, but efforts were made to improve the quality and brightness of the lamps and the control systems. Stabilization was introduced as well as remote power control. Much energy was spent in trying to develop searchlights for use against aircraft and it was not until 1932 that this was found to be impracticable and abandoned. In 1934 work was started on a larger searchlight, 44 in. in diameter with twice the candle-power of the 36 in. and 2,000 yards more range. It had been successfully developed with stabilization and power control by 1937 and was fitted in the reconstructed battleship *Warspite* and the new battleships of the 'King George V' class. It was also put into cruisers of the 'Sheffield' and 'Aurora' classes and destroyers of the 'Javelin' class. This highly successful development, however, came twenty years too late. It would have been splendid at Jutland but by the time it was in service night fighting had moved into an entirely new era.

The early thirties saw the development of a new use for electro-magnetic waves of exceptional importance, which was to affect naval warfare as much as the original introduction of radio. In his experiments in 1886 Hertz had shown that electro-magnetic waves could be reflected by metal objects in the same way as light is reflected by a mirror. In 1904 a German scientist took out a patent for a device using this principle for preventing collisions between ships in fog. In 1922 Marconi, in a lecture in New York to the Institute of Radio Engineers, also suggested the use of radio waves for detection. There are many cases on record of the reflection of radio waves being noticed during experiments and if anything it is surprising that more interest was not shown in the subject earlier. It is, of course, true that the technical problems were formidable but oddly many of the necessary ingredients were already available. The cathode ray tube dates from 1902, pulse transmissions from 1925, the magnetron from 1921 and the waveguide from 1897. As so often happens scientists in four countries developed radio waves for detection simultaneously and in secret.

In the U.S.A. the reflections from a steamer on the Potomac during an experiment by the Naval Aircraft Radio Laboratory were noticed in 1922 and some proposals were made but not followed up. In 1930 the calibration of a high-frequency direction finder by the Naval Research Laboratory was disturbed by an aircraft flying overhead and a paper was submitted to the Navy Department entitled 'Radio-Echo Signals from Moving Objects'. The Laboratory were then directed to investigate the use of radio to detect the presence of enemy vessels and aircraft. Two years later the laboratory had produced a static system to protect an area thirty miles in diameter using continuous waves. As it was obviously of little use to the Navy it was passed to the Army. In 1934 the laboratory began to experiment with a pulse system picking up an aircraft at one mile. It was another two years before they had achieved twenty-five miles and not until 1937 that they sent an experimental set to sea in the U.S.S. *Leary* with the antenna secured to a 5 in. gun mounting. Progress was then rather faster, and early in 1938 a set of 6 kw. working on $1\frac{1}{2}$ m. (200 mc.) detected a plane at 100 miles.

At this point it is necessary to take a layman's look at the technical problems of what came to be known as radar. The first problem is that of frequency. In general electro-magnetic waves will not be reflected if the size of the target is less than half the wavelength. At the same time the size of the antenna especially if it is to have a directional effect has to be greater than half the wavelength. Radar frequencies therefore have to be very high, that is above say 50 m. or 60,000 kc/s. At this frequency it was difficult in the early days to generate sufficiently high power for the echo from a target to be detected at all. For instance, for a transmitting power of 100 kw. at thirty miles, the echo from a small aircraft would only return as five billionths of a watt. An exceptionally sensitive and interference-free receiver was therefore necessary too. Then if the echo was to be detected, the pulse transmission had to be extremely short. A radar echo returns from an object 100 miles away in less than a thousandth of a second. Pulses had therefore to be measured in millionths of a second if they were not to interfere with the returning echo. It was the solution of these problems which took time. It was not until the thirties that radio techniques such as the thermionic valve and later the magnetron for transmitting power and the cathode ray tube as a way to measure the minute time intervals provided the basis of a solution.

In December 1938 the Naval Research Laboratory installed their XAF radar in the battleship *New York*. It worked on a frequency of $1\frac{1}{2}$ m. and had a seventeen foot square rotating mattress antenna. A rival radar set, the CXZ of 80 cm. designed by the Radio Corporation of America which had been brought into the secret, was installed in the battleship *Texas*. Both these sets were taken to the Caribbean with the fleet during the winter. The XAF was an outstanding success in detecting aircraft and ships as well as for navigation and spotting the fall of shot. The CXZ, except that it had a smaller antenna, was a failure. In October 1939 six more XAF sets, now called CXAM, were ordered, and this was the situation at the outbreak of the war in Europe.

In Germany it was in 1933 that the Communications Research Institute of the German Navy began to experiment with short waves to try to develop a radar rangefinder. By the following year they had produced a continuous wave set working on 50 cm. which with 50 watt power detected a 500 ton ship at just over seven miles. In 1934, too, the G.E.M.A. Company was formed to develop radar. Two years later, in 1936, a set called 'Seetakt', working on 80 cm., developed for coast defence work, was sent to sea for trials in the pocket battleship *Graf Spee*, the cruiser *Königsberg* and the torpedo boat *G10*. In the summer manoeuvres of that year it was claimed that ranges of 17 km. were obtained on a large ship and 8 km. on a cruiser. This was a gunnery set mounted in front of the main armament director, which was principally a rangefinder but had good directional properties too. It could also be used for giving warning of the approach of ships. As finally developed it could give a bearing to within 0·2 degrees, and although its power was only 7 kw. it could pick up a battleship at eleven miles, a destroyer at eight and a half, and a motor torpedo boat at three miles. It was unable however to spot the fall of shot. At the outbreak of war twelve of these sets existed but were only mounted afloat in the *Graf Spee* and the *Königsberg*, the rest being used for coast defence, but the set was put into production in 1939. The year before the German Navy had also ordered some of the air warning sets called 'Freya', which had been designed by G.E.M.A. for the Luftwaffe. They worked on 2·4 m. and could pick up aircraft at fifty miles. Yet this does not seem to have been mounted in ships but was used ashore by the Navy for air defence.

Towards the end of 1935 the French installed an 'iceberg detector' in the liner *Oregan* and later in the *Normandie*. It was a continuous wave 'interference' device with separate transmitting and receiving aerials working on 16 cm. It was of very low power with a range of only two miles. No range of the contact could be obtained and only the vaguest idea of relative bearing. It does not seem to have been installed in any other ships or to have attracted the attention of the French Navy. In 1938 four scientists produced a very low-power pulse radar, also on 16 cm., which they tried out at Le Havre and which detected a ship at five miles. Nothing seems to have come of this set either except the reading of a paper to the Societé Française des Electriciens in January 1939. At the same time the British decided to communicate their progress with radar to the French. The French Air Force in this period were installing a continuous wave interference type, 'barrages electromagnetiques', on 30 mc/s designed by a M. David of the French Air Ministry. It had widely separated transmitters and receivers and was able to give neither direction nor range. It was simply a curtain which would give a warning if an aircraft flew through it. In May 1939 the French, with British help, began to develop a high-power pulse system, but this did not come into use before the fall of France.

The development of radar (Note 13) in Great Britain dates from 1935. In that year the Air Ministry set up a committee to make a scientific survey of air defence. One of their early acts was to study a paper by Mr Watson-Watt, the Superintendent of the Radio Department of the National Physical Laboratory, which indicated that aircraft could probably be detected by short-wave wireless waves. They gave their support and in a remarkably short space of time Mr Watson-Watt had produced apparatus which detected aircraft at fifteen miles. On 11 March 1935 the Admiralty had been invited by the committee to discuss the detection of aircraft in naval warfare. The Admiralty scientific department had considered two projects for the use of electro-magnetic waves for detection in 1928 and 1931 but had turned them down as they did not believe them to be practicable at the time. Their assistance was now required by the Air Ministry as the Experimental Department of the Signal School was the only place likely to be able to produce sufficiently powerful transmitting valves for a new air defence radar under consideration. They produced the valves during the summer, and in the autumn scientists from the Signal School visited the Air Ministry's experimental station at Bawdsey and were shown radar in its early stages. In October 1935 the Admiralty approved the plan that work on the development of radar for the Navy should begin but at first only allocated a single scientific officer for the task. They decided that naval requirements were so specialized that they would undertake the work themselves at the Signal School rather than combine with the Air Ministry at Bawdsey.

In two years the Air Ministry had the beginnings of a chain of radar stations on the east coast which were detecting aircraft at 100 miles. But these CH radar stations, designed specifically for the air defence of Great Britain, could not be adapted for naval use. They worked originally on a frequency of 50 m. and later 26 m. and had huge fixed aerials with a number of masts 250 feet high. They used a pulse system with which they 'floodlit' the area to seawards over an arc of 120 degrees. The receiver by timing the echoes obtained the range and by a direction-finding system obtained the bearing of approaching aircraft.

An air defence radar to go in a ship would clearly have to have radically different characteristics. It would have to use a much shorter wavelength if the aerials were to be directional and there were many other problems, such as being able to withstand the shock of guns firing, to be solved by the designers.

The Signal School at first produced a set working on $1\frac{1}{2}$ m. and took it to sea in the minesweeper *Saltburn.* It was a failure because it was impossible at the time to obtain sufficient power on such a short wavelength. They therefore concentrated their efforts on a wavelength of 7 m. which was the longest that they believed could be used in a ship. Otherwise a directional aerial would be so large that there would be serious problems of topweight and wind resistance. They produced a prototype which they tried at sea in March 1937, with encouraging results, when they found it would pick up ships as well as aircraft. The apparatus had a pulse transmitter but did not attempt to floodlight the space round a ship; instead it transmitted a concentrated beam with which they intended to sweep like a searchlight. There were separate transmitting and receiving aerials on the fore and main masts respectively, which were rotated together by the operator. Echoes were shown on what became known as an A scope (Diagram 15). This was a cathode ray tube on which appeared a horizontal trace graduated for range from left to right and any echoes appeared as vertical deflections of the line. A fairly accurate range and a less accurate bearing could be obtained but at first no indication of height. This Type 79 radar (Note 14) was installed in the battleship *Rodney* in August 1938 and the cruiser *Sheffield* in November of the same year. It had a power of some 20 kw. and picked up aircraft at over fifty miles when they were at a height of 10,000 feet. Development of a more powerful edition of the same set had already begun and it was fitted in the anti-aircraft cruiser *Curlew* in August 1939. With a power of 70 kw. this Type 79Z set could pick up aircraft at ninety miles when flying at 20,000 feet. The Type 79Z was put into production and forty of them were ordered. At the outbreak of the Second World War, therefore, the Royal Navy had developed an air-warning radar, three ships were fitted with it and it was about to go into production.

The Royal Navy's Type 79 radar was not the only one available for maritime warfare at the outbreak of hostilities. As far back as September 1936 the new Commander-in-Chief of the R.A.F. Coastal Command suggested that an airborne radar set was required to search for ships. A year later a $1\frac{1}{2}$ m. set with a power of only 50 watts was flying in an Anson aircraft and in an exercise in the North Sea picked up the aircraft carrier *Courageous* at five miles. From this the ASV Mark I set was developed which sent a beam out from ahead to twenty-five degrees on each side of the aircraft. It was capable of picking up a small ship at four miles and a large ship at fifteen miles. This set was being fitted in a few Coastal Command aircraft in September 1939 but was really only of use for familiarization and training. There was one further maritime radar set which had been developed by the British Army for coastal defence. It was called CD and was able to pick up a 2,000 ton ship at 17,000

15. Presentation of Radar Echoes

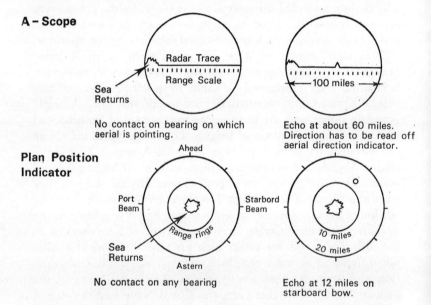

A – Scope

Radar Trace
Range Scale
Sea Returns

No contact on bearing on which aerial is pointing.

100 miles

Echo at about 60 miles. Direction has to be read off aerial direction indicator.

Plan Position Indicator

Ahead
Port Beam
Starbord Beam
Range rings
Sea Returns
Astern

No contact on any bearing

10 miles
20 miles

Echo at 12 miles on starboard bow.

yards, giving an accurate range and bearing using beam switching (Note 15). It could also pick up shell splashes and so was capable of directing coast defence guns. From this set the CHL set was developed by the R.A.F. to pick up low-flying aircraft and also ships and by the outbreak of war a chain of these covered the whole east coast.

Winston Churchill had been a member of the Air Defence Research Committee since 1935 and, after a visit to the radar stations on the east coast in the summer of 1939, wrote: 'The progress in RDF especially applied to range-finding must surely be of high consequence to the Navy. It would give power to engage an enemy irrespective of visibility; how different would have been the fate of the German battle cruisers when they attacked Scarborough and Hartlepool in 1914 if we could have pierced the mist! I cannot conceive why the Admiralty are not now hot upon this trail. Tizard also pointed out the enormous value to destroyers and submarines of directing torpedoes accurately, irrespective of visibility by night or day. I should have thought this was one of the biggest things that had happened for a long time. . . .' On arrival at the Admiralty as First Lord in 1939 he called for a programme of the installation of RDF in ships. The Admiralty undoubtedly were less far sighted than Winston Churchill but had, in fact, started the development of an air-warning radar two years after the U.S Navy and had it at sea in combatant ships slightly before the American prototypes were fitted for trial. In January 1938 the Admiralty had also begun the development of a 50 cm. set with the aim of producing a gunnery ranging system and had already tried it at sea in the destroyer *Sardonyx*. In this they were behind the Germans whose 'Seetakt' had been at sea for over a year and was now in production. Undoubtedly in their caution with radar the Admiralty were influenced by the great danger of giving away the position of the fleet by using radar. It was obvious that a ship using radar could be picked up by special receivers at several times the range at which she could obtain an echo. They were by no means certain that radar would not turn out to be a two-edged weapon.

In 1933 the German B-Dienst organization was strengthened, and two years later got its first real opportunity. The British Navy had been at peace for seventeen years, much of it under the 'ten years rule' (Note 16), in which few cipher messages were required. The cipher organization of the fleet was therefore somewhat rusty and was quite incapable of dealing with a large volume of traffic. With the Abyssinian crisis which broke in 1935 it was therefore to an extent taken by surprise. A new administrative cipher had been introduced the year before which could be used for secret messages with a reciphering table and for confidential messages straight from the book. The aim was, of course, to speed up the ciphering of the less important messages. During the crisis a British naval force was assembled at Aden and had to make considerable use of the administrative cipher. Many mitakes resulted through lack of experience and it was possible from observing the composition and activities of the squadron from the shore to guess what many of the messages were about. By intercepting this traffic the B-Dienst organization were able by 1938 to reconstruct practically the whole content of this code without the British realizing that anything was amiss. The Germans were not, however, able to make any headway with the reciphered codes used for operations. The British also changed many of their ciphers a few days before war broke out and much of the German effort was wasted. Nevertheless they had obtained splendid practice and knowledge of British methods.

A German commercial company had produced a cipher machine called 'Enigma' as early as 1923 and a modified form of this was introduced into the German armed services ten years later. In 1934 the Japanese bought an Enigma machine and used it to design their own machine for diplomatic ciphers. The U.S. Navy after years of experiments finally went over to machine ciphers of their own design in 1936. The Royal Air Force also introduced the 'Typex' machine and offered it to the Admiralty. The Admiralty rejected it as too complicated and likely to fail on service. Cipher machines normally work on a polyalphabetical system in which a different jumbled alphabet is used for each letter in a line. If the rotors and keys are changed frequently they are virtually unbreakable but are no better than the high-grade British subtraction systems. Where they are superior is in the speed with which messages could be ciphered and deciphered. This allows all messages to be ciphered in an unbreakable system instead of necessitating the use of simple low-grade ciphers for small ships and the less secret purposes. In this the Royal Navy were a long way behind Germany and the United States and began the Second World War at a considerable disadvantage.

In 1931 the U.S. Navy had only a few people engaged in crypto-analysis but by 1932 they had started to expand and were using IBM punched-card machines. Intercepts from Japan grew in volume throughout the thirties and in 1937 they set up a D/F net in the mid-Pacific. The Japanese reciprocated and built a large intercept station at Owada near Tokyo in the same year. They had little success however against the U.S. naval ciphers. It was, of course, very difficult, for lack of signal data with reduced traffic, to break into naval ciphers in peacetime. Many countries made progress against diplomatic cipher systems, however, in which much of what was secret one day was published in the form of a note the next. As early as 1921 during the Washington Naval Conference the American Black Chamber had been reading the Japanese ciphers and in 1936 the Germans had solved how the Japanese diplomatic cipher machine worked.

In Great Britain some action was taken in the late twenties to set up listening stations but these were very much on a skeleton basis. Matters did not begin to improve until the Abyssinian crisis and the Spanish Civil War made it essential to do something. In 1936 the pace was accelerated when Vice-Admiral Sir William James, who had been in charge of Room 40 in 1917–18, became Deputy-Chief of the Naval Staff. Yet two years later, personnel to man the half-dozen intercept stations were so short that the Gibraltar station had to be closed; then in 1939 a scheme was approved to man these stations with permanent civilian operators. During the Spanish Civil War it became important to identify the 'pirate' submarines which began to operate and the nucleus of an Operational Intelligence Centre was set up in the Admiralty (Note 17). At the same time new and more sensitive equipment for the intercept stations was purchased from America and the Marconi Company. By February 1939 the Operational Intelligence Centre was in full working order with direct teleprinters to the intercept and D/F stations and to the central cryptographic department. At the outbreak of war, however, the intercept and D/F organization was still really only a nucleus on which to expand (Note 18).

The greatest British advance in radio warfare in this period was undoubtedly a technical one. The D/F stations of the First World War worked on low frequency and were simple and accurate. It was now expected that signals made by ships at sea would normally be on high frequency on which, as has already been explained, it was much harder to obtain an accurate bearing. The Germans were convinced that it was impossible to obtain bearings at all, but the British, by very careful calibration and siting of the stations and by using special aerials and cathode ray tubes produced a high-frequency direction finding set which was reasonably accurate even on the 'sky wave'. These stations could at first only work on one frequency at a time and so had to co-operate closely with the intercept stations who told them when signals were being transmitted and on what frequency. Nevertheless the nucleus of a high-frequency direction-finding net was developed and established which was a considerable technical achievement. Another technical development was a device called TINA which 'fingerprinted' wireless operators and their sets and so could be used as a counter to measures such as changing call-signs to a certain extent.

By 1929 asdics was well developed in the Royal Navy. So far, it had not been widely fitted; to date only twenty-five destroyers out of a total of over two hundred had asdics. A few P-boats and trawlers had experimental sets but none of the thirty-odd sloops which would be used as convoy escorts in war were yet fitted. It had already been decided to equip all new submarines with asdics but the set in the heavy cruiser *Cornwall* had not proved a success. The Admiralty now decided to embark on a programme of expansion. All new destroyers were to be designed to take asdics whether it was actually installed or not, in fact the nine new destroyers of the 'Acasta' class were only fitted 'for' but not 'with'. The nine destroyers of the 'Beagle' class of the 1928 programme were, however, given an asdic set and were sent to the Mediterranean as the Fourth Destroyer Flotilla. The new Type 119 set with which they were fitted could be controlled remotely from the bridge and was an all-round improvement. The new 'Daring' class had a more advanced set still with a retracting dome and a new chemical recorder which considerably improved the range accuracy of asdics.

In 1932 the Admiralty reviewed their whole anti-submarine policy. They laid down that the object of all anti-submarine operations was the destruction of the enemy submarine rather than the warding off of attacks. This was because they believed that the protection of convoys at sea would have to be achieved mainly by evasion. The anti-submarine screens for them would be provided by asdic-fitted sloops or old destroyers but there would not be enough of them to provide complete protection and they would generally only be able to counter-attack a submarine after it had fired its torpedoes. In this year a very large expansion of the asidic-fitting programme was decided upon: all new destroyers were to have asdics installed on completion and plans were made to fit all older destroyers on the outbreak of war. At the same time a reserve of asdic sets was to be built up to fit in trawlers in emergency. New sloops were now all to be fitted 'for' if not 'with' asdics and two new types of ship, the convoy sloop of the 'Bittern' class and the coastal sloop of the 'Kingfisher' class, were laid down with asdics as a cardinal feature of the design.

British submarines had made good use of their asdic sets for developing anti-asdic tactics but as already told only used them passively. A new submarine Type 129 set was designed with the oscillator built into the forward end of the keel which was stronger than a retracting dome. At the same time all submarines were given 10 kc. oscillators to give them the longest communicating range so that Fessenden could be dispensed with. A new asdic set had been fitted in the heavy cruiser *Dorsetshire* and proved successful. There was some doubt about whether asdics would prove of use to cruisers but it was eventually decided that they needed a set for self-protection when by themselves, and that it must have as long a range as possible. A specially designed Type 132 set with two oscillators, one for each side, was therefore designed and first went to sea in H.M.S. *Southampton* in 1938. Other asdic developments of this period were a static harbour defence set and the supersonic echo sounder, which was extensively fitted in ships of all types.

In 1933 Adolf Hitler came to power in Germany and the next year he laid down twenty-six U-boats in defiance of the Treaty of Versailles. As a result the new destroyers of the 'Acasta' and 'Crusader' classes which had been completed without asdics were now fitted as well as a number of the older ships of the 'V' and 'W' classes. By the eve of war in 1939 the Royal Navy had over a hundred destroyers fitted with asdics as well as some forty-five sloops and old destroyers for convoy protection. Some twenty trawlers had also been taken up from trade and given asdics as well. At the same time considerable stocks of sets had now been built up so that the remaining destroyers could be fitted when war broke out. In general the position *vis-à-vis* the German U-boats which now numbered fifty-seven was considered to be well in hand. Indeed the Admiralty at this time believed that the threat of German surface raiders, especially the pocket battleships was more serious.

During the period of asdic expansion in the thirties, there was little material development. Asdic sets of the kind fitted in the 'D' class destroyers were considered fully satisfactory and this was the type put into production. In 1935 there was a slight setback when trials showed that the 300 pound depth charge would only destroy a modern deep-diving submarine at twenty feet. Analysis of exercises showed that, even so, an asdic-controlled depth charge attack had a fifty per cent chance of success and that asdic-fitted destroyers on a fleet screen had a seventy per cent chance of detecting a submarine attempting to pass through it. In June 1938 Winston Churchill visited Portland to see the asdic, 'the system of groping for submarines below the surface' as he called it. Afterwards he wrote to the First Sea Lord: '. . . I am sure the nation owes the Admiralty, and those who have guided it, an inestimable debt for the faithful effort sustained over so many years which has, as I feel convinced, relieved us of one of our great dangers.'

The Royal Navy remained right up to the outbreak of war in 1939 practically the only navy with an effective anti-submarine device. The U.S. Navy were the only rivals and they were a very long way behind. By 1934 they began to manufacture sonar sets with magnetostriction transducers which they had developed in 1927 and also produced a rubber streamlined dome which permitted operation at speeds up to ten knots (Note 19). Sonar sets of this type were then installed in Destroyer Division Twenty, consisting of U.S.S. *Rathburn*, *Waters*, *Talbot*, and *Dent*. These sets were manufactured at the rate of fourteen a year and by September 1939, when war broke out in Europe, some sixty destroyers had been equipped. The training of operators was, however, a long way behind; the first 'Sound School' at San Diego had only commissioned in 1936.

On the eve of the outbreak of war in 1939 the Admiralty had direct high-frequency wireless communication with seventeen stations throughout the world (Map 16), from Esquimault in British Columbia to Simonstown in South Africa and Hong Kong on the China Station (Note 20). The messages were sent at routine times and were normally keyed in Whitehall itself by land-line to transmitters at Horsea and Cleethorpes, the receivers being at Flowerdown near Winchester. On each station there was a broadcast to send routine general messages to all ships but signals for individual ships were normally sent direct on low or medium frequency. In war, to prevent the ship having to answer, it was planned to use the 'I' method. For instance, for a ship somewhere in the Pacific the message might be sent from Wellington in New Zealand and acknowledged by Esquimault in British Columbia, the ship addressed intercepting the message without answering. For ships to pass messages to the shore there were one or more high-frequency wavelengths allotted to each station. High frequency was often necessary to obtain sufficient range and was obviously desirable in war as it was much harder for the enemy to use direction finders. In general results were poor; ships often failed to get through and tended to wait until they were close enough to use a low or medium frequency wave. In theory there was two-way wireless communication between the Admiralty and the Commanders-in-Chief and their ships throughout the world. It was independent of the cable system but it must be admitted that coverage was poor in places and high frequency often unreliable (Note 21).

Within a fleet the Commander-in-Chief and all ships including destroyers and naval reconnaissance aircraft kept watch on a low- or medium-frequency fleet wave which was ready for use for enemy reporting, fleet manoeuvring and general intercommunication in action. Wireless silence was normally in force at sea but this wave could be used on very low power when cruising. There was in addition an auxiliary wave kept by all large ships which was intended for passing administrative messages but could be used as an alternative for manoeuvring or general inter-communication in action. Each squadron or flotilla had its own gunnery fire-control wave and battleships and cruisers each had a high-frequency aircraft-spotting wave but these were not manned until action was imminent. For receiving messages from the shore all large ships kept continuous watch on an Area Operational Broadcast but destroyers were only able to listen to 'general' periods in which messages for them were concentrated. The Royal Air Force Coastal Command had its own reconnaissance wave and anything relevant was sent out to the fleet on the broadcast. Messages were sent to the shore using the area high- or low-frequency waves and the

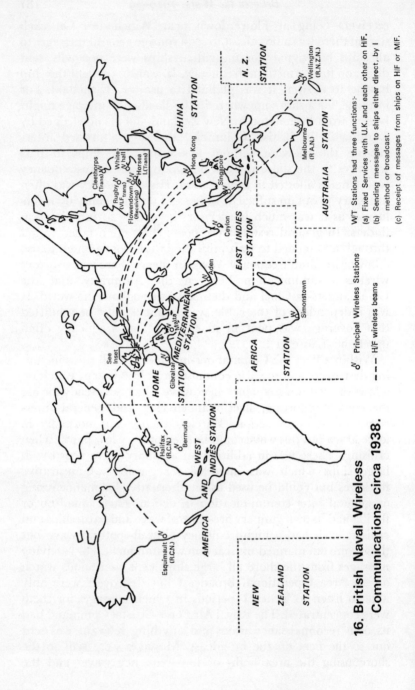

W/T Stations had three functions:-
(a) Fixed Services with U.K. and each other on H/F.
(b) Sending messages to ships either direct, by 1
    method or broadcast.
(c) Receipt of messages from ships on H/F or M/F.

o Principal Wireless Stations

- - - H/F wireless beams

16. British Naval Wireless Communications circa 1938.

CHINA STATION

N. Z. STATION

Wellington (R.N.Z.N.)

Hong Kong

Singapore

Melbourne (R.A.N.)

AUSTRALIA STATION

Ceylon

EAST INDIES STATION

Aden

AFRICA STATION

Simonstown

Cleethorps (Trans)

Rugby (VLF trans)

White (W'hall)

Flowerdown (Receiving)

Horsea I.(Trans)

See Inset

Gibraltar

Malta

MEDITERRANEAN STATION

HOME STATION

Halifax (R.C.N.)

Bermuda

WEST INDIES STATION

AMERICA AND

Esquimault (R.C.N.)

NEW ZEALAND STATION

large ships in the fleet kept constant watch on both these waves which were also used by detached ships and groups to communicate with the Commander-in-Chief and each other if necessary. Aircraft carriers had an additional high-frequency channel for communicating with their strike aircraft and fighters had a high-frequency voice radio.

A large ship had therefore to keep watch on at least five frequencies and in action two more. To compete with this organization ships had to have a considerable number of wireless sets. A battleship had eight transmitters, half of them of high power, and nine receivers as well as a medium-frequency direction-finding set. A destroyer had four transmitters, two of medium power and two of low power and eight receivers of various types. All these sets used morse: voice transmission was not used or indeed liked and was only used in single-seater fighters. Communication was, however, rapid and positive and was well tested in exercises. Yet the majority of the wireless sets in the fleet were obsolescent, did not give good performance on the higher frequencies and lacked frequency stabilization. New sets of improved design were just coming into service at the outbreak of war.

A special broadcast was planned for submarines in war on the very low-frequency transmitter at Rugby and a new standby station at Criggion in Wales. This could be received when the submarines were submerged and so enabled them to keep touch with the situation by day. This broadcast was backed up by a high-frequency broadcast at night which could be received by the submarines while they were on the surface. Submarines reported the enemy by using the ordinary high-frequency ship–shore waves.

Beside the great advances in high-frequency radio, in radar and in asdics, the progress in applying electricity for power in warships was small. For instance the new battleships *Nelson* and *Rodney* completed in 1927 had six generators of 300 kw. each, which was a total of 200 kw. more than the much larger *Hood* completed in 1919. The most extensive use of electricity was in the huge American aircraft carriers *Lexington* and *Saratoga*, converted from battle cruisers on the slips and also completed in 1927. They had turbo-electric propulsion and with 209,000 h.p. had at the time the most powerful engines ever installed in a warship. Four shafts were driven by eight electric motors of 22,500 h.p. each and all were controlled from one central position. In 1936 the U.S. Navy began to instal diesel-electric propulsion in their new fleet submarines as well. These large submarines had 6,400 h.p. giving them a speed of twenty knots. Diesel-electric propulsion was, after some teething troubles, very successful in these submarines which had four main diesel generators each, but few other navies followed suit. The batteries of submarines on which they depended for submerged propulsion showed little improvement between the wars. The submarines of the late thirties had much the same submerged endurance as their predecessors of the First World War.

In general, however, the influence of the electron on sea power during the period between the wars was substantial. The range of radio communication and the increase in the number of channels made world-wide communication possible without having to rely on cables. The invention of asdics was of exceptional importance as an anti-submarine measure in spite of the fact that it was of comparatively short range. Nevertheless Winston Churchill's description of it as a 'system of groping for submarines' was not far off the mark and the British un-doubtedly overestimated the effect that it would have on naval warfare. The invention or rather the development of radar was probably to be in the end the greatest advance of this period. The total number of sets at sea in the British, American and German Navies was seven but its great potential was recognized although it was realized that, in the same way as wireless transmissions in the First World War, it could give away the position of the user.

VIII

The Second World War, 1939-41

THE FIRST SEVEN MONTHS of the Second World War are often known as the 'phoney' war from the inactivity of the armies and the leaflet raids by bombers. It was however far from a phoney war at sea and in the air over the sea. On the second day of the war, an R.A.F. reconnaissance plane sighted German warships in the Schillig Roads and off Brunsbüttel and a striking force of fourteen Wellington and fifteen Blenheim bombers was sent to attack them. The interest of this operation for our subject is that the Heligoland Bight was covered by a network of 'Freya' radar stations with a range of fifty miles. The bombers were detected approaching and so failed to achieve surprise. They caused little damage and were received by heavy anti-aircraft fire and also by fighters; seven aircraft were lost.

At the outbreak of the war the British Home fleet had two ships with Type 79 radar, the battleship *Rodney* and the cruiser *Sheffield*. On September 25 the fleet put to sea to help the submarine *Spearfish* which was returning from patrol damaged and unable to dive. This sortie led to the first clash with the Luftwaffe. Dornier DO 18 flying-boats first found and shadowed the fleet and one of them was shot down by Skua aircraft from the *Ark Royal*. *Ark Royal* had no radar and the *Rodney* and *Sheffield* no voice radio sets with which they could communicate with aircraft. There was therefore no possibility of directing fighters by radar. The three Skuas were in fact carrying out a standing fighter patrol over the fleet and sighted the flying-boat themselves. The use of radar at this time was confined to the passing of the equivalent of air-raid warnings to the fleet and in this way prevent surprise. In the subsequent series of air attacks on the fleet, *Ark Royal* was near-missed and the *Hood* hit by a bomb but remained undamaged. The fleet's anti-aircraft fire was heavy but failed to bring any aircraft down.

The fitting of the forty Type 79 radar sets ordered at the outbreak of war took some time and was carried out as ships and sets became available. The installation could only be done in a dockyard and so the early sets were allocated to ships refitting (Note 1) and new ships building (Note 2). Later, opportunity was taken to fit any ships which were in the yards to repair action damage (Note 3).

When the German battle cruisers *Scharnhorst* and *Gneisenau* made their first sortie towards the end of November, *Rodney* and *Sheffield* were still the only two ships in the Home fleet with radar. Both German ships had been fitted with the latest version of Seetakt radar just before sailing, but the possession of radar by the German squadron proved less of an advantage to them than the dearth of it proved a disadvantage to the Home fleet. No initial detections were made by Seetakt and the armed merchant cruiser *Rawalpindi* which was sunk between Iceland and the Faeroes on November 23 was sighted visually. No doubt Seetakt was used for ranging during the action but at 8,000 yards against such a large target it can scarcely have made much difference. On the other hand when the cruiser *Newcastle* with no radar found the two German ships picking up survivors, she soon lost them in rain squalls and was never able to regain contact. Three days later the *Scharnhorst* and *Gneisenau* passed right through the British cruiser patrol line off the Norwegian coast on their way home. Furthermore they passed through it in daylight although the weather was very bad. If the British cruiser line had had radar they would have had a far better chance to detect the German ships. The only available British radar was, it is true, an air warning set whereas Seetakt was designed for surface work. Nevertheless Type 79, although it worked on a lower frequency, had ten times the power and its performance for surface work was probably as good as Seetakt. Three weeks later at the Battle of the River Plate, the *Graf Spee* had an earlier form of Seetakt radar while the three British cruisers had no radar at all. The *Graf Spee*'s gunnery was extremely accurate and she began to hit the *Exeter* soon after opening fire at 19,400 yards; this was no doubt due to radar ranging.

In the early months of 1940 the anti-aircraft cruisers *Curacoa* and *Carlisle* were fitted with radar. The *Curacoa* was given an improved Type 79 (Type 279) which had a range-finding device with which it was possible to fire anti-aircraft guns as a barrage. The *Carlisle* was fitted with Type 280 which was the GL Mark I set developed by the British army for anti-aircraft gun control. It was a 3½ m. set which was of considerable value for air warning as well as fuze prediction. It could not however be adapted completely to the naval anti-aircraft fire control.

Surface and air operations in which radar was involved were, however, of less importance in the 'phoney' war period than underwater operations. There were fifty-seven German U-boats at the outbreak of war and they were all propelled below the surface by electric motors and batteries and had no better submerged performance than the U-boats at the end of the previous war. They had, however, an electric torpedo (the type G7e) using secondary batteries which, although it had a comparatively poor performance (3,000 yards at thirty knots) was completely trackless. Ships could not therefore see the torpedoes coming and so take avoiding action: furthermore destroyers could not run down the tracks and counter-attack with depth charges. The torpedoes also had magnetic instead of contact pistols to explode their warheads. The advantage of this was that the damage caused by a torpedo exploding right under a ship's bottom was much more serious than against the side. At the same time the torpedoes could be set to run deeper and so could be used in rougher seas. Alternatively they could be set to run just below the surface so that small ships of shallow draught could be attacked which would otherwise be immune to torpedo attack.

The Germans knew of the existence of asdics from their intelligence but did not know very much about it. In the first seven months they lost a total of eighteen U-boats, eleven of which were detected by asdics. Only thirteen U-boats were completed in the same period and so the total strength began to fall. Admiral Dönitz was not unduly perturbed and pointed out that this was a reasonable price to pay for their successes. They had sunk the battleship *Royal Oak,* the aircraft carrier *Courageous* and the destroyers *Exmouth* and *Daring* as well as 222 merchant ships of 764,766 tons. Furthermore U-boats had on three occasions been able to get within effective range of fleet units screened by asdic-fitted destroyers and on two occasions had survived the counter-attacks.

The British for their part were confident that once they really got contact with a U-boat in reasonable conditions it had little chance of escape. Contacts were however not very frequent. The vast majority of the merchant ships sunk by U-boats were unescorted or had straggled from convoys. British strategy at the outset was to form independent hunting groups of destroyers wherever possible and to try and take the offensive against the U-boats whilst convoy escorts were often reduced to one or two ships. But the short detection range of asdics meant that few results were obtained by searching for U-boats; the average range being just over a thousand yards meant that it was rather like searching for a small ship in fog. By contrast the U-boat could see the destroyers at ten miles or so and had time to manoeuvre to keep out of asdic range. Where a convoy was escorted, the U-boat, in order to attack, had to risk closing within asdic range.

The number of U-boats available at the outset was so small that they simply attacked independent ships whenever there was an opportunity. Admiral Dönitz realized, however, that he would have to be able to attack and defeat the convoy system if a submarine campaign against trade was ultimately to succeed. To do this he needed above all, numbers so that attacks could be made with packs of submarines simultaneously. One or two attempts were made to form 'wolf-packs' in this early period without much success but a decision on principle which was to be extremely important later was made. This was that wolf-packs against convoys would be controlled from the shore and not by a senior officer embarked in one of the U-boats. 'My primary functions' wrote Dönitz 'were to pass on to U-boats at sea all the information regarding the enemy which I received from a variety of intelligence sources, to correct or clarify any wrong or misleading information sent by the U-boats themselves, to issue orders to individual U-boats or groups, to co-ordinate the duties of maintaining contact and to intervene in the event of contact with the enemy being lost.

My control, therefore, extended up to the moment of the launching of an attack . . .' (Note 4).

The U-boat strategy therefore depended heavily on wireless communications. The Germans realized the value that the British direction-finding network had been to them during the First World War but believed that it was not possible to obtain bearings on high-frequency signals of sufficient accuracy to be of any use and that by frequency changing and using short signals they would give little away. The British shore H/F D/F network was, in fact, rapidly expanding and was already able to get sufficiently accurate bearings to fix danger areas and divert convoys. In addition the use of intercept stations listening on a number of frequencies in co-operation with the D/F stations was able to compete with frequency changing by the U-boats.

The U-boats were also used as in the First World War to lay mines, but the mines were now of a completely new type. Instead of the conventional moored contact type they were ground mines actuated by a magnetic device as a ship passed overhead. This kind of mine was not new, indeed a few had been used towards the end of 1918. They could however only be used in shallow water, the TMB in fifteen fathoms and the larger TMC in up to twenty fathoms. Altogether thirty-four small minefields were laid by U-boats before March 1940. The U-boats were joined in mid-November by the Luftwaffe laying additional mines from aircraft. At the outbreak of war the Royal Navy had a substantial force of minesweepers but these were only equipped to sweep moored mines and were of no use at all against the magnetic ground mine. In the absence of any counter-measures the German mining campaign, considering the very small number of mines laid, was a substantial success. The battleship *Nelson*, the cruiser *Belfast* and the minelayer *Adventure* were all seriously damaged and the destroyers *Blanche*, *Gipsy* and *Grenville* were sunk as well as 129 merchant ships totalling, 430,054 tons. In November 1939 it became so bad that the Thames estuary and therefore the Port of London nearly had to be closed.

The British had, in fact, also developed a magnetic mine which was just ready for production at the beginning of the war. They had also studied counter-measures and had already tried a magnetic sweep which proved effective against the British mines but not against the German. Before a new sweep could be devised it was essential to discover how the German mines worked. As soon as the Luftwaffe started using mines it was only a matter of time before one was dropped on land. On November 23 a mine was found off Shoeburyness and was successfully taken to pieces by the staff of H.M.S. *Vernon*. It was found that it was fired by a 'dip needle' when there was a vertical change of magnetism which would be activated by ships built in the northern hemisphere. This was quite different from the British mines which had a long coil in them which fired the mine when there was a certain rate of change of the magnetism in the horizontal plane.

Counter-measures were then actively pursued and took five different forms. First it was decided to try and neutralize the vertical magnetism of all ships by a process known as 'de-gaussing'. In this either coils carrying a small current were wound round the hull or the ships were subject to a process known as 'wiping' (Note 5). The other four counter-measures were methods of exploding the mines. One method thought out before the war, was to mount a huge electro-magnet in the bows of a small merchant ship in the hope that it would explode the mine well ahead and before the ship passed over it. A second was to instal a large coil of wire carrying a small current in an aircraft which then flew over the minefield. A third method was to tow a skid astern of a mine-sweeper on which was mounted a coil energized by an electric current. The final method was the 'LL' sweep in which mine-sweepers towed floating electric cables into which a heavy current was pulsed and which fired the mines well astern of the minesweepers (Note 6).

The first form of these counter-measures began to achieve results in the early months of 1940 and at the end of March 'LL' sweeps towed by trawlers started work with success. Fifteen mines were exploded in March alone by these methods and so counter-measures now existed, but the real reason that casualties were not higher in this early period was that the Germans only had a stock of 1,500 magnetic mines and had no more to lay. But British counter-measures were, in any case, only partly effective. The aircraft only swept a very narrow channel which it was impossible to mark. The mine destructor ships were often badly damaged by explosions of mines very close ahead and the skids were generally lost every time a mine went up. The 'LL' sweep was the best but the trawlers towing it had to risk passing over the mines first and although they were carefully 'de-gaussed' this could be a dangerous business.

On the outbreak of war the British were getting no information at all from German signals. The Germans, it will be recalled, used the Enigma cipher machine with frequent changes of rotors and it could not be broken. Just before the war no indication whatever was received that the pocket battleships *Graf Spee* and *Deutschland* and eighteen U-boats had put to sea. The sortie of the *Scharnhorst* and *Gneisenau* in November which led to the sinking of the *Rawalpindi* was also undetected. On the other hand the German B-Dienst in Berlin, with the modest strength of fifty, soon began to obtain results. After a setback ten days before war was declared when the British changed their ciphers they soon got into their stride again. In November they were able to read some of the messages during the *Rawalpindi* sortie and claimed that they helped the German battle cruisers to evade the patrols which had been established to block their return. They also knew that the Home fleet had shifted its base to Loch Ewe and a U-boat was sent to mine the entrance, damaging the *Nelson*. From the British mine warnings they also obtained a picture of the effectiveness of the magnetic-mine campaign. They were, however, unable to break the British high-grade operational ciphers.

In the middle of March 1940 a concentration of fourteen British submarines off the south-west coast of Norway and in the Skagerrak was detected by B-Dienst monitoring of British signals. The Germans sent eight small coastal submarines to operate against them, resulting on April 10 in the sinking of H.M.S. *Thistle* by *U4*. Before this had happened, however, Admiral Horton, commanding the British submarines, had increased the concentration in anticipation of a German invasion of Norway and nineteen boats were at sea. This move was based on intuition rather than intelligence. It is true that the British detected a change in the pattern of the German wireless signals but their general intelligence appreciation was that the concentration of ships in German ports was part of 'the war of nerves'. The Home fleet was therefore caught in harbour when the German invasion began on April 7.

The Germans, on the other hand, had obtained some information of the British intention to lay mines off Norway and of the proposed disposition of the Home fleet to cover the operation. Throughout the Norwegian campaign, B-Dienst continued to receive British messages and deciphered between thirty and fifty per cent of them. They knew of the approach of the troop convoys for the Narvik area and diverted U-boats to intercept. Later on, between June and August, B-Dienst was able to obtain a great deal of information about the British submarine patrols off the Norwegian coast. This was in part responsible for the sinking of the *Shark* by aircraft on July 5 and of the *Spearfish* by *U34* on August 1. The Admiralty had, however, set up a special section of the Naval Intelligence Divison to check on signal security. In August both the Administrative and Operational ciphers were changed and B-Dienst could get no more information for some months. This was regarded by the German command as a serious set-back.

Although the German magnetic mine had proved a great technical success, the opposite was true of their other magnetic device, the torpedo pistol used by their U-boats. That the magnetic pistol was not altogether satisfactory became apparent from premature explosions early in the war – an attack on H.M.S. *Nelson* by *U56* on 30 October 1939 failed for this reason. The U-boats had an important part to play in the German invasion of Norway. They were to take up positions to defend the landings against counter-attacks. Strategically they were well placed and made nearly forty torpedo attacks, half of which were on battleships and cruisers but all were failures except that they sank one transport. The main reason was the complete failure of the magnetic pistol in high latitudes (Note 7). The situation was aggravated by the poor depth keeping of the torpedoes, for when set to fire on contact, they generally ran underneath their targets. It was subsequently found by an inquiry that the magnetic pistols had been accepted for service prematurely and with insufficient trials. The German U-boat fleet was therefore impotent in the Norwegian campaign and its effectiveness was not restored until they had reverted to contact firing and the depth keeping of the torpedoes had been checked in the late summer.

In the Norwegian campaign, there were still only half a dozen British ships fitted with radar. Three of these were the anti-aircraft cruisers *Curlew, Carlisle* and *Curacoa,* the first of which was sunk at Narvik and the last badly damaged at Andalsnes. They found that in the fjords with high land on both sides their radar was of very little use. None of the aircraft carriers used in the campaign had radar and so there was no fighter direction. The few radar-fitted ships with the main fleets were able to give warning of the approach of enemy aircraft on the occasions when they were attacked. There were no radar sets on either side in the two Battles of Narvik but in the action with the *Renown* on April 9 off the Lofoten Islands, the *Scharnhorst* and *Gneisenau* made use of their Seetakt. Nevertheless the *Renown* with no radar had the advantage of the light and sighted the enemy first. Later when the two German battle cruisers sank the aircraft carrier *Glorious* they used radar ranging at 28,000 yards. In general, although on occasions they were useful, in this early phase of their development the few radar sets available cannot be said to have made very much difference and the campaign would have taken the same course whether they had been there or not.

After Norway the German minelaying campaign continued. More mines were laid but at the same time the number of minesweepers to cope with them rose and by the end of 1941 stood at nearly a thousand. The problem was complicated by the fact that the Germans laid both magnetic and moored mines which had to be swept separately by different types of minesweeper. The complexity too of influence minesweeping (Note 8) was considerable as the enemy began to use new types of firing mechanism. Mines of reversed polarity had already been introduced to catch ships which had been 'over de-gaussed'. They then began to use delay action mechanisms and so the mines were often inactive while sweeping was in process but would come alive after the sweepers had passed. In August 1940 it was clear to the British that some entirely new firing mechanism was being used. In September one of these mines was recovered and found to be of the acoustic variety which fired as the noise of the ship's engines and propellers passed overhead. This development had been anticipated; a sweep introduced in November exploded acoustic mines in the Thames estuary on the 24th of that month.

The acoustic sweep was a simple electrically driven hammer in a metal container lowered into the water in the bows of the minesweeper. It was at first possible to sweep both magnetic and acoustic mines together, the acoustic mines being set off by the hammer box ahead and the magnetic mines by the 'LL' sweep astern. Towards the end of 1941, however, the Germans produced a mine which required both influences simultaneously and would not go off if only one influence was present or if they came one after the other. Some mines were designed to catch the sweepers, for instance there was a very coarsely set acoustic mine which would go off when the hammer box was right overhead.

The British had begun to lay their magnetic mines from the air during the Norwegian campaign. The same battle of wits went on between the British mining experts who prepared the mines laid by the R.A.F. in enemy waters and the German minesweeping specialists. The British had a coarse magnetic mine specially designed to blow up the German mine destructor ships with their huge electro-magnets in the bows. They laid 'mixed bag' minefields with mines of all types including delayed action settings and mines which required to be actuated several times before exploding – these last could be swept more than once before going off and so it was extremely difficult to know when an area was safe.

When Italy entered the war on 11 June 1940 there was only one ship in the Mediterranean fleet fitted with radar. This was the anti-aircraft cruiser *Carlisle* and she was almost at once ordered to convoy duty in the Red Sea. The early operations in the Mediterranean, notably the actions off Calabria and Cape Spada, were therefore conducted without radar. The Italian Navy had no radar either but Admiral Cunningham was left to face the whole Italian metropolitan air force with no better detecting device than binoculars. Force H which was based at Gibraltar, on the other hand, had the *Valiant* and then the *Sheffield* with radar although the aircraft carrier *Ark Royal* was not yet fitted. At the end of August the Admiralty included four radar-fitted ships in their reinforcements for the Mediterranean fleet. These were the new aircraft carrier *Illustrious*, the battleship *Valiant* and the anti-aircraft cruisers *Coventry* and *Calcutta*, all of which had Type 279. The fitting of radar in the *Illustrious* was probably the most important step taken with this new device since it was introduced into the Navy. It has been seen how available radar sets had been fitted in ships building and whenever they came into dockyard hands. If any priority was given it was to anti-aircraft cruisers. Aircraft carriers were considered far too busy to be taken away from operations to be given this priceless aid to the air defence of the fleet. The *Illustrious* also had a squadron of twelve of the most modern Fairey Fulmar fighters on board. The captain of the *Sheffield*, who was a naval aviator, had made efforts to develop fighter direction and had made some progress. The *Illustrious*, however, was the first ship in which this really became possible. On passage through the Western Mediterranean her fighters succeeded in shooting down several reconnaissance aircraft and no serious air attacks developed.

Fighter direction was still in a very early stage of development. Voice radio communications with the fighters were not very good and the Type 279 radar had considerable limitations. The aerials were trained manually and the presentation was by A-scope. This meant that it was impossible to track more than two or three aircraft at a time. Plotting had to be by hand and while this was going on the watch for new contacts suffered considerably. There was, moreover, little indication of height which was all important in directing fighters. Radars, such as the Type 279, working on metric wavelengths suffered a substantial distortion of the transmitted beam because of reflections from the sea (Diagram 17). The result was a series of lobes in which aircraft would give an echo but there were considerable gaps in the coverage. Aircraft flying low were unlikely to be detected until very close, but the pattern of lobes made it possible to a certain extent to estimate height, and the combination of Type 279 and voice radio into a system of fighter direction was a substantial advance on what had been possible before: aircraft could be vectored to the attack which they could make well clear of the fleet and they could actually prevent potential shadowers gaining contact at all. The former standing patrols over the fleet, which often became involved in dog fights and so interfered with the anti-aircraft gunnery, were now a thing of the past (Note 9).

On October 12 the cruiser *Ajax*, which was fitted with Type 279 radar and had joined the Mediterranean fleet by the route round the Cape, became involved in a night action with Italian destroyers to the east of Malta. Under a full moon they were sighted and engaged visually; two of them, *Ariel* and *Aerione*, were sunk and a third, the *Antiglieri*, was disabled. During the action the *Ajax's* radar was hit and put out of service. In this first night action in which radar was present, it cannot be claimed that it had much influence. The value of Type 279 for surface work was limited and its real contribution was for the air defence of the fleet by day against shore-based aircraft. In this the radar-fitted ships continued to give good service, including contributing to the success of the passage of an important convoy through the Mediterranean and the Battle with the Italian fleet off Cape Spartivento on November 27.

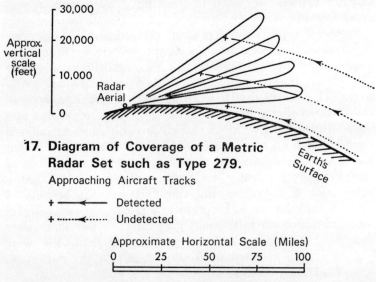

17. Diagram of Coverage of a Metric Radar Set such as Type 279.

Approaching Aircraft Tracks

+ ◄——— Detected

+ ·······◄······· Undetected

Approximate Horizontal Scale (Miles)

0   25   50   75   100

During the last quarter of 1940 the Home fleet also received substantial reinforcements of radar-fitted ships. These included the new battleship *King George V* and the new cruisers *Kenya*, *Dido* and *Phoebe* while the *Nelson* returned to the fleet after her repairs with Type 279. *Dido* had a new Type 281 set which had been developed from the Army Type 280 set fitted in the *Carlisle*. It also worked on a wavelength of $3\frac{1}{2}$ m. (90 mc/s) but had the greatly increased power of 350 kw. It was able to detect aircraft at over 100 miles when flying at 20,000 feet and was designed to be of use for surface and anti-aircraft gunnery as well. It could pick up a battleship at eleven miles, had 'beam switching' which gave a bearing accuracy of a half-degree and it could find the range within about thirty yards. In the last quarter of 1940, too, the development of 50 cm. radar for gunnery fire control came to fruition. Early in the year the power had been raised to 25 kw. An experimental set mounted in the *Nelson* gave ranges of 18,000 yards on a cruiser and 12,000 yards on a destroyer. This basic radar set was fitted in the fleet in four different forms. The first of these was the Type 284 for surface gunnery and the aerial was mounted on the main armament directors of battleships and cruisers. It was, however, really only a range-finder and had a maximum range of 20,000 yards. This was enough for 6 in. gun cruisers but could not help modern battleships and 8 in. gun cruisers at their maximum ranges. Nevertheless, when it gained contact there was no reason now why naval gunfire should not straddle for range with the first salvo, but as correction would probably be needed for line, hitting should begin with at least the third salvo. With optical range-finders hitting would probably not be achieved on average until the sixth salvo. This set was first mounted in the cruiser *Birmingham* (Plate II) and in other ships, including the *King George V*, as opportunity offered. The second set was the Type 285 designed for anti-aircraft gunnery and its aerial, which could be elevated as well as trained, was mounted on the anti-aircraft gun directors. Again this was mainly a range-finder and could pick up aircraft at 17,000 yards. Continuous accurate range made the setting of time fuzes very much more precise than before and was the greatest advance in anti-aircraft gunnery since the introduction of directors and fire-control systems in the thirties (Note 10). The Type 285 was first fitted in the destroyer *Southdown* in September 1940 and also in H.M.S. *King George V* and later ships. The third set was the Type 282 for close-range anti-aircraft weapons and the fourth the Type 283 which provided a way to use the main armament for anti-aircraft barrage fire. These two last sets were introduced into the fleet rather later. The *King George V* had therefore on completion six radar sets, one Type 279 for air warning, one Type 284 for main armament control and four Type 285 for the anti-aircraft batteries.

In the summer and autumn of 1940 the U-boats returned to their attack on trade in the Atlantic. They found plenty of unescorted ships and realized that all the convoys were weakly escorted. Admiral Dönitz knew that he must press on with his 'wolf-pack' tactics against convoys and he therefore ordered U-boats to report the position of convoys by wireless whenever they sighted them. He was still receiving information about British convoys from B-Dienst although at this stage he did not have much success; concentrations of U-boats were ordered on three occasions during the summer of 1940 as a result of radio intelligence but they did not make contact. Nevertheless from June to October 274 merchant ships totalling 1,395,398 tons were sunk by an average operational strength of twenty-seven U-boats which were only able to keep six or eight of their number in the Atlantic at a time. In September B-Dienst deciphered the position of the rendezvous at which a convoy was to meet its escort. Four U-boats concentrated and sank five ships. In October they did better still and in three convoys sank thirty-eight ships.

The basic principle of the 'wolf-pack' attack was to oppose the concentration of escorts round a convoy with a corresponding concentration of attacking U-boats. To achieve such a concentration it was essential to make use of the surface mobility of the submarine – U-boats could sustain speeds of sixteen knots on the surface but only two to three knots submerged. On the surface therefore they had twice the speed of the average convoy whilst submerged they had at best only a third. To carry out such tactics it was essential that the U-boats should not be forced to submerge by ships or aircraft or they would lose their mobility. Night was therefore preferable for the concentration period and essential for the final attack phase. As they often had to press on on the surface by day it was also necessary to operate where there were no air patrols.

Escorts and air patrols were very short in the summer and autumn of 1940 when Great Britain was threatened with invasion and so conditions were ideal for 'wolf-pack' tactics, which they were able to carry out only a couple of hundred miles north-west of Ireland. In this period three-quarters of the ships sunk were destroyed at night. The procedure was generally that a patrol line of U-boats would be organized by Admiral Dönitz, based on radio intelligence, with the aim of intercepting a particular convoy. The first U-boat to make contact would report at once by high-frequency wireless to the shore and would make medium-frequency signals to home the other U-boats to the convoy. When all U-boats were in position, the U-boats would attack individually as soon as it was dark. They were able to do this on the surface, relying on their small silhouettes to avoid being seen; they found they could elude escorts and attack individual merchant ships at point-blank range. They would hang on and attack again and again until they had no torpedoes left. These tactics were also a very effective counter to asdics. The asdic beam is not good at picking up submarines on the surface, and with its slow sweep rate was in any case liable to miss U-boats moving at high speed. If a U-boat was sighted, however, it could be forced to dive by gunfire and would then be heavily counter-attacked by asdic and depth charges. In the period June to October of 1940 in fact only two U-boats were destroyed in this way. The situation was therefore one of grave danger to the British who could well lose the war if sinkings on this scale continued.

The British, realizing their peril, took energetic counter-measures. They substantially increased the number of escorts (Note 11) and diverted air patrols to the Atlantic. Fortunately sinkings declined in the winter because of bad weather and the U-boats' operations being forced to the westwards by the Coastal Command air patrols. Information about British convoys acquired by B-Dienst had also fallen off (it was not until January 1941 that they began to get results again). At the same time the British D/F stations which included M/F as well as H/F direction finders were more numerous and began to get into their stride. The Admiralty tracking room, using the information they provided and without being able to decipher any of the German messages, began to be able to route the convoys clear of the U-boat concentrations.

On the outbreak of war there were only twelve Hudson aircraft in Coastal Command fitted with ASV Mark I radar. It was not very efficient, only gave a very short range on U-boats and had many technical deficiencies, and as at the same time Coastal Command aircraft were armed with a poor anti-submarine bomb which was of little use, they were therefore not a very great threat to U-boats in the early stages. Nevertheless they often sighted them, especially on passage round the north of Scotland. In September 1940 the new ASV Mark II was fitted in two squadrons of Whitley bombers allocated to

Coastal Command and this was a considerable improvement. This set operated on a frequency of $1\frac{1}{2}$ m., as did its predecessor, but it also transmitted two narrow beams on each side which could pick up a surfaced U-boat at about twenty-five miles. It was therefore capable of searching a substantial area. On 19 November 1940 a Sunderland flying-boat fitted with the old ASV Mark I made an attack on a U-boat but did not sink it. On 10 February 1941 a Whitley with ASV Mark II attacked another, but during 1941 it was still ships which caused nearly all the U-boat casualties. During the year thirty-six German and Italian U-boats were sunk by ships and in most cases it was asdics that was responsible. To compete with pack attacks, however, something was required which would detect submarines on the surface. Starshell had been tried but this tended to reveal the position of the convoy too.

In November 1940 a naval version of ASV Mark II was fitted in a destroyer. It was a somewhat primitive installation known as Type 286 and had fixed aerials. It covered an arc both sides from fine on the bow to just abaft the beam but could only give very rough bearings without swinging the ship. Nevertheless it often enabled destroyers to detect U-boats on the surface at night and many sets were fitted early in 1941. It was responsible for the sinking of *U100* on March 17 by H.M.S. *Vanoc* (Plate III) and *Walker*. By midsummer ninety-seven escorts out of a total of 247 in home waters were fitted with Type 286. Moreover a very much better set was just coming into service.

It had been realized from the start that for detecting small surface targets the best results would be obtained by a higher frequency radar set. The problem had always been that it was very difficult to get sufficient power at such frequencies. The best valves could only produce about 75 watts at a frequency of 3,000 mc/s (10 cm.) which was of little value. In February 1940 Birmingham University experimented with a device known as the Resonant Cavity Magnetron and produced a power of over 5 kw. on a wavelength of 10 cm. A development team was formed in the autumn at the Admiralty Signal Establishment and by March 1941 they had produced a prototype centimetric set, Type 271 (Plate III), which was sent to sea in the Corvette *Orchid*; it proved able to detect a surfaced U-boat at 5,000 yards. By July twenty-five ships were being fitted and by September it was accepted for general service. Before long an increase in power from 5 to 90 kw. was made possible by the development of the Strapped Magnetron and this increased the range at which a surfaced U-boat could be detected to 8,000 yards.

The U-boat campaign continued unabated throughout 1941 and there is no space in this book to follow it in detail. In general, while both the number of escorts and aircraft available to the British was greatly increased and the convoy system was extended until (with American co-operation) it covered the whole Atlantic, so also did the number of U-boats – by the end of 1941 there were eighty of them operational against the twenty-two of the beginning of the year. In spite of the increase of the number fitted with radar, aircraft failed to achieve much success but this was also because of the ineffectiveness of the weapons they were using. A Wellington aircraft with ASV II did make an attack on a U-boat by radar in September and in November a Whitley sank *U206* in the Bay of Biscay. Aircraft radar was generally most disappointing and at this time many more U-boats were sighted visually than were picked up by it.

Although as already stated surface escorts disposed of thirty-six German and Italian U-boats during the year, they failed to finish off many others which they attacked. The German U-boats had found that diving as deep as they could was very effective. At first this may seem surprising as the distance at which a depth charge is lethal to a submarine increases with depth, but the asdic sets of those days had no way to measure the depth of a submarine, and asdic contact was always lost at close range as the U-boat passed below the asdic beam. The deeper the U-boat the greater the range at which it disappeared, and so the longer the 'blind' run-in before dropping the depth charges. The depth charges then took longer to sink and the accuracy of the attack suffered appreciably. Finally the latest U-boats could dive to 600 feet and the deepest setting on the British depth charges was 550 feet. It is true that many destroyers and escort vessels were now able to fire patterns of ten and even fourteen depth charges instead of the original five and could to a certain extent spread them for depth. In spite of this the lethality of the asdic-controlled depth-charge attack against a deep-diving German U-boat was probably not much more than ten per cent.

The Battle of the Atlantic became a hard slogging match in

which each side had its successes and failures. In May 1941 convoy OB 318 lost five ships but its escorts sank *U110* and two weeks later HX 126 was caught by a wolf-pack nine U-boats strong before it had any escort at all and lost nine ships. In June HX 133 was attacked by ten U-boats while it had only four escorts but reinforcements of another nine escorts arrived. In a running battle lasting several days five merchant ships were sunk for the loss of *U556* and *U561*. In September SC 42 and SC 44 lost twenty ships for two U-boats destroyed but SL 87 lost seven ships and HG 73, in spite of a strong escort of ten ships, lost nine merchantmen. It is interesting that the heavy losses of HG 73 were attributed to radar failure in the escorts. Finally SC 42 was attacked by a concentration of seventeen U-boats and in battles lasting several days lost seventeen ships. Reinforcements then arrived from Iceland and *U501* and *U207* were sunk.

During 1941 the Admiralty tracking room really got into its stride and was nearly always able to predict where the U-boat danger areas were. The direction-finding stations were their main source of information, the number of which had again increased. At the end of the year there were sixteen stations covering the North Atlantic in the United Kingdom, Iceland and Newfoundland, five in the Mediterranean, three in the West Indies and three in the South Atlantic. A watch was kept by many stations on the medium frequencies too, so as to pick up the homing signals made by U-boats to help other U-boats to concentrate against convoys. It seems probable that British cryptographers obtained some results during the year, as in February in the Lofoten Islands raid they captured some rotors for a German Enigma cipher machine. In May and June the Home fleet captured two German weather reporting trawlers off Jan Mayen Island and obtained some more valuable cryptographic material.

In January 1941 the Germans decided to send the *Scharnhorst* and *Gneisenau* out into the Atlantic to raid shipping. Intelligence of their passage through the Great Belt reached the British, and the Home fleet put to sea to intercept them south of Iceland. Eight cruisers were spread on patrol in patchy visibility and at dawn on January 28, one of these, the *Naiad*, fitted with Type 279 radar, sighted the two battle cruisers south of Iceland. The

British cruiser line had however already been detected by the German ship. The Germans at once hauled round to the north-wards and retired at high speed and the *Naiad* never regained contact. The *Scharnhorst* and *Gneisenau* refuelled in the Arctic and later broke out through the Denmark Strait. This incident was the most important success of German shipborne radar so far. On this occasion it outranged the Type 279, which never seems to have gained contact at all, and was responsible for the escape of the two ships from the waiting Home fleet.

In January 1941 the Luftwaffe arrived in Sicily just as an important convoy was being passed through the Mediterranean. This was convoy 'Excess' and six ships, that is about a third of the total number of cruisers and above involved in the operation, had radar. Amongst its escort was the new anti-aircraft cruiser *Bonaventure*, with Type 279. The *Sheffield* with her veteran Type 79 was still the only radar-fitted ship in Force H. The convoy was met by the Mediterranean fleet from the east which was divided into several separate forces. The main body had *Illustrious* and *Valiant* with radar, another force, which included the *Barham* and the *Eagle*, had the radar-fitted *Ajax* with it, while the *Calcutta* brought away a convoy from Malta to the eastwards. The cruisers *Southampton* and *Gloucester*, however, made the passage from Alexandria through the Sicilian narrows to meet the convoy with no radar at all. All went well until Fliegerkorps X located Admiral Cunningham's force just west of Malta on 10 January 1941. Radar gave plenty of warning of the approach of the dive-bombers but *Illustrious* had time neither to recall some of her fighters which were pursuing some Italian torpedo aircraft nor to fly off more fighters. She was hit by six heavy bombs and very seriously damaged. The battleships *Warspite* and *Valiant* were also attacked but survived. Next day, however, the *Southampton* was dive-bombed and became a total loss. The *Southampton* and the *Gloucester* were in company east of Malta and, having no radar, were completely surprised by dive-bombers attacking out of the sun.

On March 25 information reached Admiral Cunningham that a sortie by the Italian fleet against the convoys to Greece was imminent. There is little doubt that this was obtained by cryptography (Note 12) as it was long before any movement could have been detected by reconnaissance. He was therefore able to arrange air patrols which sighted the Italian fleet and thus to engage it. At the Battle of Cape Matapan on 28 March 1941 which resulted there were only three radar-fitted ships with Admiral Cunningham: these were the battleship *Valiant* the aircraft carrier *Formidable* and the cruiser *Ajax*; all had Type 279. The early part of the Battle of Matapan need not concern us except to recall that at nightfall it had become a pursuit by the British of the Italian fleet which had been attacked all day by aircraft from the *Formidable* and from Greece and Crete. The Italian ships were in general faster than the British, and Admiral Cunningham's only hope was that some of them had been damaged and that he could overhaul them during the night. He had good reason to believe that some of the enemy ships had in fact been hit by his torpedo bombers and he determined to risk a night action to finish them off. At 2015 the *Ajax* with the cruisers ahead of the battlefleet detected a ship six miles away to port by her radar. Admiral Pridham-Wippell who commanded the light forces decided simply to report the contact and to press on after the Italian fleet. Admiral Cunningham decided to investigate the contact with the battlefleet and altered course towards it at about 2115. An hour later the *Valiant*'s radar had contact with the stopped ship on the port bow at six miles and held it until at 9,000 yards she had her in sight. Simultaneously the flagship *Warspite*, ahead of the *Valiant*, sighted two ships on the starboard bow crossing ahead. *Valiant*'s radar was at once put on to the new targets, the range being 9,500 yards, and the battlefleet turned to bring its guns to bear. The destroyer *Greyhound* then illuminated the enemy with her searchlight and the *Warspite* opened fire with 15 in. broadsides at 2,900 yards. Her lead was followed by the *Valiant* and *Barham*, all of whom now used searchlights and starshell. The enemy were the Italian cruisers *Zara* and *Fiume*, which had turned back to help the stopped ship which was the *Pola*. In four and a half minutes *Zara* and *Fiume* were blazing wrecks but as an Italian destroyer fired torpedoes, the battlefleet turned away and the main action was over. The *Pola* was torpedoed and sunk by the destroyers *Jervis* and *Nubian*.

The night action phase of the Battle of Cape Matapan was a considerable victory in which radar certainly had a share, but the main credit must go to the development of night fighting by the Royal Navy between the wars and the excellence of their training. While radar made the initial contact with the *Pola*, the battle itself was fought visually with the assistance of searchlights and starshell. The Italian Navy still held to the policy of avoiding action at night so that the main armament guns of the *Zara* and *Fiume* were not even manned when the British battle fleet opened fire.

In May 1941, when the new German battleship *Bismarck* with the cruiser *Prinz Eugen* broke out into the Atlantic, practically every large ship of the Home fleet was fitted with some kind of radar. Five ships had both air warning and gunnery radars, the most modern installation being in the brand new battleship *Prince of Wales* with a dozen sets. These included a Type 281 air warning radar as well as a Type 284 for control of her main armament. The cruiser *Suffolk* had the older air warning Type 279 and a Type 284 for her 8 in. guns. Four ships had air warning sets only and another four, including the battle cruiser *Hood*, had a single Type 284 for the control of the main armament. Two cruisers, one of which was the *Norfolk*, and eleven of the fleet's twenty-five destroyers had the Type 286 fixed aerial set developed from ASV Mark II with which Atlantic escort vessels were being fitted on a large scale. Force H at Gibraltar was not so well equipped. The battle cruiser *Renown* and the aircraft carrier *Ark Royal* had no radar at all and reliance had to be placed in the cruiser *Sheffield*, with her pre-war Type 79. Some of the *Ark Royal*'s Swordfish aircraft, however, had ASV Mark II and this was also so of the *Victorious*'s aircraft with the main body of the Home fleet. Sixty of the total of 400 general reconnaissance aircraft in R.A.F. Coastal Command also had ASV Mark II.

When the *Bismarck* was known to have sailed, therefore, the cruisers sent to patrol the Denmark Strait and the Iceland–Faeroes Gap all had some form of radar. First contact with the enemy was, however, obtained visually by the *Suffolk* at 1922 on May 23 in the Denmark Strait at the range of seven miles which was dangerously close, but she was able to turn back into the mist and hold contact with her Type 284 gunnery radar without being seen. The *Norfolk* with her fixed 286 radar hurrying to gain contact on *Suffolk*'s report also sighted the enemy before obtaining an echo. She was closer still: the *Bismarck* fired upon her but she too managed to disengage successfully.

For the next ten hours the two cruisers shadowed the *Bismarck*, losing contact for an anxious period of two and a half hours in the early morning of May 24. During this time a force consisting of the battle cruiser *Hood*, the battleship *Prince of Wales* and six destroyers were steering to intercept, guided by the signals from the *Norfolk* and *Suffolk*. In spite of bad visibility during the night, Vice-Admiral Holland in the *Hood* imposed a rigid wireless and radar silence upon his force. Even gunnery radar was not to be used until action was imminent. After 0200 on May 24, when the cruisers had lost contact, he directed the *Prince of Wales* to use her Type 284 to search an arc for the enemy, but when told that it would not bear he refused permission to use Type 281. At 0535 the *Bismarck* was sighted at a range of seventeen miles which was considerably greater than contact could have been established by radar using either Type 281 or 284. The *Hood* opened fire first at 26,500 yards followed almost at once by the *Prince of Wales* and both German ships. It seems highly unlikely that the *Hood* used radar ranging. The maximum range of Type 284 was 22,000 yards at best. The *Prince of Wales* certainly obtained no results from her 284 or 281 during the action and her first salvo fell 1,000 yards over. She took six salvoes to cross the target. The *Bismarck*'s first salvo, on the other hand, was exactly right for range and fell just ahead of the *Hood*. The third salvo hit and penetrated the magazine and the *Hood* blew up and sank. The *Prince of Wales* continued to close until at 14,600 yards she was suffering serious damage and she then turned away under smoke. She had by this time succeeded in hitting the *Bismarck* with two heavy shells. The accuracy of the *Bismarck*'s fire suggests that she was using her Seetakt radar for ranging. The power of this set had been increased since the outbreak of war and ranges were claimed to be seventy-five per cent of the extreme optical range. The ineffectiveness of Type 284 in both British ships was disastrous.

There had, of course, in the previous six months been a staggering increase in the number of radar sets in the fleet and there was obviously a lack of experience in operating, adjusting and maintaining them. The rival squadrons were in sight of each other for eighteen minutes before fire was opened and this should have been long enough to warm up and prepare Type 284 for action. Admiral Holland's policy of radar silence is interesting as it shows, if nothing else, the belief held at the time that radar was very likely to give away one's position. It is true that it was very important that the *Bismarck* should not realize that Admiral Holland's force was approaching or she might have turned round and with her superior speed avoided action altogether. Except during the night, visibility was in any case greater than the range of the radar sets, and as there was no enemy air threat there seemed little point in Admiral Holland risking compromising his position.

After the sinking of the *Hood*, the *Norfolk, Suffolk* and *Prince of Wales* continued to shadow the German ships, the *Suffolk*'s Type 284 being mainly responsible for keeping contact. The Commander-in-Chief in the *King George V*, with the Home fleet, which included the aircraft carrier *Victorious*, was now doing his best to intercept. During the afternoon he decided to detach the *Victorious* with an escort to launch an air striking force to try and slow the *Bismarck* down. At 2200 a striking force of Swordfish torpedo bombers and Fulmar fighters was flown off. One of the Swordfish was fitted with ASV Mark II and found the *Bismarck*; in the subsequent attack one torpedo hit was obtained. The aircraft then, thanks to ASV Mark II, found their way back to the *Victorious*. Three hours later the *Bismarck* decided to make for Brest and altered course to the south-east. The *Suffolk* was zigzagging and at the time turning to an outward leg and so lost contact. A rapid search by the *Norfolk* and *Suffolk* was organized but was in the wrong direction and contact was not regained. the *Bismarck* did not at once realize her good fortune. Five hours later, believing the shadowers to be still in contact, she transmitted a long cipher signal giving her intentions. It was at once picked up by the British direction-finding stations and when plotted indicated she was making for France. By an error in staff work, this information was passed out to the C.-in-C. Home fleet in a form which gave him the impression that *Bismarck* was taking the northern route home. Most of the Home fleet was therefore redisposed accordingly but fortunately the Admiralty realized that she was making for Brest. They were therefore able to organize, in co-operation with Coastal Command, patrols and movements to intercept. The *Bismarck* was next located at 1030 on May 26 by a Catalina flying-boat of Coastal Command which was fitted with ASV Mark II radar. Shortly afterwards she was found by one of the *Ark Royal*'s aircraft, and the *Sheffield*, the only radar-fitted ship in

Force H, was detached to shadow. At 1450 a striking force was flown off the carrier consisting of fourteen Swordfish torpedo bombers, one of which had ASV Mark II. This aircraft gained contact by radar from above the clouds and the others dived down to attack. The ship was then found to be the *Sheffield*; and a number of torpedoes were aimed at her but fortunately missed. A second strike three hours later was ordered to locate the *Sheffield* first, who then directed it to the *Bismarck*. This time the *Bismarck* was hit in the rudder and the wound proved mortal. That night and next morning her destruction was completed by units of the Home fleet.

If the British had not possessed radar there is no doubt that the *Bismarck* would have broken out on to the trade-routes without being brought to action. ASV Mark II was of great value for the purpose for which it had been designed: on the other hand, Type 284 was a conspicuous failure as an aid to gunnery but a great success for shadowing. The elderly Type 79 in the *Sheffield*, which had provided Force H with air warning for nearly a year, was also used for shadowing at the end. Radar certainly proved of more value to the British than the Germans. If Seetakt was responsible for the remarkable accuracy of the *Bismarck*'s gunnery against the *Hood*, then it proved itself superior to Type 284, but it seemed to be very little use for surface warning or any other purpose.

Space in this book does not permit us to follow every operation in which radar was involved at sea. We can, however, note some of the more important occasions when it was used. The *Tiger* convoy carrying essential armoured reinforcements to General Wavell through the Mediterranean in May 1941 arrived successfully. It was lucky with the weather but an important feature was fighter protection controlled by radar over the whole route. The Mediterranean fleet was also reinforced by the battleship *Queen Elizabeth*, and the cruisers *Naiad* and *Fiji*, all fitted with Type 279 radar which accompanied the convoy. In the duel round Crete between the Mediterranean fleet and the Luftwaffe immediately following the evacuation from Greece, it needed more than radar to win. Of the fourteen large ships involved, nine had air-warning radar, two only had the fixed aerial of Type 286 and three, the *Warspite*, *Barham* and *Gloucester* no radar at all. Radar, of course, ensured that ships were not surprised by dive-bombers but could not help against sustained and heavy attacks when ammunition was running short.

It is of interest that the British cryptographers gave no warning of the sailing of any of the German surface raiders or of the sortie of the *Scharnhorst* and *Gneisenau* in January or indeed of the *Bismarck* in May. Intelligence certainly knew the *Bismarck* was putting to sea but this was by photographic and ordinary air reconnaissance and sighting as she passed through the Belts. Radio intelligence certainly picked up the long signal made by the *Bismarck* as she turned for France and established her position by direction-finding stations. At the same time a considerable shift of radio activity from the German Group North to Group West was noticed. None of the German messages could be deciphered, but the correct deduction was made that she was heading for Brest. After the *Bismarck* had been sunk, radio intelligence was mainly responsible for the sinking of a number of her supply ships.

The British pre-war world-wide wireless organization was able to cope in the first part of the war, but it was badly overloaded, especially the I Method (referred to in Chapter IV) of contacting ships at sea. It was found necessary to use area broadcasts instead and to get sufficient coverage these had to be on more than one frequency. Instead of broadcasts being at specified times they became practically continuous and in some areas there had to be more than one broadcast to handle the traffic. The passing of messages from ships to the shore on high frequency was not as efficient as it should have been. Messages often took a long time to get through and sometimes failed altogether.

The internal wireless organization in the fleets stood the test of war. The fleets were, however, small and operated fairly close to their bases. The greatest deficiency was voice communication with aircraft especially in the failure to provide rapid communication in ships for fighter direction and the co-ordination of air defence. Another serious deficiency was in convoy communications. It had been thought before the war that visual signals would suffice but a need for voice inter-communication among the escorts soon became apparent as well as voice channels to Coastal Command aircraft. During 1941 low-power high-frequency voice sets were introduced for convoy escorts and they were used without restriction. It was believed that good communication was essential and that the risk of interception by the enemy must be taken. In fact the German intercepting stations obtained a very great deal of information from this source.

Most of the German radio developments during the war were for communication with U-boats. Broadcasts to U-boats were on very low frequency which they could receive submerged. They were backed up by high-frequency broadcasts as well. Messages from U-boats were on high frequency which seemed to be more efficient than the British system and communication proved rapid and reliable in spite of the fact that the frequencies were often changed to try to baffle the British direction-finding system.

In the narrow seas the co-operation of escorts of convoys with R.A.F. fighters steadily improved. Very high-frequency voice sets of R.A.F. design were used for this purpose but the fighters were generally controlled from the shore, using the shore radar stations. In this area it was soon found that the German E-boats communicated freely in plain language on very high-frequency voice sets. Radio interception stations were set up ashore and sets were taken to sea in destroyers, and it was often possible to obtain warning of E-boat attacks, the position of minefields and what casualties they had sustained.

This book has now reached chronologically the eve of Pearl Harbor and it is relevant to review the technical progress of the U.S. Navy during their period of neutrality. We left them in September 1939 with two ships fitted with radar and six sets on order. The CXAM sets ordered in October 1939 were fitted in May 1940 in the battleship *California*, the aircraft carrier *Yorktown* and the cruisers *Chicago*, *Pensacola* and *Northampton*. During 1940 fourteen more improved CXAM-1 sets were ordered and fitted in the other seven aircraft carriers, in five other battleships and the cruiser *Augusta*. Work also started on a number of new projects: Western Electric were given a contract to develop a 60 cm. surface fire-control radar (Type FA) and the Naval Research Laboratory to develop a surface search set. For surface search a short wave was obviously desirable but at the time the greatest transmitting power available was by the use of the Klystron valve which produced only 10 watts. The SC radar was therefore designed with a wavelength of 50 cm. It was compact enough to fit in small ships and proved rather better for air than surface warning. Finally an omni-directional telescopic air warning radar (Type SD) on a metric wavelength was developed for submarines. By the end of 1940 the FA was accepted for service and ten were ordered to fit in the heavy cruiser *Wichita* and nine light cruisers.

This was the situation when in the autumn of 1940 a British mission under Sir Henry Tizard visited the U.S.A. to exchange information. This mission brought with them a magnetron, and this has been described as one of the most important cargoes to cross the Atlantic during the Second World War. With the information about the magnetron, which made powerful microwave radar possible, came also details of the British 175 cm. airborne search radar (ASV Mark II). The U.S. Navy at once set to work to design microwave sets for fire control and warning radar. They also designed their own air-borne ASB set, which was ready for production by the end of 1941. The FA fire control set in the *Wichita*, although designed mainly as a range-finder, was found to be very useful for giving warnings of the approach of surface vessels. It was not accurate enough, however, for blind fire, and the design of two new microwave sets (Type FC and FD) was begun for surface and anti-aircraft fire control respectively.

The FC was fitted in U.S.S. *Philadelphia* in October 1941 and ten more were ordered. They proved a great improvement over the FA and made blind fire possible. The FD started trials in August 1941 in U.S.S. *Roe* where it was married to the new Mark 37 fire control system for 5 in. guns. This was, however, the only ship fitted before Pearl Harbor. During the year the SC warning radar was fitted on a large scale to both big and small ships, and in March 1941 the new microwave set (Type SG) started trials. It went into production during the summer but did not immediately replace the SC sets, many of which remained in service for the rest of the war. At the end of 1941 the Plan Position Indicator was developed (Diagram 15). This showed all echoes simultaneously as though on a map with one's own ship at the centre, thus making it very much easier to see the situation at a glance; it was an important development.

Turning now to sonar, in September 1939 the Navy Department decided to fit it in all destroyers within six months, although the fifty old destroyers transferred to the Royal Navy in the autumn of 1940 had no sonar at all. At the same time as the destroyer deal, an exchange of information with the British took place. From this the U.S. Navy quickly adopted the British streamlined dome and the chemical range-recorder so that their sonar sets then became equivalent to the asdics in the Royal Navy.

The United States Navy was involved in neutrality patrols from the middle of 1940, and from September 1941 began to assist with the escort of convoys in the Western Atlantic. On September 4 the U.S. destroyer *Greer* had a brush with *U652*. She had sonar but of the type that could not operate above ten knots and the U-boat escaped. On October 10 the U.S. Destroyer *Kearney* was torpedoed and seriously damaged while escorting convoy SC 48 and three weeks later the U.S. destroyer *Reuben James* escorting convoy HX 156 was torpedoed and sunk by a U-boat. The American unit involved in these operations was the Support Force of twenty-seven sonar-fitted destroyers commanded by Admiral Bristol. By the end of 1941, however, only about one in five of them had radar. Their communications at first became overburdened and gave a great deal away to the German cryptographers. This then was the situation in the U.S. Navy at the time of Pearl Harbor.

Of the four nations which developed radar independently, the British were the last to do so. They then rapidly assumed the lead and by the outbreak of war were ahead of their competitors, yet there was something in Winston Churchill's criticism before the war and there is no doubt that he foresaw what radar would become much more clearly than the Admiralty. The Admiralty realized how useful it could be for the air defence of the fleet and as a gunnery range-finder, but they were very slow to follow up its obvious value for fighter direction and were dilatory in fitting radar in aircraft carriers.

The *Ark Royal* fought in home waters and in Force H for two years without it and had still not been fitted when she was sunk towards the end of 1941. The *Eagle* was not given even the small Type 291 set until 1942. The U.S. Navy on the other hand had all their aircraft carriers fitted by the end of 1940. As a way to detect surface ships the Admiralty showed remarkably little interest until the surface tactics of the U-boats forced them to take action. It was the R.A.F. who first asked for radar for detecting ships in 1935, and it was their set which was first put in escort vessels to pick up surfaced U-boats. Once the Admiralty had decided that Type 286 was essential to defeat the U-boats, however, their performance was remarkable and over a hundred ships were fitted within six months. Their production of large numbers of the 10 cm. Type 271 and its fitting to practically all types of ship as a surface warning set was also very rapid. No doubt they had serious material problems in fitting radar in the early stages which had to be overcome and they were deterred to a certain extent by the fear that it would give away a ship's position to the enemy. The narrow directional beam and high frequency of naval radar sets made it difficult to detect, and before long the use of radar became practically unrestricted. Its value in any case far outweighed the fact that it might give away a ship's position. The German development of radar was slower still and by the end of 1941 they were little more advanced than they had been in 1939. On balance radar proved of enormous value to the British for air defence, anti-submarine purposes and gunnery, and without it the Allies would have been well on the way to defeat in the Battle of the Atlantic and would probably have been unable to pass any ships through the central Mediterranean at all.

The invention of asdics, which was practically a British monopoly did not prove to be the 'answer' to the U-boat mainly because of its short range. Asdic contact frequently led to the destruction of a U-boat once it was found but did not prove to be much good as an area sweep. This was the principal reason why it always proved better to use anti-submarine vessels to escort convoys rather than to hunt for submarines independently. Nevertheless asdics was responsible for sinking 68 of the 104 U-boats disposed of in the first two years of the war. Without it the British would also have lost the Battle of the Atlantic.

The German magnetic ground mine proved a remarkably effective weapon in the early stages of the war. The British researches in this field soon enabled them to find the countermeasure however, and as each new type of mine appeared they were equal to it. Nevertheless it needed a huge effort to counter the influence mine which was out of all proportion to the effort required to manufacture and lay it. Its near relation, the magnetic firing mechanism for torpedo warheads, on the other hand was a disastrous failure. If it had been effective in the Norwegian campaign the German U-boats would have inflicted losses on the Royal Navy as serious as the Luftwaffe was later able to do off Crete.

Probably the most interesting revelation of this period of the war was the way the 'cryptographic' boot was on the other foot. Supreme in this field in the First World War, the British had their communications exploited to the full by the Germans in the Second World War. The British received no advance warning of any movement of importance except possibly the Italian fleet sortie which led to the Battle of Cape Matapan. The Germans on the other hand gained priceless information of British operations during the Norwegian campaign and in the Battle of the Atlantic. This was done without breaking the high-grade British ciphers at all. The British direction-finding network on the other hand was able to exploit the U-boats' need to use wireless for their 'wolf-pack' tactics and it gained valuable information, as in the First World War, which enabled them to route many of their convoys clear of danger.

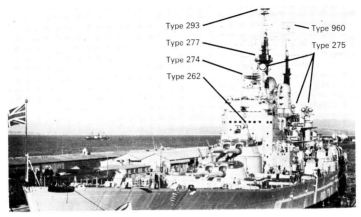

H.M.S. *Vanguard* (Battleship)
Fitted with air warning type 960, surface warning and target indication type 293, main armament fire control type 274, anti-aircraft fire control type 275, close-range fire control type 262 and height finding type 277.

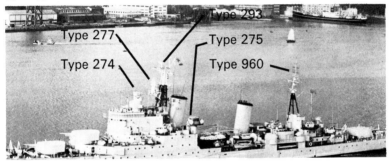

H.M.S. *Birmingham* (Cruiser)
Fitted with air warning type 960, surface warning and target indication type 293, main armament fire control type 274, anti-aircraft fire control type 275, height finding type 277 and navigational radar type 972.

H.M.A.S. *Anzac* (Destroyer)
Fitted with type 293 for combined air and surface warning and target indication, type 962 for navigation, type 275 for anti-aircraft and surface fire control and type 262 for close-range anti-aircraft guns.
(Photos: Imperial War Museum)

PLATE V

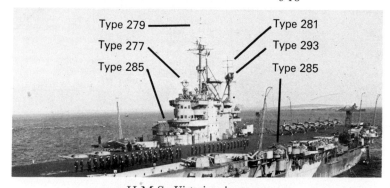

H.M.S. *Victorious* in 1945

Fitted with air warning radars types 279 and 281, height finding radar type 277, surface warning and target indication radar type 293 and anti-aircraft fire control radar type 285.

H.M.S. *Ark Royal* in 1957

Fitted with air warning type 960, low air warning type 982, height finding type 983, surface warning and target indication type 293, navigational radar type 972, anti-aircraft fire control type 275 and close-range anti-aircraft control type 262 (this last is not visible in the photograph).

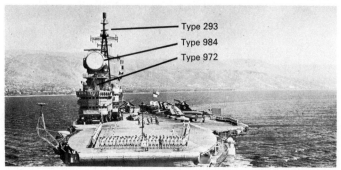

H.M.S. *Hermes* in 1962

Fitted with the all purpose air warning radar type 984, surface warning and target indication radar type 293 and navigational radar type 972.

(Photos: Imperial War Museum)

PLATE VI

IX

The Second World War, 1942-3

As THE AMERICAN State Department had no crypto-graphic service this function was performed for them by the Army and Navy. In 1941 they had constructed a replica of the Japanese 'Purple' cipher machine and could read the messages passing between the Japanese Embassy in Washington and Japan. They were also able to read parts of the Japanese fleet cipher in the Pacific and were well practised in analysing their wireless traffic. For the attack on Pearl Harbor, however, the Japanese issued their orders in writing and no signals referred to it at all. When Admiral Nagumo's carrier force assembled in the Kurile Islands they kept rigid wireless silence and left behind their normal wireless operators in Japan to continue signalling as if they were still in the Inland Sea. American traffic analysis was, nevertheless, able to detect the move southwards of the Japanese invasion forces for Malaya and the Philippines. They noticed too that the Japanese carriers had not put to sea with them but believed they were simply being kept in reserve to counter any movement by the U.S. Pacific fleet (Note 1).

On 1 December 1941 the Japanese changed all their call signs which made matters very much more difficult. When Admiral Nagumo put to sea for the attack on Pearl Harbor he still kept rigid wireless silence for the whole outward voyage. The Japanese had, however, sent a naval officer to the Consulate in Honolulu to report the movements of the U.S. Pacific fleet; on December 2 they ordered all high-grade cryptographic material to be destroyed and so the Americans were able to decipher this officer's final report on the ships present in Pearl Harbor, which was in a low-grade code. The U.S. Navy intercepted and deciphered in full the Japanese instructions to their Ambassador in Washington telling him to break off diplomatic relations. Furthermore, they knew that this note was to be delivered at an exact time which was also the time of dawn in the Philippines. The message to the Japanese Ambassador, however, said nothing about a surprise attack on Pearl Harbor or anywhere else. In spite, therefore, of their very considerable progress with breaking Japanese ciphers, the Americans were still surprised at Pearl Harbor with disastrous results.

By 7 April 1942 the Combat Intelligence Unit at Pearl Harbor had deciphered messages revealing a Japanese plan to seize Port Moresby in New Guinea early in May. Admiral Nimitz at once took advantage of this information and assembled a task force round the aircraft carriers *Yorktown* and *Lexington* in the area. The result was the Battle of the Coral Sea in which *Lexington* was sunk on May 8. Three days earlier Japanese Imperial Headquarters decided to occupy the Western Aleutians and Midway Island. This was to be a major operation involving practically the whole Japanese fleet. As time was very short it had to be organized entirely by wireless as the Japanese ships were spread all over the Western Pacific. At this juncture the Combat Intelligence Unit could read ninety per cent of the messages sent in the Japanese fleet code but they knew a change of cipher was overdue and might occur at any minute. In fact the Japanese had not completed the distribution of the books and the change had had to be put back to June 1.

Indications from decrypted messages began to tell Admiral Nimitz what was in the wind from May 10 onwards and on the 14th he declared a state of 'Fleet Opposed Invasion' in the Hawaiian Area. On May 20 Admiral Yamamoto, the Japanese Commander-in-Chief, sent an important operational order and eighty-five to ninety per cent of this was deciphered by the Americans. The missing parts, however, included the vital time and place of the attack. Admiral Nimitz then recalled the task force built round the carriers *Hornet* and *Enterprise* which had just left for the Coral Sea and ordered the damaged *Yorktown* at full speed to Pearl Harbor. He also despatched a task force of cruisers and destroyers to the Aleutians and reinforced Midway with as many troops and aircraft as it would hold. Finally he placed his carriers to the north-west of Midway where they were unlikely to be sighted by Japanese reconnaissance planes and where they were poised ready to counter-attack. The Battle of Midway, of course, ranks with the great sea fights of history and there are many claimants for the credit for this resounding victory. Nevertheless, it would never have been possible without the breaking of the Japanese codes, and this stands as the supreme achievement of cryptography in both world wars.

There is no space in this book to follow the Battles of Coral Sea and Midway in detail. It is relevant, however, to discuss the arrangements for fighter direction which involved the use of radar and radio. When the U.S. Navy entered the war all their aircraft carriers had either CXAM-1 or SC radar and their aircraft were well practised in using voice radio. The first chance to test their arrangements came on 21 February 1942, when the aircraft carrier *Lexington* was approaching Rabaul to make an attack. *Lexington's* CXAM-1 radar detected a Japanese reconnaissance flying-boat forty-three miles away and Wildcat fighters were vectored out to shoot it down. Later eighteen Japanese planes approached and were detected seventy-six miles away. More fighters were launched and most of the enemy were shot down in sight of the task force. This minor victory for radar-controlled fighters showed that perhaps, contrary to experience in the war so far, ship-borne aircraft could compete with shore-based aircraft.

In the four great carrier battles in the Pacific in 1942 radar controlled fighters had their influence. At the Battle of the Coral Sea in May *Lexington* was entrusted with the fighter direction of the *Yorktown's* aircraft as well as her own. She detected a heavy attack from the Japanese aircraft carriers *Shokaku* and *Zuikaku* at sixty-eight miles. There were ony eight fighters airborne and another nine were launched at once, but there were too few of them. The *Lexington* was sunk and the *Yorktown* badly damaged. Subsequently the fighter directors were criticised but for tactical rather than technical reasons. At Midway in June all three American carriers had radar, the *Hornet* and *Yorktown* Type SC and the *Enterprise* CXAM. The American carriers put three Japanese carriers out of action and there was only one counter-attack; this was by the only remaining undamaged Japanese carrier *Hiryu* and the target was the *Yorktown*. It consisted of eighteen dive-bombers which were detected by

Yorktown forty miles away. She had twelve fighters airborne which succeeded in destroying half the attackers, but the rest seriously damaged her, putting her radar out of action. A second attacking force from *Hiryu* was detected by the cruiser *Astoria*'s radar, again at forty miles, when there were only four fighters up. Eight more were launched but they were short of fuel and four of the ten Japanese planes dropped torpedoes, two of which hit *Yorktown* and she subsequently sank (Note 2).

At the Battle of the Eastern Solomons in August, *Saratoga*'s fighters shot down a Japanese flying-boat detected by radar before the battle had really begun. The *Enterprise* was the fighter-direction ship for the force and in the late afternoon of August 24, a strong force of aircraft from the Japanese carriers attacked. They were detected at eighty-eight miles and fifty-three fighters were ready to oppose them. There was, however, only one radio channel for two fighter-direction officers and indeed for all other purposes to do with aircraft. As the Japanese striking force deployed into a large number of groups for the attack, it became impossible to sort out the radar picture and to tell friend from foe. The radio channel soon became choked, many of the attackers got through and the *Enterprise* was badly damaged by dive-bombers.

In October at the Battle of the Santa Cruz Islands, the Americans were outnumbered by four carriers to two. The *Enterprise* and *Hornet* remained ten miles apart with their escorting vessels but *Enterprise* was given the fighter direction. When the first attack sixty-five planes strong came in there were thirty-eight defending fighters in the air. There were problems with identification and by the time they were sorted out the Japanese were only forty-five miles away. The defending fighters were in any case too close and did not make contact before the Japanese dive-bombers were attacking and already under anti-aircraft fire. The *Hornet* was heavily damaged by both bombs and torpedoes, and totally disabled. A second attack of forty-four planes also damaged *Enterprise* but not so badly. The *Hornet* was abandoned and sunk by Japanese surface forces during the night but the *Enterprise* managed to recover some of her planes and retire. The fighter direction was again heavily criticized by the U.S. Navy in this battle and steps were taken to improve their methods, training and material.

.   .   .   .   .   .

On the other side of the world, by the autumn of 1942 the British had made considerable advances in their fighter defence for Malta convoys. The 'Pedestal' convoy which sailed from Gibraltar for Malta on 10 August 1942 was accompanied by the aircraft carriers *Indomitable*, *Victorious* and *Eagle* carrying seventy-two Sea Hurricane, Fulmar and Martlet fighters. Fighter operations were co-ordinated between the carriers, all of which now had radar, and, in addition, cruisers and battleships had the equipment to direct fighters too. The German and Italian air opposition to the convoy consisted of no fewer than 600 aircraft in Sicily and Sardinia. Many of these aircraft were short-range fighters but they were able to attack with some 263 sorties in all. The fighter defence suffered a serious blow early on when the *Eagle* was sunk by a U-boat and later when the *Indomitable* was badly damaged by dive-bombers and her flight deck put out of action. Yet they fought the convoy through the western basin with small losses, shot down thirty-nine enemy aircraft and damaged as many more, but of the fourteen merchantmen which started only five got to Malta. Most of the casualties were from E-boats and aircraft in the last stages of the voyage after the cruiser *Cairo* had been sunk and the *Nigeria* damaged so that there was nobody to direct the shore-based fighters from Malta. Indeed this was the largest scale fleet fighter defence operation so far by the Royal Navy and when the odds are taken into account was a considerable success. The success was based not only on a larger number of fighters than ever before with the fleet but more radar and voice communications which enabled them to be efficiently controlled.

We now turn from fighter defence to the use of radar in the surface battles round the Solomon Islands in the Pacific during autumn 1942. On 9 August 1942 the U.S. and Royal Australian Navies suffered a serious defeat at the Battle of Savo Island. This was the U.S. Navy's first surface fleet action since the Spanish–American War of 1898. It was a night action in which many of the Allied ships had radar while the Japanese had none. In all except one ship the radars were early types such as SC or FA which worked on metric wavelengths; the exception was the light anti-aircraft cruiser *San Juan* which had the new centimetric SG set, but she was to the eastward and did not take part in the battle. H.M.A.S. *Canberra* had no radar at all and

H.M.A.S. *Australia* the small Type 286. In the Battle of Savo Island the Allied navies were covering the disembarkation of the U.S. Marines at Guadalcanal where some nineteen transports were unloading. They took up a defensive posture with three cruiser-destroyer forces guarding the three main approaches to the landing area. Two destroyers fitted with SC radar, U.S.S. *Blue* and *Ralph Talbot*, were thrown out in the likely direction of the enemy's approach to act as pickets. The effectiveness of the radar of the cruiser-destroyer forces themselves was seriously decreased by land echoes.

As the Japanese force of seven cruisers and a destroyer approached, it launched float planes to reconnoitre. They were able to ascertain the Allied dispositions without opposition. Both the destroyers *Blue* and the cruiser *Quincy* detected them on radar but the general opinion was that they were friendly. The first surface contact was when the Japanese flagship *Chokai* sighted the destroyer *Blue* at about seven miles. The *Blue*'s SC radar should have picked up the Japanese at ten miles but failed to do so, and they passed astern of her without being detected at all. The Japanese then sighted the southern force consisting of the cruisers *Chicago* and *Canberra* at 12,500 yards. They closed and fired torpedoes and had just been sighted by the *Canberra* and the destroyer *Patterson* when the Japanese float planes dropped flares over the transport area, silhouetting the Allied ships. The Japanese then opened fire with their guns. Both cruisers were hit by gunfire as well as by torpedoes, the *Canberra* being put completely out of action. The Japanese next turned their attention to the northern force whose position they knew from the reports of their float planes. They sighted them first and engaged with guns and torpedoes using searchlights at 5,000 to 6,000 yards. The result was the destruction of the heavy cruisers *Vincennes*, *Quincy* and *Astoria*. The Japanese force then retired at high speed.

There were many contributory factors to the disaster such as fatigue and fear among the U.S. ships that they were firing at each other, but nevertheless a force without radar had completely defeated another which was fitted with it. The Japanese night-fighting tactics, using float planes with flares, powerful binoculars and splendid lookouts as well as superbly trained gun and torpedo crews were outstanding; if the American metric radar had been working properly it should have detected the

Japanese at a greater distance than their lookouts could see. The advantage of accurate range which the American gunnery radars should have conferred on them was nullified by the closeness of the action and the fact that the Japanese began to hit before the Americans opened fire. A subsequent inquiry numbered among its findings that the defeat was partly caused by depending too much on inefficient radars and also by poor communications. The U.S. Navy used voice radio a great deal but a lack of method led to confusion (Note 3). It was obvious that the whole problem of night fighting using radar and voice communications needed urgent attention. As it was, the Japanese development of First World War tactics to the ultimate was still superior to the new electronic methods.

In the two months following the Battle of Savo Island the struggle ashore on Guadalcanal continued. Both sides landed reinforcements, the Japanese doing so by warships after dark. The Japanese also took to bombarding the airfield with surface task forces at night. It was to interfere with these operations that an American task force of cruisers and destroyers under Rear-Admiral Scott approached the island in October.

Task Force 64 had several advantages over the victims of Savo Island: they waited until air reconnaissance reported a Japanese force advancing before they took up their position; surprise was therefore on their side and they had learned a great deal from Savo Island. They had been together for several weeks, had time to exercise themselves in night tactics and planned to use their float planes in the Japanese fashion. Last but not least the cruisers *Boise* and *Helena* had the new centimetric SG radar. The *San Francisco*, Admiral Scott's flagship, however, only had SC radar as had the fourth cruiser *Salt Lake City* and the five destroyers. To complicate matters, Admiral Scott believed the Japanese had search receivers which could pick up the transmissions of the SC radars and so ordered that they should not be used.

The Japanese bombardment force of three heavy cruisers and two destroyers under Admiral Goto advanced without any idea that an American task force was in the area. The American float planes were launched but were used to search near Guadalcanal and did not play a significant part in the action. The first contact was by *Helena*'s SG radar at a range of 27,700 yards but for some reason she kept the information to herself and simply plotted the enemy. The flagship *San Fransicso* was using her fire-control radar to sweep but picked up nothing. It was thirteen minutes later before *Boise*'s SG picked up the enemy. *Boise* reported on voice radio at once, but confusion was caused by bad communication drill and Admiral Scott was not sure that the report did not refer to his own destroyers. By this time the range was down to 5,000 yards and the Japanese lookouts had still seen nothing. The *San Francisco*'s fire-control radar then gained contact by which time the *Helena* could see the enemy and was asking permission to open fire. Again voice procedure was faulty, causing a delay, and if Admiral Scott had realized what the *Helena* was asking he would have refused. *Helena*, however, believed she had permission and opened fire with accurate radar-controlled salvoes, catching the Japanese completely by surprise and hitting the *Aoba* at once. The action then became general at 4,000 yards and the Japanese turned and fled. As the Japanese flagship swung round, Admiral Goto was mortally wounded. At this point Admiral Scott lost his nerve and ordered cease fire. He was by no means certain that the American cruisers were not engaging his own destroyers. It took four minutes to sort things out on voice radio, and when *San Francisco* received permission to reopen fire all doubt was removed: she used a searchlight and illuminated the Japanese destroyer *Fubuki*. At 1,500 yards *Fubuki* was soon despatched but the range of the main Japanese squadron was opening fast. The U.S. task force then took up the chase. Their radar-controlled gunfire finished off the *Furutaka* and further damaged the *Aoba*. *Boise* picked up a new target on her radar and was rash enough to illuminate it with her searchlight. Two Japanese cruisers then concentrated on her and she was heavily damaged.

The Battle of Cape Esperance, as this action came to be named, was however a success for the Americans and a serious check to the Japanese. The SG radar proved greatly superior to the Japanese lookouts and the American fire control radars directed their gunnery which did much damage. Communications in the form of voice radio were again confusing, not because the messages failed to get through but because communication procedure and the content of the messages themselves was bad. It also proved very difficult to tell friend from foe. The new type of electronic night action showed some improvement over Savo Island but there was still much to be done.

With the battle still raging on Guadalcanal, the rather odd situation obtained where the sea was commanded by American air power by day and by Japanese surface ships by night. It was at night therefore that the Japanese brought up reinforcements and tried to cut down American air strength by bombarding Henderson Field. In spite of American radar, Japanese night-fighting techniques were still well able to compete.

In mid-November both sides planned a supreme effort to gain mastery on the island. The Japanese intended to bring up substantial reinforcements and bombard Henderson Field with battleships. This was the broad situation on the night of November 12–13 when an American cruiser-destroyer force under Rear-Admiral Callaghan took up a position to try and prevent a Japanese battleship division from bombarding the airfield. Admiral Callaghan had five cruisers and eight destroyers which had been hastily scraped together and had had no time to exercise as a task force. The cruiser *Helena* and the destroyers *O'Bannon* and *Fletcher* had SG radar; the two flagships only had SC sets. To make matters worse the ships with SG were not put in positions where they could use it best. *Helena* was in the centre of the cruiser line and the two destroyers brought up the rear of their respective divisions. The Japanese force, consisting of the battleships *Hiei* and *Kirishima* escorted by the light cruiser *Nagara* and eleven destroyers, was, as usual, depending on lookouts.

The two forces met just north of Guadalcanal, first contacts being by *Helena*'s SG radar at ranges of 27,000 and 32,000 yards. The two forces continued to close at a combined speed of forty-three knots; the Japanese with no idea that an American task force was close ahead of them and Admiral Callaghan in the *San Francisco* trying to use *Helena*'s radar to tell him what was happening through the medium of voice radio. There was only one VHF voice radio channel, which, fortunately for the Americans, the Japanese did not know about, but it inevitably became clogged while the situation developed very rapidly. As a result the two forces virtually ran head-on into each other and a point-blank devastating mêlée resulted, the Americans ploughing right through the middle of the Japanese formation. In under a quarter of an hour the *Atlanta* was totally disabled the *San Francisco* seriously damaged and both *Portland* and *Juneau* hit by torpedoes, four of the American destroyers were either sunk or sinking and both Admirals Callaghan and Scott had been killed. On the Japanese side the battleship *Hiei* was seriously damaged and limping away, two destroyers were sunk or sinking and three others damaged. The Americans had understandably as the weaker force lost more heavily, but they prevented the bombardment of Henderson Field and next day its planes finished off *Hiei*. By engaging in such a close mêlée, however, the Americans sacrificed the whole advantage of radar. The Japanese and, to a certain extent, the Americans used searchlights which allowed a devastating concentration of gunfire to be developed on the target. As always, however, the ships using the searchlights drew fire on to themselves. Voice radio again came in for criticism but the root cause of the trouble was not really in defective communications; it was that all the best SG radars were in private ships and both flag officers and both destroyer division commanders were virtually blind. If Admiral Callaghan had been in *Helena* and Captain Tobin and Commander Stokes in *Fletcher* and *O'Bannon* they would at least have been able to see what they were doing.

The remnants of both forces engaged in the first part of the naval battle of Guadalcanal, as it was called, withdrew; consequently during the next night a Japanese force of two heavy cruisers was able to bombard Henderson Field without opposition. Admiral Halsey, who now commanded in the South Pacific, had already decided to send in his two new battleships *Washington* and *South Dakota* but they could not get there in time to stop the bombardment. They arrived for the night of November 14/15 on which the Japanese intended to bombard Henderson Field yet again, this time using the battleship *Kirishima*, the heavy cruisers *Atago* and *Takao* and the light cruisers *Nagara* and *Sendai* with nine destroyers. The American task force under Rear-Admiral Lee, with the two battleships escorted by four destroyers, arrived off Guadalcanal as soon as it was dark. They swept round Savo Island and were in the area of the battle of two nights before when the Japanese advanced forces of light cruisers and destroyers entered the sound.

Washington picked them up on her SG radar at 18,000 yards and both battleships engaged and drove them out again. While this was going on, the battleship's screen became engaged at much closer range with another larger group close south of Savo Island. Three of the four American destroyers were sunk or put out of action by guns and torpedoes and the fourth was seriously damaged. The two battleships had difficulty distinguishing the radar echoes close to the land and then *South Dakota* suffered an electrical failure which put all her radar and radio sets out of action. She became separated from *Washington* and was missed by a large number of Japanese torpedoes. As the two battleships emerged separately from between Savo Island and Guadalcanal they met the Japanese bombarding force on its way in. *South Dakota*, her power just restored, was illuminated by searchlights at 5,000 yards and engaged by *Kirishima*, *Atago* and *Takao*. She returned the fire but was hit repeatedly, practically every radar and radio set being put out of action. The damage to her upper-works was serious but the Japanese ships being equipped only for the bombardment had no armour-piercing shells and her vitals remained intact. Meanwhile *Washington*, unobserved by the enemy, developed an accurate radar-controlled fire at 8,400 yards on *Kirishima* and completely disabled her. Both battleships, having saved Henderson Field again, retired to the southward, successfully dodging more torpedo attacks by Japanese destroyers. *Kirishima* was later sunk by the Japanese and they also lost a destroyer.

This was the first night action between battleships in the history of modern naval warfare. It is true that the two American battleships were brand new whereas the one Japanese was, although modernized, of First World War vintage. The fact remains that the use of radar both for warning and for fire control was decisive and of great value in helping the two American battleships to know when destroyers were likely to fire torpedoes at them. Admiral Lee understood radar and its capabilities better than the task force commanders involved in the earlier actions in this area, as well as having the advantage of being in the same ship as an SG radar set. Without radar it is doubtful that Admiral Halsey would have committed these new and valuable ships to a night action, and it is probable that without it the superior Japanese night-fighting techniques would have gained yet another success. As it was the two phases of the naval Battle of Guadalcanal tipped the scales in favour of the Americans.

Before the Japanese evacuated Guadalcanal there was one more surface night action at the end of November. At the time the Japanese were still trying to reinforce the island by using destroyers to run supplies through at night, throwing these over in drums off the beaches. On November 30 a U.S. cruiser-destroyer force arrived off Guadalcanal to try to prevent the Japanese reinforcing the island any further. It was under the command of Rear-Admiral Wright, who had only just arrived in the area. It consisted of five cruisers and six destroyers and they at least had time to hold a conference and decide upon their tactics. The force was divided into three groups, two of cruisers and one of destroyers, each of which included a ship with SG radar. The destroyers were to make an independent torpedo attack using radar and then to clear the range for the cruisers to use radar-controlled gunfire at over 12,000 yards (Note 4). Searchlights, after what happened to *Boise* at Cape Esperance, were not to be used at all. The Japanese force consisted of eight destroyers under the command of Rear-Admiral Tanaka, and at 2300 on November 30 it was approaching Guadalcanal. The American task force had just reached the usual battle area between Savo Island and Guadalcanal when the flagship *Minneapolis* picked up the enemy at 23,000 yards. *Fletcher*, the leading destroyer also soon had contact and at 7,000 yards asked permission to fire torpedoes. Admiral Wright hesitated, and by the time he gave permission the enemy were past and it was too late. At 10,000 yards Admiral Wright ordered 'open fire' and the whole American line, except one or two ships with SC radar who couldn't find a target, complied. The Japanese were taken completely by surprise but recovered instantly and fired twenty torpedoes in the next few minutes, followed by more later. The Japanese destroyer *Takanami* was the main target of the Americans and was smothered by fire. Six of the Japanese torpedoes then hit four out of the five American cruisers, causing serious damage and putting them out of the battle. All but one of the Japanese destroyers therefore got away although very little of their stores reached the army ashore. Of the torpedoed American cruisers only *Northampton* was lost; *Minneapolis*, *New Orleans* and *Pensacola* reached Tulagi but all were in a very poor state.

The Battle of Tassafaronga, as it was called, was a serious defeat for a greatly superior radar-fitted force of American cruisers and destroyers by Japanese destroyers alone, which had no radar and were encumbered by troops and drums of stores. Without question the leadership of Admiral Tanaka and the night tactical training of his ships was superb. On the American side many of the faults of previous actions such as inexperienced commanders and task forces quickly scraped together without tactical training were repeated, but for the first time the senior officers were in ships with SG radar and most of the original battle plan was sound. The principal reasons for the defeat were indecision which threw away the value of early radar contact, an over-optimistic assessment of the effectiveness of radar-controlled gunfire and a substantial underestimate of the effective range of the Japanese 24 in. oxygen propelled torpedoes (Note 5). The early FA gunnery control radars gave accurate range and could spot fall of shot at medium ranges but were of little value for laying and training. Even though the correct range was set, the spread of the salvoes was such that there were few hits (Note 6). The use of long snaking columns at night made the American task forces ideal torpedo targets. Nothing came of exhaustive inquiries by the American higher commanders and they remained puzzled. Hope was put in the more general fitting of SG radar and the new FC centimetric fire-control set.

Guadalcanal was evacuated by the Japanese early in February and there were no further night surface actions for five months. The Americans won the Guadalcanal campaign: they did so because their superior air power by day allowed them not only to support their troops better but to reinforce and supply them faster than the Japanese were able to do by night. The American surface forces could not claim that they had obtained command of the sea at night although they certainly disputed it, but they were able to limit the supplies and reinforcements that could be brought in and this turned the scales. It was radar which made it possible for them to do this. Without it they could not have competed at all with the superior Japanese night-fighting techniques and tactics.

We now change the subject somewhat abruptly to communications. In 1942 the British made a substantial improvement in their high-frequency wireless network for receiving messages from ships at sea. It will be recalled that with two wavelengths on each station reception had not proved very reliable. In this year five general ship-to-shore waves were established to be used on all stations. These were in the 4, 6, 8, 12 and 16 megacycle bands. The number of receiving stations was increased and all, including those of the G.P.O., were pooled. Charts were produced to show ships, according to where they were, which was the best wave to use. The system then became excellent and it was unusual for a ship not to be answered at once by some receiving station in the world (Note 7). This station would take the message and send it to its destination by the fixed services between shore stations. This system was soon joined with the American ship-shore organization into a single system. The sending of messages from the shore to ships was by 1942 in most places by multiple frequency continuous broadcast and the I Method had practically disappeared.

With the entry of the U.S.A. into the war, the German U-boats moved across to the American coast and in the first half of 1942 sank the huge total of 585 ships amounting to 3,080,934 tons with very little opposition. By the autumn, however, countermeasures were in force and it became more economical for the U-boats to attack trade nearer home in the Atlantic. By this time their numbers had grown substantially and in July out of a total of 331 boats, 140 were operational. Apart from the fact that activities were on a very much larger scale, the U-boats and their weapons (Note 8) were the same as at the beginning of the war and they still worked in 'wolf-packs' on the surface; yet the U-boats in this period had a priceless advantage in the success of their cryptographers. They were intercepting about 2,000 messages a month, and from February 1942 were able to read the British convoy cipher. This gave them a great deal of information about the movements of convoys and the routes of independent merchant ships. They also learnt much about British successes against U-boats but, what was most dangerous of all, they could read the British daily U-boat summary which showed them the results of the labours of the Admiralty tracking room. While they still could not read the British high-grade operational ciphers, they were often able, as already related, to read the British high-frequency voice communication channel between the escorts of convoys. The results obtained by B-Dienst, however, varied from month to month

and every time a cipher was changed they suffered a set-back;
but by October 1942 they had broken another cipher from
which they found they could get information of convoys more
in advance.

The main Allied improvement in their opposition to the U-
boat at this time was the increase in numbers of escorts and
aircraft available. The ships were also better equipped, and the
more powerful Type 271Q radar with a Plan Position Indicator
was widely fitted. A new anti-submarine weapon called the
Hedgehog had also been introduced. This was developed to
overcome the weakness of the asdic which lost contact well
before the depth charges had to be dropped and the last part of
an attack had to be made blind. With the Hedgehog a number
of small spigot mortar bombs were thrown ahead of the ship
while she was still holding contact by asdics. The bombs sank
much more rapidly than depth charges but were small and had
actually to hit the U-boat to sink it. This had the advantage
that they could secure a kill without having to set the depth as
in a depth charge, but the disadvantage that if they missed the
submarine would not even be damaged. Hedgehog was not
widely fitted in this period and the depth charge remained the
normal anti-submarine weapon. Some progress had also been
achieved in making attacks more effective against deep-diving
U-boats. The maximum depth charge setting was increased to
750 feet and a special attachment was developed for asdic sets.
This 'Q Attachment,' as it was called, was a second oscillator
which projected a fan-shaped beam downwards in the vertical
plane and was able to hold contact to close range when U-boats
were so deep that they would otherwise be below the asdic
beam.

The British had produced a high-frequency wireless direction-
finding set for fitting in ships before the war but its performance
was very disappointing and most of them were landed to make
way for radar. In the summer of 1940 the Admiralty had sent an
investigation team into the Atlantic in a merchant ship to
listen to U-boat wireless transmissions. As a result a renewed
effort was made to fit H/F D/F in the escorts of convoys. By
July 1941 a new set FH3 with aural reception was fitted in a
ship but the results were still disappointing. In October a new
set with visual presentation went to sea in H.M.S. *Culver* and
was a great improvement; in March 1942 it was first used in

action in H.M.S. *Leamington* escorting convoy WS 17 and thereafter it became an important anti-submarine device. It enabled convoy escorts to obtain a bearing whenever U-boats used their high-frequency radio to report the position of a convoy. If more than one ship with 'Huff-Duff', as it was called, was present, cross-bearings could establish the U-boat's approximate position; ships could then be detached to drive off the U-boat and force it to submerge and lose contact. Often they were able to gain contact by radar and then by asdics and sink the U-boat. The number of sets available in 1942 was small, but in 1943 there were enough for two or three ships fitted with it to sail with each convoy. The U.S. Navy produced their own version of 'Huff-Duff' in 1942 and it was fitted in their escorts in much the same way.

Although the escorts *Vetch* and *Stork* had sunk *U252* in April 1942 with the help of Type 271 radar, the Germans did not realize that radar was being used against them until the middle of the summer. In June it was the opinion of the top U-boat captains that no special device was being used by the British escorts. Coastal Command air patrols over the Bay of Biscay using ASV II increased during the early part of 1942 and Admiral Dönitz noticed that they were beginning to surprise U-boats on the surface by day much more often than before. In May a device known as the Leigh Light was fitted in some Wellington aircraft. This was a searchlight in the aircraft's nose which was used in conjunction with ASV II. When contact was made at night by radar, the aircraft would approach to attack and switch on the light at close range to give a point of aim. In June aircraft succeeded in severely damaging three U-boats in this way on a dark night. Admiral Dönitz then realized that the British must be using radar and asked that U-boats should be fitted at once with search receivers to detect the approach of radar-fitted aircraft. In the longer term he asked for the U-boats themselves to be fitted with radar and experiments to be made to 'insulate' a U-boat against detection by radar. He then gave orders for U-boats crossing the Bay of Biscay to proceed submerged by day and night and only to surface when essential to recharge their batteries.

In the autumn of 1942 the battle raged mainly in the gap in the centre of the Atlantic which could not be reached by shore-based aircraft and the U-boats were able to continue their surface tactics. In August eighteen U-boats attacked convoy SC 94 and sank eleven ships for the loss of *U210* and *U379* and three others damaged. Next month in a four-day chase seven ships and the destroyer *Ottawa* were sunk from ON127 and no U-boats were lost. Surprisingly none of the escorts of this convoy had yet been fitted with radar. Between July and September 302 ships totalling 1,505,888 tons were sunk. In August the FuMB search receiver began to be fitted in U-boats. They could now tell when an aircraft with ASV II was approaching and had time to dive. To a certain extent therefore this instrument restored the surface mobility of the U-boats and at the same time the 'Bay Offensive' by Coastal Command ceased to be able to sink U-boats.

Operations during the winter were interrupted by the North African landings but were resumed at the end of the year when thirteen ships were sunk out of one convoy. In the new year of 1943 merchant ship casualties steadily mounted until in March they reached 108 ships amounting to 627,377 tons. In the middle of the month forty U-boats, acting on information from B-Dienst set upon the two convoys HX 229 and SC 122 (Note 9). In four days they sank twenty-one ships for the loss of one U-boat. Two thirds of the ships sunk in March were in convoy and the Admiralty subsequently believed that the U-boats came nearest to victory at this point in the whole war. In the middle of May however four groups of U-boats concentrated against convoy SC 130 and in a battle lasting five days sank no ships at all and lost five U-boats. The U-boat casualties for the whole of May totalled forty-one which substantially exceeded the rate of building. By May 24 Admiral Dönitz had already conceded defeat and withdrew his U-boats from the North Atlantic. Only two months after the crisis therefore the situation was completely reversed and the U-boat campaign collapsed.

The reasons for this sudden change of fortune were many and in some of them the electron was involved. Without doubt the most important reason was the spread of efficient airborne radar. In December 1942 the 10 cm. ASV Mark III began to be fitted in Coastal Command aircraft for trials. It was available in a few operational aircraft in February and began to be used on patrols in early March. The ASV III was not only a very much better radar set than ASV II but it could not be picked up by the FuMB search receiver fitted in U-boats. The U-boats no longer knew they were about to be attacked and surprise was restored to attacking aircraft. In the two months of April and May 1943, of the fifty-six U-boats sunk, over thirty were destroyed by aircraft. Roughly half of these were sunk on the transit routes in the Bay and elsewhere and half round the convoys. The elimination of the Atlantic air gap by the use of very long-range aircraft and escort carriers was, of course, also of major importance. In addition to the U-boats they sank in the air gap, aircraft forced many more to submerge and so sacrifice their mobility and lose contact with the convoy. If these aircraft had not had radar they would only have been able to do this by day, but with radar they could virtually deny the surface of the sea to U-boats round the clock.

Since March 1942 the British had obtained no information by deciphering German signals but it seems that in the spring of 1943 they began to have more success. What was more important was that early in 1943 they realized from the frequency with which U-boats countered the diversion of convoys that the Germans must be reading their signals. In May they introduced changes with which even B-Dienst could not compete. Admiral Dönitz, after being fed daily with first-class information about British convoys, routes, diversions and where the British thought his U-boats were, suddenly went blind. With the security that still surrounds the details of cryptography it is impossible to assess just how decisive this change in cryptographic fortunes was. It can only be an informed guess to say that it was probably as important as the closing of the Atlantic air gap. One of the other major tactical changes which brought about the defeat of the U-boats in May 1943 was the formation of support groups. These were not independent hunting groups as used early in the war but were well-trained first-line escorts sent in groups to reinforce the normal escorts of threatened convoys. When U-boats concentrated against convoys they found themselves opposed sometimes by double lines of defence and an escort strength that could always spare ships, once they gained contact with a U-boat, to hunt them until they were destroyed. There seems little doubt that the astonishing success of these groups in being with the right convoy at the right time relied heavily on cryptography as well as the normal intelligence work of the Admiralty tracking room based on direction finding.

It is seldom in war that great victories can be attributed to one or even two factors. Certainly in this case it was many things and we must not forget the centimetric radar in escorts, the improved methods of attacking deep-diving submarines, the use of high-frequency direction finders by the escorts and the great improvement in convoy communications. What we can say is that the electron was involved in practically every one of these and it cannot be denied that it had a major part in the victory in the Battle of the Atlantic.

The result of the American submarine campaign in the Pacific against the Japanese was very different. During the first year the U.S. submarines were plagued, as had been the Germans, by a defective torpedo which ran too deep and had an unreliable magnetic exploder. The submarines themselves were, however, excellent for the Pacific: they were larger than the German U-boats and were fast on the surface – their four diesel engines propelling through electric drive gave them a speed of twenty knots. At the outbreak of war a number of them were fitted with SD radar which had been designed as an air-warning set for use on the surface. It would give the range of an approaching aircraft but not its bearing. Its performance in a rough sea was poor, it was suspected that the Japanese could home on it and it was little used. A new radar set, the centimetric Type SJ, was under development and began to be fitted in the autumn of 1942; this was a search set for use when on the surface and was capable of picking up merchant ships at 10,000 yards, sometimes considerably more. The SJ radar was ideal for making night surface attacks as it was able to find ships over a wide area. The targets could be detected before they could be seen and the submarine could use its surface speed to get into an attacking position without fear of being sighted. The course and speed of the target could then be ascertained accurately by plotting and so when the torpedoes were fired they were more likely to hit.

The first submarine to take an SJ radar on patrol was U.S.S. *Haddock* in August 1942. She sank two ships in night attacks and from then on Japanese merchant ship casualties increased dramatically. In January 1943 the *Wahoo* sank three ships and damaged a fourth in a ten-hour running battle with a convoy; this sort of performance was repeated by many other submarines. In September 1943 the U.S. submarines began to work in 'wolf-packs'. Their 'wolf-pack' tactics were, however, quite different from those of the German U-boats. Packs of two to four submarines would leave harbour in company under the command of the senior officer. They would communicate freely on very high-frequency voice radio and would keep together for the whole patrol, returning to harbour in company. Control from the shore was limited to the allocation of the area in which they were to work. At night the pack would be spread to search for targets. If a convoy was found the submarines would close to attack, communicating as necessary on voice radio. Generally one submarine would attack from each side, the first one to finish then dropping astern to shadow and pick off any damaged ships. The attacking submarines were known as flankers and the one astern as the trailer. As they did not use high-frequency radio in the pack attacks they gave nothing away to the Japanese shore H/F D/F network. The VHF voice radio had a short range and could not be picked up much beyond the horizon. Sometimes the submarines would use their radar and surface speed at night to get into a favourable position to make a submerged attack as soon as it was light.

The Japanese anti-submarine measures were well behind those of the Allies. Japanese destroyers and escort vessels had an echo-ranging set similar to asdics but by the end of 1943 they had not fitted radar. Radar sets were doing trials and by the end of 1943 they had produced sixty 10 cm. sets. These were not very good as they were of low power (2 kw.) and had a long pulse. None of them had been fitted in escort vessels by the end of 1943. The Japanese also had search receivers but these were not yet fitted in escort vessels either. Their shore H/F D/F network was efficient, with a dozen stations from the Aleutians to Rabaul, and they were able to tell roughly how many U.S. submarines were at sea and in which areas they were working. In all they succeeded in sinking fifteen U.S. submarines during 1943 for the loss of 308 merchant ships totalling 1,366,362 tons. The Japanese intelligence was otherwise bad. They were unable to break any American codes and believed that their own were secure. In this they were quite wrong. On 29 January 1943 the Japanese submarine *I.7* was sunk off Guadalcanal with new code books for distribution which were captured. From then on cryptography yielded an immense amount of information about Japanese merchant ship movements and convoys which was used to help the U.S. submarines find their targets. Admiral Lockwood, commanding the U.S. submarines in the Pacific, has estimated that they sank some thirty per cent more tonnage because of radio intelligence.

It is now generally accepted that victory in the Battle of the Atlantic came in May 1943. At the time, however, the Germans looked upon it as a temporary breathing space until they could renew the battle with improved equipment. In the long term they hoped to develop U-boats with greatly increased submerged characteristics which could carry out pack tactics and concentrate against convoys without surfacing. This was a long way away, however, and so they pinned their hopes on three ways to make it possible for the existing U-boat fleet to attack convoys without crippling losses. The first of these was a new search receiver to detect centimetric radar. The British ASV III was adapted from the H2S radar designed for Bomber Command and was very similar. It was therefore only a matter of time before a bomber was shot down and a centimetric radar set fell into the hands of the Germans. This in fact happened in February 1943 near Rotterdam, but the Germans were very reluctant to believe that it was possible to produce sufficient power on such a high frequency and took some time examining the H2S. By May however they had begun to design a new search receiver but it could not be ready before the autumn. The second German advance had been under development for some years. This was the 'Zaunkönig' acoustic homing torpedo (Note 10). This torpedo was attracted by the noise of a vessel's propellers and made torpedo attack on small ships such as escorts possible. The U-boats would therefore be able by attacking the escorts to render a convoy defenceless. The 'Zaunkönig' was a complicated weapon and precautions had to be taken to ensure that it did not turn and chase the U-boat which had fired it. Development was now well advanced and the 'Zaunkönig' would also be available in the autumn. The third advance, if it can be called an advance, was to mount more anti-aircraft guns in the U-boats.

During the summer the U-boats suffered two more defeats. The first was in the Bay of Biscay where they tried to fight it out with the radar-fitted aircraft using their anti-aircraft guns. This was very unwise and although in May, June and July, fifty-seven Coastal Command aircraft were lost in the Bay, so were twenty-eight U-boats, and another twenty-two were damaged. The second defeat was in the Central Atlantic where a group of U-boats had been sent to harass convoys from the U.S.A. to the Mediterranean and where U-boats bound for more distant areas refuelled from U-tankers. In June, July and August aircraft from the American escort carriers *Core, Card, Santee* and *Bogue* disposed of sixteen U-boats, eight of them U-tankers. This success not only prevented attacks on convoys in this area materializing but was directly responsible for the collapse of U-boat operations in distant seas by the disruption of their fuelling arrangements. Most of the attacks were by carrier-borne aircraft by day and were heavily opposed by anti-aircraft fire. The carrier operations were based on H/F D/F on the many German signals needed to organize the fuelling programme with the U-tankers. There is little doubt too that the Americans were obtaining plenty of information from deciphering German messages as well. Some of the U-boats were sunk by a new 'Mark 24 Mine' – this was in fact a small acoustic homing torpedo – which the U.S. Navy introduced into service just before the Germans.

Admiral Dönitz resumed the attack on Atlantic convoys in September. U-boats, equipped with the new 'Hagenuk' search receiver able to give warning of the approach of centimetric radar and with the 'Zaunkönig' homing torpedo, crept submerged through the Bay of Biscay without loss. They also had heavy anti-aircraft armaments and a radar decoy balloon. On September 20 twenty U-boats attacked convoys ONS 18 and ON 202, and in an action lasting four days they sank six merchants ships with ordinary torpedoes and hit four escorts with the 'Zaunkönig', three of which sank. This was for the loss of two U-boats.

This phase of the U-boat campaign continued for four months after which it also collapsed. During the period they only sank sixty-seven ships of 369,800 tons for the loss of sixty-two U-boats. The British were ready for the 'Zaunkönig' torpedo and had a counter-measure in the form of a towed noise-maker ready to send to sea (Note 11). Few more escorts were sunk and this new weapon failed to live up to Admiral Dönitz's expectations.

The new German search receiver was effective and told the U-boats when to dive: this reduced their losses in the Bay of Biscay but did not restore their mobility in the vicinity of convoys. The new devices therefore failed to restore the potency of the conventional U-boats. The only hope of victory now lay in new types of U-boat with high submerged speed, and until these could be produced all that could be done was to continue operations to tie down the huge air and surface forces deployed against them by the Allies and to prevent them being used for any other purpose.

The attack on trade continued in other places than the Atlantic and it is of interest to our subject to see what was going on in the narrow seas between Great Britain and Europe. The R.A.F. CHL stations of the coastal radar chain were able to pick up ship echoes from the beginning of the war. They were, therefore, very useful in counter-measures against German E-boats whether they were used for minelaying or attacking convoys with torpedoes. The East Coast is generally low and so they could only detect E-boats at about seventeen to twenty miles in most places. Near the Humber the war shipping channel was so far out that it could not be covered by radar from the shore. At Dover, on the other hand, the Straits right across to the French coast were within range. At some places where it was important to the Navy to have coverage, special CDU radar sets were placed, notably in forts across the entrance to the Thames estuary. The shore radar was used not just to give warning but actually to direct coastal forces craft to intercept the enemy.

On the night of 24–25 October 1943 a typical action was fought off the Norfolk coast. Two coastal convoys, one northbound and one southbound, were on passage in the war channels, each escorted by a destroyer. Four other destroyers patrolled fifteen-mile stretches of the war channel and sixteen coastal craft (Note 12) were disposed to seawards in pairs roughly ten miles to the eastwards. Five motor torpedo boats were kept in reserve at instant readiness at Lowestoft. On this particular evening about thirty E-boats left Ymuiden to attack the northbound convoy. They split up into three main groups which approached the war channel at points about ten miles apart. At 2318 the destroyer *Pytchley* escorting the northbound convoy obtained a radar contact with five or six E-boats of the northern group. She at once sent a radio warning and succeeded in driving them off by gunfire, damaging one severely. As a result the E-boats failed to locate the convoy. The Commander-in-Chief at the Nore at once moved all the coastal force groups and the patrolling destroyers about twenty miles northwards, parallel to the war channel, and ordered the five motor torpedo boats in Lowestoft to put to sea. The shore radar stations now began to report numerous contacts immediately east of the war channel and the destroyer *Eglinton* was ordered to join the escort of the northbound convoy. As a result of these moves the destroyers *Worcester* and *Mackey* both engaged groups of E-boats, sinking one, and subsequently five of the coastal force groups made contact, sinking another three E-boats. These operations directed almost entirely by radar either in ships or ashore protected both convoys from attack, although a trawler which had straggled was sunk.

Away in the Pacific we must take note of another substantial success by the American cryptographers. In April 1943 Admiral Yamamoto, the Japanese naval Commander-in-Chief, made a tour of inspection of the southern area. His programme was sent in cipher by wireless and intercepted and decoded by the Americans. They were able to dispatch a number of long-range fighters from Henderson Field on Guadalcanal and shoot down his plane in flames into the jungle on Bougainville Island. The Japanese at the time never even suspected their codes were being broken and remained in ignorance of the reason for the death of their Commander-in-Chief.

There were no significant contacts between surface forces in this same area until the American invasion of New Georgia in June 1943. This led to the battles of Kula Gulf and Kolombangara in the middle of July. The strategic stiuation was very similar to that at Guadalcanal with the Japanese trying to interfere with the landings and to run in supplies. By this time all the American cruisers and destroyers had been fitted with SG radar and also with combat information centres. The cruisers had the new FC centimetric fire-control radar with which complete blind fire was possible. In the Battle of Kula Gulf these technical advances seemed to make little difference. An American task group under Rear-Admiral Ainsworth of three cruisers and four destroyers was sent to prevent Japanese destroyers landing reinforcements on New Georgia. The Japanese used ten destroyers divided into three groups, and one of these destroyers, the *Niizuki*, had an early type of Japanese radar set (Note 13). First contact was, as usual, made by SG radar at 24,700 yards, but by the time the Americans had assumed their battle formation the range had fallen to 12,000 yards and the *Niizuki* had sighted them visually. Admiral Ainsworth then decided to engage with full radar control but the range was closing so fast that it was down to 6,800 yards before he opened fire. The whole American line concentrated on *Niizuki* and smothered her, new radar, force commander and all, and she was unable to fire her torpedoes. Two other destroyers launched all sixteen of their torpedoes and hastily retired and escaped. Three torpedoes then hit and sank the cruiser *Helena*. Skirmishes with the other Japanese groups also took place but the only result was that the destroyer *Nagatsuki* ran ashore. *Niizuki* sank and *Nagatsuki* was sunk by American aircraft next day, but the Japanese had landed most of their troops.

The Battle of Kolombangara a week later was also fought by Admiral Ainsworth's task force but he had the New Zealand cruiser *Leander* in place of the *Helena* and ten instead of four destroyers. The Japanese were again running in troops in destroyers but were using the cruiser *Jintsu* and five destroyers as a covering force. First contact was made this time by the Japanese using a radar search receiver (Note 14) which picked up the American radar impulses at something of the order of 100 miles and tracked them accurately at fifty miles. When the two forces were twenty-six miles apart, an American Catalina flying-boat sighted and reported the Japanese and at 30,000 yards SG radar in the task force picked them up too. Admiral Ainsworth believing the enemy were unaware of his presence continued to close and then ordered his van destroyers to attack with torpedoes. The Japanese were ready with their torpedoes too and the moment they saw the Americans they fired. The American torpedoes were launched practically simultaneously the range being about 10,000 yards. Both sides then opened gunfire, the Americans firing blind in radar control and the Japanese using searchlights. As usual all the Allied fire fell on one ship, this time the *Jintsu*. She was also hit by two torpedoes and was disabled. The Japanese torpedoes then arrived and hit the *Leander*. In a later phase of the action, the Japanese destroyers had reloaded and succeeded in torpedoing the cruisers *Honolulu* and *St Louis* and the destroyer *Gwin*. All three Allied cruisers got back to Tulagi whereas the *Jintsu* sank. At the time the U.S. Navy believed their radar-controlled gunfire had sunk much more than proved to be the case. It was not clear to them that SG and FC radars and combat information centres, excellent though they were, still could not compete with the long-range 24 in. torpedoes.

There was a battle involving destroyers at Vella Lavella in October but the next surface action in which cruisers took part was not until November immediately after the landings on Bougainville. The Japanese sent a force of two heavy and two light cruisers with six destroyers to try to destroy the transports which were still unloading in Empress Augusta Bay. Defence was entrusted to Task Force 39 under Rear-Admiral Merrill consisting of four cruisers and eight destroyers. Some of the Japanese ships had primitive radar sets but they still relied mainly on their lookouts. In this action Admiral Merrill kept at long range and engaged with radar-controlled gunfire, making frequent alterations of course as an anti-torpedo measure. In this he was successful and his main force evaded all the torpedoes fired at them. The cruiser *Sendai* was damaged and subsequently sunk by American torpedoes. In this battle the U.S. Navy found the answer to the 24 in. torpedo which was to keep at the limit of its range and by radical manoeuvring make the control problem almost impossible. Such tactics however made their own gunnery difficult. At these ranges radar ranging was more accurate than the guns and hitting was infrequent. Their gunnery at 19,000 yards obtained some twenty hits out of more than 4,500 rounds fired. These tactics depended entirely on radar and the enemy was only seen on the radar screens. In this battle, too, destroyers made their torpedo attacks entirely by radar. At these ranges the Japanese could not see their enemy at all and attempts to use long-range heavy calibre starshell were countered by the use of smoke. With these new tactics Admiral Merrill at last got the measure of Japanese night surface tactics. The Battle of Empress Augusta Bay was a victory for the U.S. Navy as they were able to protect the transports with very little damage or casualties to themselves.

.   .   .   .   .

While these battles were being fought in the Pacific at night without the contestants seeing each other, there were no night surface actions in European waters. Electronic development however did not stand still and the British, except for the development of total blind fire for gunnery, in general kept pace. It had become clear during 1941 that the gunnery radar sets of the 284/5 series had many deficiencies. Probably the greatest of these was that 284 for surface fire control had a shorter range than the main armaments of battleships and heavy cruisers. To improve matters the power of the Type 284 was progressively increased until it was doubled. With 50 kw the Type 284M was able to pick up targets at 30,000 yards. Although the Types 284/5 could obtain a bearing and were of great assistance in finding a target, a visual point of aim was still essential. Obviously the next step was to try to achieve full blind fire using radar. It would then be possible to engage ships which could not be seen at all. These sets were therefore given beam switching which achieved a bearing accuracy of a quarter of a degree, but this was not really good enough for accurate fire at long range and in the Type 285 it was not possible to get sufficiently accurate elevation for anti-aircraft work. It was clear that to get satisfactory results these fire control sets would have, as in the U.S. Navy, to be completely redesigned to work in the 10 centimetre band. Work was begun accordingly.

During 1942 arrangements for fighter direction and air defence were greatly improved. They were still based on the 281 and 279 radars which gave reasonable coverage out to 100 miles. The 281 now had a single aerial for transmitting and receiving, and the Plan Position Indicator began to be used. Voice radio was greatly improved both between aircraft and ships and between ships themselves. It was possible now to 'tell' an air defence situation to other ships and cruisers, and battleships were able to direct fighters. Every aircraft carrier now had radar and also every large ship. Better radar also spread rapidly among small ships. The Type 286 was modified to use a rotating aerial and became a very useful set for combined warning of air and surface targets (Plate III). The set was then redesigned and as Type 291 gave ranges of thirty-five miles on aircraft and 17,000 yards on a large ship. This set was from the second half of 1942 fitted in all operational British submarines as well as other small surface warships.

During 1942–3 all ships as they came into refit had radar fitted or brought up to date. Battleships and cruisers were given sets for air warning, fighter direction, surface warning and fire control of all types of guns (Plate IV). Destroyers had surface warning and small air warning sets as well as gunnery fire control sets. Atlantic escorts generally had surface warning only but East Coast escorts had small air warning and anti-aircraft fire control sets (Note 15).

At the end of 1943 the German battle cruiser *Scharnhorst* sortied from her base in North Norway to attack convoy JW 55 B on its way to North Russia. The convoy, in addition to its own close escort, was covered by a force consisting of the three cruisers *Belfast*, *Norfolk* and *Sheffield* which was in its turn supported by the battleship *Duke of York* with the cruiser *Jamaica* and four destroyers. The large British ships all had the latest radar described in the last few paragraphs.

The *Scharnhorst* was not so up to date. She had two radar sets, one high up on the foremast and the other lower down abaft the main mast. The forward radar was the usual G.E.M.A. Seetakt with large mattress aerial working on 80 cm.; the after set may have been similar but is more likely to have been a 'Hohentwiel', a Luftwaffe ASV set which had been adapted for use in the German Navy during 1943. It was smaller and worked on 55 cm. and had a power of 30 kw. It could give up to 40 km. range on aircraft but only 7 km. on ships.

The conditions facing the convoy in this Arctic winter were rigorous in the extreme. A moderate gale with heavy seas was blowing, temperatures were very low and it was almost perpetual night. The sun never rose above the horizon and day consisted of a few hours of twilight. Conditions for look-outs were almost impossible but the performance of radar, with its operators in reasonable comfort was unimpaired. The first contact was between the *Scharnhorst* and the three cruisers of the covering force. It was at 0840 on December 26 by *Belfast*'s 273 at a range of 35,000 yards. The squadron closed in until at 0921 the *Sheffield* sighted the *Scharnhorst* at 13,000 yards. Three minutes later the *Belfast* opened fire with starshell and the *Norfolk* engaged with her 8 in. guns, the range by then being 9,800 yards. The *Scharnhorst* knew nothing until the starshell burst overhead and the shell splashes rose close on the beam.

Her Seetakt radar then obtained contact and she turned away at full speed and opened fire with her after turret; the range opened rapidly as in the prevailing sea conditions she had a substantial speed advantage. The action only lasted ten minutes but in that time the *Norfolk*, with her guns aimed visually in the light of the starshell but with range and fall of shot being given by 284M radar, hit the *Scharnhorst* at least twice. One shot caused a fire amidships and the other put the Seetakt radar out of action. The enemy battleship being only able to see the flashes of the British guns obtained no hits and disengaged to the south-east at high speed, but she next decided to work round to the north and make another attempt to attack the convoy. When she believed she had shaken off the British cruisers, she altered course. The British were however still in radar contact and noted the move. They lost contact eventually at 1030 at 36,000 yards when *Scharnhorst* was steering north-east at twenty-eight knots. Admiral Burnett was then able to head her off and keep between her and the convoy.

The *Scharnhorst* was next detected at about noon by the *Belfast*'s (Note 16) and *Norfolk*'s Type 273 radars at 30,500 and 27,000 yards respectively as she approached the convoy again. The range decreased rapidly and at 1221 the *Sheffield* and *Scharnhorst* sighted each other simultaneously. The *Scharnhorst* turned to disengage at once and as she did so her after radar gained contact. She opened fire, being able to see the British ships against the southern horizon in the twilight. She made good practice and hit the *Norfolk* in 'X' turret, putting it out of action, and again amidships, destroying all her radar sets except the Type 284M on the forward director. The range then opened until at 12,400 yards she could no longer see the target and ceased fire. The British ships obtained no hits in this skirmish and Admiral Burnett now decided to confine himself to shadowing to ensure that the *Duke of York*, which was still some way off but fast approaching, made contact. The *Scharnhorst* had received a somewhat obscure signal indicating Admiral Fraser's approach from a Luftwaffe air reconnaissance report and now decided to abandon the attack on the convoy and return to base. Admiral Burnett's cruisers fell in astern as she steamed for home and they kept contact by radar at 13,400 yards, which was just outside visibility distance. The pursuit lasted three hours during which *Norfolk* fell astern to deal with action damage and *Sheffield* to repair an engine defect. The *Belfast*, however, held contact without difficulty and kept Admiral Fraser informed by wireless of the *Scharnhorst's* every move.

There was a distinct possibility that the navigational reckonings of the *Belfast* and the *Duke of York* would show a considerable disparity. The *Duke of York*, however, made good use of her H/F directional wireless to check the relative positions of the two forces. At 1617 the *Duke of York's* Type 273 radar picked up the *Scharnhorst* at 45,500 yards. The range closed rapidly and at 1632 the Type 284M had an echo at 29,700 yards. Eight minutes later the *Duke of York* had contact with the *Belfast* and *Norfolk* at 40,000 yards. The *Belfast* was ordered to illuminate with starshell and at 1647 she did so, followed a minute later by the *Duke of York* herself. The *Scharnhorst* appeared to be caught completely by surprise, probably because her only remaining radar set had a substantial blank arc ahead. As the starshell burst she was seen to have her turrets trained fore and aft. The *Duke of York's* first salvo, aimed visually with radar range, was fired at 12,000 yards and hit as did her third salvo, putting *Scharnhorst's* foremost turret out of action. The *Scharnhorst* turned to the eastward and increased to full speed to escape. She began to draw away almost at once and the action continued at gradually increasing range. *Scharnhorst's* fire was at first wild but improved between 17,000 and 20,000 yards by which time she was using her remaining radar set for ranging.

The destroyers *Savage*, *Saumarez*, *Scorpion* and *Stord* had been ordered to get into a position to attack with torpedoes and, in pairs, were very slowly overhauling the target on each side of her. The destroyers were fitted with the rotating Type 286Q radar for combined warning and 285M for fire control and were already in contact. At about 1820 *Duke of York* obtained a hit in *Scharnhorst's* forward boiler room and her speed fell to eight knots. At the same time she ceased firing at *Duke of York*, the range being about 20,000 yards; she was soon able to increase speed again to twenty-two knots but the destroyers gained on her rapidly and were already at 12,000 yards.

The *Duke of York* then altered to the southward to head *Scharnhorst* off from her base. At 1844, the range being 21,400 yards, the *Duke of York* also checked fire. At this time it seemed possible that *Scharnhorst* might escape, but the destroyers had reached a firing position and between 1849–55 they launched twenty-eight torpedoes from between 1,800 and 3,500 yards, obtaining at least three hits. The *Duke of York* was now able to close rapidly and at 1901 she re-opened fire at 10,400 yards obtaining many more hits. Between 1925 and 1934, the cruisers *Jamaica* and *Belfast* and the destroyers *Musketeer*, *Opportune* and *Virago* (Note 17) fired twenty-eight torpedoes and obtained another five hits, as a result of which *Scharnhorst* sank.

In his despatch Admiral Fraser reported: 'In general the speed of wireless communication and the exceptional performance of radar reflects the greatest credit on the personnel concerned and in this night battle contributed in great measure to its success.' In this writer's opinion this is a considerable understatement where radar is concerned. There is little doubt that without radar the battle would never have been fought at all, let alone won. As it was, radar turned the Arctic night into day for the British but for the Germans it remained an Arctic night. Their radar was greatly inferior for surface search and gunnery and was no better than their lookouts and optical range-finders. The British Type 271–3 centimetric radars with Plan Position Indicator presentation showed them the whole situation at ranges which would need very good visibility to be equalled by day, with the added advantage that relative positions, courses and speeds could be accurately calculated. For gunnery the Type 284M gave accurate ranges to maximum gun range and spotted fall of shot. Starshell had to be used to give a point of aim but the starshell was accurately controlled by radar so as to illuminate the right place at the right time. Starshell was used from 6 in. and 5·25 in. guns at very long ranges, far greater than could be illuminated even by the 44 in. searchlights of the *Duke of York*. Searchlights were in fact only used at the very end for confirming that *Scharnhorst* had sunk and for picking up survivors. Radar was also of great value for torpedo control. Although the torpedoes were fired with a visual point of aim sometimes with the aid of starshell, radar plotting gave the enemy's course and speed and ensured that friendly ships were not endangered.

It is interesting that the use of radar by both sides was completely unrestricted. There were no fears such as Admiral Holland felt in the *Bismarck* action, that radar might prove more of a disadvantage than an advantage. In fact neither side seems to have used search receivers or to have benefited in any way from the enemy's transmissions. Admiral Fraser was very free with his wireless transmissions too. He sent a number of signals before contact was made with the *Scharnhorst*, to co-ordinate the movements of his forces and to establish exactly where they were. One signal made as the *Duke of York* was opening fire was intercepted and decoded by the German Group North which gave her position. It was sent to *Scharnhorst* at 1763 but it was of little value as she had been in action with her for over half an hour. In general Admiral Fraser's free use of wireless paid off. It gave the enemy little information and was responsible for the splendid team work of the various British units. *Scharnhorst* also made a number of signals before action was joined, some of these were necessary to try and control the movement of the five destroyers which sailed with her, but one gave away the fact that she was at sea. It was made at 2355 soon after sailing and was unnecessary. It was to try and obtain confirmation that the German High Command agreed that, if need be, *Scharnhorst* should go on with the operation without the destroyers.

By the end of 1943 radar had become essential equipment in all warships from battleships to coastal forces. It was also widely used in aircraft. It was used not only for directing fighters and night surface action but for gunnery range-finding by day. It was also the key to the battle against the U-boats and was widely used by coastal forces in the narrow seas. In the hands of the Americans it was proving very effective for submarine warfare. All these craft also found it invaluable for navigation and station keeping. Counter-measures to radar hardly existed and its use was practically unrestricted. Cryptography in this period continued to be of priceless value to the side which was successful with it. The battle for supremacy was continuous and the results were very varied. For instance, while the Germans were well informed about convoys in the Atlantic in the autumn of 1942 they did not receive an inkling of the Allied invasion of North Africa. In general it can be said that the electron had penetrated naval warfare to an extent that it was essential in order to wage it at all.

Type 992
Navigational Radar
Gunnery Radar
Type 965
Type 277
Type 901

H.M.S. *Devonshire* in 1962
This guided-missile destroyer has type 965 for air warning, type 277 for
height finding, type 992 for surface warning and target indication, type 901
for control of the Seaslug missiles, gunnery radar and a modern commercial
navigational set.

Type 965
Navigational Radar
Type 293

H.M.S. *Gurkha* in 1963
A general-purpose frigate with type 965 air warning radar, type 293
surface warning and target indication radar and a commercial navigation
radar.

(Photos: Imperial War Museum)

PLATE VII

U.S.S. *Enterprise*

This nuclear-propelled super carrier has the SPS32 air warning radar and the SPS33 tracking radar. The fixed flat surface aerial arrays can be clearly seen.

(Official U.S. Navy Photograph)

PLATE VIII

X

The Last Two Years of the
Second World War

THE MOST IMPORTANT advance in wireless communications during the last two years of the war was in the tactical use of voice radio in fleets. By 1944 the British Home fleet had a high-frequency voice wave for the exchange of tactical information between action information centres in ships. This wave could, of course, be intercepted by the enemy at considerable distances and could therefore only be used in action when the position of the fleet was already known to the enemy. High-frequency voice radio was also used by aircraft carriers for fighter direction. Of greater importance was the introduction of a few voice channels using the American TBS sets on very high frequency. The advantage of VHF was that it behaved in the way that Hertz had established towards the end of the last century. Its range was optical and it did not extend beyond the horizon. Furthermore it was not reflected by the ionosphere. It was therefore safe to use at sea before contact with the enemy was established. Two VHF circuits were initially introduced in the British Home fleet. The first was a general inter-communication circuit which was used for manoeuvring and reporting surface radar and asdic contacts. The second was an air plot control wave for large ships to exchange information on the air situation. All these voice circuits were backed up by the old morse channels such as the admiral's wave on high frequency and the fleet and auxiliary waves on low or medium frequency (Note 1). Communication with the shore was maintained as before by area operational broadcasts and the high-frequency ship-to-shore network.

With the movement of much of the Royal Navy eastwards at

the end of 1944 to form the British Pacific fleet there came an urgent need to standardize communications with the U.S. Navy. The British Pacific fleet in any case needed better communications as it was larger than the forces used in European waters. The growth of fleet aviation and the need to control complicated replenishment operations required much more sophisticated communications too. The result was a very great increase in the employment of VHF which came to be used at sea almost without restriction. Some six VHF channels were used by ships and another four between ships and aircraft. These included two general tactical inter-communication channels, another for communication between groups, one for air warning and others for inter-communication between fighter-direction officers and for aircraft carriers for briefing and intelligence. At the same time there were two area operational broadcasts from the shore, a special intelligence broadcast, an administrative broadcast and yet another for senior officers. To cope with all this the British Pacific fleet included the *Montclare*, a liner converted into a wireless base ship; she could work some twenty channels simultaneously.

During the war the British shore wireless station network expanded a great deal. It had to be able to cope with a vast increase in traffic and to give better coverage in many areas which had been little used by H.M. ships in peacetime. By the end of the war there were some sixty-five stations throughout the world whereas in 1939 there were only seventeen. Technical improvements were also made such as better transmitters, directional aerials and arrangements for sending and receiving high-speed morse. The wireless equipment in ships too was roughly doubled during the war. A battleship at the beginning had nine transmitters and receivers while at the end it had sixteen transmitters and twenty-three receivers. By the end of the war all naval aircraft had some kind of wireless, fighters having VHF sets instead of H/F, with a choice of four fre-frequencies. At the same time the wireless interception and direction-finding network for picking up enemy signals continued to expand. By 1945 there were some twenty interception stations and sixty-nine direction-finding stations from the United Kingdom to such remote places as the Faroe Islands, the Cocos Islands, Port Darwin, Fiji and Iceland. As an example the South Atlantic was covered by H/F D/F stations at Tristan da Cunha, St Helena, Ascension Island, Accra, Freetown and Simonstown. The radio intelligence service traffic became so great by the end of the war that it had its own fixed wireless service to pass its information back to the United Kingdom or the naval headquarters where it was required.

It was seen in the last chapter how the attempt by the U-boats to renew the campaign in the Atlantic using search receivers, homing torpedoes and anti-aircraft guns failed at the end of 1943. Admiral Dönitz now pinned his faith in the new kind of U-boat which was to operate submerged rather than on the surface but which could not be available in quantity for some time. In the interim period he decided to continue operations as best he could and to fit 'Schnorchel' tubes so that the existing U-boats would not have to surface to charge their batteries. The Schnorchel was a purely mechanical device which provided air for the diesel engines so that they could be run with the submarine submerged. It had an automatic valve at the top of the tube which shut to prevent the sea coming in if its top went under inadvertently. The first operational U-boats fitted thus were equipped in the spring of 1944 and by the end of May teething troubles had been overcome. It proved an immediate success and in June Admiral Dönitz decided not to use any boats on operations which were not fitted with it. The fitting of Schnorchel provided immunity from detection by radar from ships or aircraft. The radar sets of the day could not pick out the Schnorchel head from the sea returns. Soon the U-boats adopted the practice of diving as soon as they left their bases and remaining submerged for a patrol lasting many weeks and only surfacing to enter port again. U-boat casualties from aircraft fell dramatically but the price for this immunity was substantial. The U-boats could proceed submerged using their Schnorchels and diesel engines continuously at about five knots, or alternatively they could run totally submerged on batteries at say three knots for eight hours and then recharge using Schnorchel and taking four or five hours to do so. In both cases their speed was reduced to a fraction of their former seventeen knots on the surface. There could be no question of concentrating in 'wolf-packs' against convoys, which now had twice the speed of the U-boats. So that although U-boat casualties were greatly reduced by the Schnorchel so were the sinkings of merchantmen by them.

The first operation in which the Schnorchel U-boats took part was to oppose the Allied landings in Normandy. They had therefore to operate in the Channel. They soon found that it was possible to operate in such enclosed waters and to do so with moderate success. It was easier to find convoys and they did not need to use their wireless if they were not going to work in 'wolf-packs'. At the same time they found that asdic-fitted vessels were often unable to distinguish their echoes from among the tide-rips, wrecks and shallow bottom of the area. The U-boats however took a very long time to get to their patrol areas and to return to base afterwards. Once they had revealed their position, with their very low speed they were comparatively easy to evade. During the second part of 1944 they sank very few merchant ships and their own casualties, although well below the rate at which U-boats were being built, were substantial. The Allied counter-measures depended almost entirely upon asdic-fitted ships. Aircraft, although by their presence they prevented the U-boats surfacing to use their speed, seldom made detections. As the U-boats kept wireless silence the direction-finding stations, the cryptographers and the Admiralty tracking-room had little to go on. The first indication that a U-boat was at sea was often obtained only when it made its first attack on a convoy. The U-boat would then find it very difficult to shake off the asdic-fitted escorts, and many were lost in this way.

In the last phase in 1945, the Allies were able to master the U-boat inshore campaign by a substantial use of deep mine-fields and a huge concentration of some 400 escorts in British coastal waters. Asdic sets had not improved very much during the war but by the end a new anti-submarine weapon had come into service. This was the 'Squid', a new and more effective ahead-throwing weapon. Six fast-sinking heavy depth bombs were thrown from mortars while the asdic set was still in firm contact. A new small asdic set which sent out a horizontal fan-shaped beam, which could be depressed and which could find the depth of the U-boat, was part of the new system. An improvement on the 'Hedgehog' was that the pattern always exploded and could damage a U-boat even if it was not accurately placed.

Two new anti-submarine devices for use by aircraft were also developed in the U.S.A. and came into service in this period. The first was a small hydrophone buoy which was dropped into the sea and which transmitted what it heard by radio back to the aircraft. The second was the Magnetic Airborne Detector which could detect a submarine if the aircraft flew low right over the top of it. A 'retro-bomb' was devised to work with the Magnetic Airborne Detector so as to project the bomb to the rear and counter the forward motion of the aircraft. Both of these systems made it possible for aircraft to detect totally submerged submarines but their use was very limited and in no way made up for the neutralization of airborne radar by the Schnorchel.

Aircraft radar continued however to improve, and it had always been realized that the Germans might find out about ASV Mark III on 10 cm. and two developments were followed in anticipation. The first of these was to increase power to 200 kw. instead of 50 kw. to double the range but also to fit an attenuator which would automatically decrease the power as the aircraft approached the U-boat and so give the impression that the range was constant. This set was the ASV Mark VI and was delivered to Coastal Command at the end of January 1944 just before the Schnorchel came in after it had been realized that U-boats had a 10 cm. search receiver. Another line was to convert ASV Mark III to work on a wavelength of 3 cm. This was the ASV Mark VII which later proved able to locate a Schnorchel at short range. Nevertheless the role of aircraft had fallen from that of the prime U-boat killer of 1943 to the passive one of keeping U-boats submerged so that they could not use their surface mobility.

The new Type XXI U-boat on which Admiral Dönitz relied to restore mobility and renew the Battle of the Atlantic was not in service before the Allied armies had over-run Germany. They had been, however, produced in substantial numbers and many were just completing their trials. These submarines still used diesel engines with electric storage batteries and motors for propulsion, but the design was altered to give absolute priority to submerged performance at the expense of surface performance. A cardinal feature was an improved telescopic Schnorchel with which a speed of ten knots submerged using the diesel engines was possible. A battery three times the weight of the usual one in a conventional U-boat was installed; it was also of greatly increased capacity although this was obtained at the expense of its life. The result was the storage of 5,000 h.p./hours instead of 1,100 h.p./hours (Note 2), allowing a submerged speed of seventeen-and-a-half knots for one hour or five knots for over twenty-four hours. The Type XXI also had a substantial endurance and would be able to patrol from Germany for several weeks to as far off as Capetown.

A new hydrophone system also made it possible to fire torpedoes accurately at a depth of 150 feet and a new reloading system allowed several attacks in quick succession to be made on a convoy. Finally a search receiver was carried on top of the Schnorchel and a radar set with a telescopic aerial was fitted. There is no doubt that the Type XXI U-boat was the greatest advance in submarine construction since the early years of the century and it provided a chance to renew the Battle of the Atlantic with success. Its mobility was not as good as a conventional U-boat on the surface but was very much better than that of a conventional Schnorchelling boat. Its submerged mobility would make it possible to close with convoys and its heavy armament to deliver a devastating attack. Its high submerged speed would make it almost impossible to attack with depth charges and difficult even with the new 'Hedgehog' and 'Squid'.

In 1944 the American submarine campaign in the Pacific really got into its stride. In January U.S. submarines using SJ radar sank fifty ships of 240,840 tons and exceeded this again in February. The submarines *Tang* and *Seawolf* both scored over 20,000 tons sunk in this period. In May the Japanese put all their shipping into convoy and at the same time the American submarine command changed its strategy. Much greater use was made of 'wolf-packs' and they were disposed to take advantage of the excellent radio intelligence being obtained of Japanese convoy movements. By midsummer the Japanese were suffering from severe shortages of raw materials, especially oil. In June a 'wolf-pack' consisting of the submarines *Shark*, *Pilotfish* and *Pintado* disposed of 35,000 tons of shipping and at the end of July *Parche* and *Steelhead* sank 39,000 tons out of one convoy. In August and September *Picuda*, *Redfish* and *Spadefish* sank thirteen ships totalling 64,448 tons. The peak month was October when sixty-eight ships of 328,843 tons were disposed of. During 1944 American submarines halved the Japanese merchant marine, leaving less than was required to support civilian needs in Japan let alone the war effort. The great majority of the attacks were made on the surface at night using SJ radar. SJ radar was also used on occasions with the submarine submerged to 'radar-depth' that is with the radar array just above the surface. Many of the submerged attacks were the result of a first contact at night by radar followed by the submarine proceeding fast to a submerged intercepting position in daylight. During 1944 too, U.S. submarines achieved considerable successes against Japanese warships. While these results were not achieved without loss, nineteen U.S. submarines being sunk during the year, they took the same number of Japanese destroyers with them and a submarine hunt proved as dangerous for the hunters as the hunted.

All Japanese escorts had asdics by this time and many also had radar, but their sets were technically and operationally inferior; they were often unserviceable and easily put out by shock or vibration, and even when working with their low power and long pulse they were not really satisfactory.

It was not only in submarine operations in the Pacific that the U.S. Navy excelled. The Battle of the Philippine Sea in June 1944 is famous as a carrier victory as well as a substantial success for U.S. submarines. No less than twenty-one Japanese submarines were deployed mainly as scouts or on patrol lines to cover the sortie of the Japanese fleet. Four more were used to run supplies to Bougainville and other beleaguered Japanese garrisons. Of these twenty-five submarines, no fewer than seventeen were sunk, thirteen by American destroyers and escorts, two by aircraft and one shared between them. The cause of loss of the seventeenth is unknown. Most of the Japanese submarines succumbed to sonar attacks using 'Hedgehog'; some were detected initially on the surface at night by radar. Six of the submarines were sunk by the destroyer escort *England* thereby creating a record unsurpassed in the Second World War. So many of the contacts were made by sonar in the wide open Pacific that it would be stretching our credulity too much to suppose that this was chance. There seems little doubt that the positions of all these submarines had been revealed by crypto-analysis and the American ability to read Japanese signals continued to the end.

There is not enough space in this book to follow fighter direction from ships through every operation. Fighter direction from ships was used more and more by both Great Britain and the U.S.A., especially during landing operations when special ships were employed. There is room, however, for a description of the U.S. Navy's fighter control at its zenith in the Pacific. This was in June 1944 during the Battle of the Philippine Sea in which the most notable difference from the carrier battles of 1942 was one of scale. The Japanese produced a force of nine aircraft carriers with 222 fighters out of a total of 430 aircraft and the U.S. Navy fifteen carriers with 475 fighters out of a total of 891 aircraft. The battle was brought about by a Japanese high command decision to resist any further encroachments of the U.S. forces towards Japan. When the Americans invaded Saipan the Japanese mobile fleet therefore advanced across the Philippine Sea to counter-attack. Admiral Spruance with the Fifth fleet took up a defensive posture to await the Japanese, and it is this phase of the action which is of interest to us. Admiral Spruance divided his fleet into five task groups, four centred on aircraft carriers and one on battleships. Three of the carrier groups were stationed twelve miles apart on a north-south line and the battleships with the fourth carrier group were thrown out fifteen miles to the westwards towards the enemy. The whole was disposed to cover the landings on Saipan and Tinian.

The organization for controlling the 475 odd fighters had advanced greatly since the carrier battles of 1942. A new air warning SR radar was fitted in the latest ships and could obtain echoes at 150 miles. Most other ships had at least SC radar. New VHF radio sets were in process of being fitted in the fleet and many channels were available. Overall control was invested in the task force fighter-direction officer in the aircraft-carrier *Lexington* (Note 3). He was in touch with four group fighter-direction officers who were in their turn in touch with the fighter-direction officers of the individual ships of their groups. The force fighter director allocated raids to groups and saw that enough reserves were kept back for emergencies. Group fighter directors allocated individual interceptions to ships.

Conditions were excellent, the sky was clear and the vapour trails of attacking aircraft could be seen clearly. The Japanese attacks were spread piecemeal over a period of four hours from 1030 to 1430. The first raids were detected by radar at the full 150 miles and the whole task force was turned into the trade wind so that fighters could be operated continuously. The vast majority of raids were intercepted by fighters before they reached the task force and no fewer than 243 Japanese aircraft were shot down. Only 130 escaped whereas the Americans lost but twenty-nine aircraft. The Japanese did not sink or seriously damage a single ship. The worst casualties were in the battleship *South Dakota* and carrier *Bunker Hill*, but both were operating at full efficiency again before long. This defensive phase of the battle was therefore an outstanding success. The contribution of the new Hellcat fighters and the splendid training of their pilots must take much of the credit as well as the tactical handling of the force by Admiral Mitscher. The radars in the fleet and the greatly improved voice communications which made the highly efficient direction of such a very large number of fighters possible must also be allocated a substantial share of the credit.

The increase in the distance of warning of the approach of aircraft by radar sets did not solve the problem of low fliers. Centimetric radars were capable of detecting aircraft flying low above the horizon but could not compete with the curvature of the earth. In 1944 the U.S. Navy in the Pacific began to use destroyer pickets for this purpose. Destroyers fitted with air-warning radar were thrown out from ten to fifty miles in the direction of the enemy to report the approach of low-flying aircraft. The destroyers *Stockham* and *Yarnall* were used in this way in the Battle of the Philippine Sea by Admiral Lee commanding Task Group 58.7. Destroyers so employed were very vulnerable and *Stockham* was attacked several times but was lucky in not being hit. When the Kamikaze or suicide plane attacks began at the end of the Leyte campaign in 1944 the need for pickets was greater still; these were used extensively in the Okinawa campaign, a number of picket stations being established round the island to give an outer radar screen from ten to 100 miles away. To help with their protection they were given fighter direction teams to control patrolling fighters but nevertheless, with Kamikaze planes, it was dangerous work.

On 16 April 1945 the *Laffey* survived twenty-two attacks while on picket duty including hits by six Kamikaze planes and four bombers. Nearly twenty destroyers were sunk on this duty and many more damaged. The Kamikaze planes were liable not only to approach low down and so achieve some surprise but were wont to attach themselves to returning American formations. A special kind of picket destroyer was used to meet this problem called a 'Tom-Cat'. 'Tom-Cats' were stationed some sixty miles away to the flanks and all returning strike aircraft had to pass close to them to check that they were not being followed. Fighters overhead controlled by the 'Tom-Cats' were available to take a closer look. The use of 'Tom-Cats' also cleared the radar screens in the direction of the enemy and made the detection of normal raids easier. Radar-controlled fighter defence was one of the main answers to the Kamikaze attack and the complement of fighters in all aircraft carriers was substantially increased to compete.

It has been seen how radar ranging and then radar blind fire had improved anti-aircraft gunnery. It had for many years been realized, however, that what was really required was a fuze to explode the shell when it came within lethal range of the aeroplane. Time fuzes, although the accuracy with which they could be set had been enormously improved by radar, still had to be set before the gun fired and could therefore never allow for an alteration of course and/or height by the target during the time of the missile's flight. In the summer of 1940 the U.S. Navy decided that some sort of electronic proximity fuze should now be a practicable proposition. They were spurred on by the knowledge that the British were ordering large numbers of very small valves from an American firm. In September 1940 the British Scientific Mission to the U.S.A. under Sir Henry Tizard revealed that they had by no means solved the problem. Knowledge was, however, pooled and early in 1941 the U.S. Navy dropped its consideration of magnetic, acoustic, photo-electric and thermal lines of research and concentrated on one using electro-magnetic waves. By the end of the year this was showing promise and in trials in January 1942 half of the experimental fuzes fired from a gun went off successfully. It was not until August that they were ready for a sea trial and then the cruiser *Cleveland* shot down three drone targets (Note 4) with four rounds. After this astonishing success the fuze, known as the VT fuze, was at once put into mass production. It was in fact a tiny C.W. radar set powered by batteries and crammed into a space the size of a milk bottle. It had to stand the shock of discharge of the gun and the spinning of the projectile and still work and was a remarkable technical achievement.

By the beginning of 1943 5,000 rounds of VT-fuzed ammunition had been rushed to the South Pacific area where most of the fighting was going on at the time. On January 5, the U.S.S. *Helena* brought down a Japanese dive-bomber near Guadalcanal with her second salvo. Next month an American troop convoy was attacked at night in the same area by twelve torpedo bombers. It was defended entirely by radar controlled anti-aircraft guns using VT fuzes which shot down five of the attackers who secured no torpedo hits at all. In July 1943 during the Sicily landings the U.S. destroyers *Swanson* and *Roe* with FD radar and VT fuzes shot down a Ju 88 with an expenditure of only thirteen rounds. During the whole of 1943 some 9,100 VT-fuzed rounds were fired in action and proved three times as effective as time-fuzed ammunition using the latest radar fire control. From 1944 onwards the use of the VT fuze became standard practice. Probably its greatest achievement in naval warfare was its part in the defeat of the Japanese Kamikaze or suicide plane campaign from April to June 1945 (Note 5).

We must now return to the use of radar in surface actions. On the night of the 24–25 October 1944 was fought the Battle of Surigao Strait. This was one of several actions collectively known as the Battle of Leyte Gulf. Two Japanese forces under Vice-Admirals Nishimura and Shima attempted to penetrate through this strait to attack the American landing craft off the beaches on Leyte Island. The first Japanese force under Admiral Nishimura consisted of the battleships *Fuso* and *Yamashiro*, the heavy cruiser *Mogami* and four destroyers. Admiral Shima, with the cruisers *Nachi*, *Ashigara*, *Abukuma* and four destroyers, was following about forty miles astern. The American carrier forces were fully committed to the north and so the defence of the beachhead had to be left to the American bombarding and supporting forces under Rear-Admiral Oldendorf. These were strong, consisting of six battleships, four heavy and four light cruisers, twenty-eight destroyers and forty-five motor torpedo boats. The battleships and cruisers were however short of ammunition and what they had was mostly of the high explosive kind for bombarding the shore rather than armour piercing for engaging other battleships. They had, however, the priceless advantage of centimetric radar for surface warning and fire control which was fitted in all ships.

The Japanese forces had been sighted by air reconnaissance and were known to be approaching Surigao Strait. The night was calm but very dark. What radar sets were fitted in the Japanese ships is not known. By this time they had certainly developed several types of radar, including the Mark II Model 2 working on 10 cm. (3000 mc/s); sixty of these sets were fitted in the fleet but they were only of 2 kw. power and never really satisfactory. Both Admirals Nishimura and Shima decided to advance boldly through the Strait and attack, the two forces operating completely independently of each other. Admiral Oldendorf organized three lines of defence. The first of these was composed of thirteen groups of motor torpedo boats mostly in the approaches to the Strait. The second line was composed of the destroyers in three main groups and the third line was the battleships and cruisers at the northern end. The motor torpedo boats were all fitted with radar and in a series of attacks fired a large number of torpedoes without securing any hits. Their reports by wireless of the enemy's approach were, however, most valuable.

The first destroyer attack was by three destroyers on the eastern side and two on the western side of the Strait. They detected the enemy's approach at 36,000 yards and using radar entirely (Note 6) fired no fewer than forty-seven torpedoes. Some of them were seen and engaged by the Japanese ships but at an average range of 8,000 yards they hit both Japanese battleships and three of their destroyers. The battleship *Fuso* and destroyers *Yamagumo* and *Michishio* sank and the battleship *Yamashiro* and destroyer *Asagumo* were damaged. This was followed almost at once by the attack of another fifteen destroyers in five groups firing some seventy-seven torpedoes, hitting *Yamashiro* with three more and hitting the *Asagumo* again. There was now not much left of the Japanese force, but *Yamashiro*, *Mogami* and the destroyer *Shigure* continued the advance. *Yamashiro* was engaged by the three battleships *California*, *Tennessee* and *West Virginia*, all firing by radar at

22,800 yards with the latest Mark 8 control system. The other three battleships *Maryland, Mississippi* and *Pennsylvania*, with an older system, had difficulty in identifying targets. The cruisers also joined in and the *Yamashiro* was repeatedly hit and capsized and sank. The *Mogami* was heavily damaged but managed to stagger away to the south accompanied by the destroyer *Shigure*.

Meanwhile Admiral Shima's force was approaching and the *Abukuma* was hit by a torpedo from a motor torpedo boat. The rest of his force advanced through the Strait and fired sixteen torpedoes by radar at two echoes and retired without scoring any hits. As she turned the *Nachi* collided with the *Mogami* without very serious consequences and all retired together, pursued by the gunfire of American cruisers. *Mogami* later sank and all that survived of Admiral Nishimura's force was the destroyer *Shigure*, but Admiral Shima got away with only the loss of *Abukuma* and a destroyer. The Battle of Surigao Strait was fought almost entirely by radar. The U.S. Navy did not attempt to use searchlights or starshell and would have been quite happy if they had never seen the Japanese. In fact the Japanese used starshell and searchlights and the burning ships and explosions lit up the scene so that the American ships saw quite a lot. Nevertheless the Battle of Surigao Strait was a radar battle fought on a pitch-black night at ranges which would, a year or two before, have been considered long by day. Furthermore the results in hits by gun and torpedo were devastating.

The U.S. Navy was considerably ahead of the Royal Navy at this time in fire-control radar. The new British gunnery radar sets on the 10 cm. band, however, began to come into service before the end of the war. The Type 274 which was to replace the 284 as a surface fire-control set was the first to be completed. It had a power of 500 kw. and with it complete blind fire was possible. The fall of shot for range could be spotted by the echoes of the splashes but it was not possible to tell how much a salvo was left or right for direction. A special Type 931 set of 40 kw. working on 1·25 cm. was under development in Canada to meet this requirement but was not completed by the end of the war. With this set the exact position of the fall of shot relative to the target could be seen on a P.P.I. type display. To replace the anti-aircraft Type 285 set, the Type 275 was produced also on 10 cm. with a power of 400 kw., but it only began its trials at sea in early 1945 and so missed the war. The Type 275 was completely integrated with the anti-aircraft fire control system and complete blind fire was possible. The Type 262, which was the successor to the Type 282 radar for close range anti-aircraft fire control, was a more advanced radar still. It only had a power of 30 kw. as long range was not required but worked on 3 cm. This set was not only capable of complete blind fire but was able to 'lock on' to a target, in other words it could follow a target on its own. It was normally an integral part of a twin 40 mm. Bofors mounting. The new gunnery sets necessarily had very narrow beams both in azimuth and elevation and so had difficulty in finding a target. It was therefore necessary to have some way to indicate it to them, and the Type 293 radar was developed especially for this purpose. It was a 10 cm. set of 500 kw. and was capable of picking up an aircraft flying between 200 and 20,000 feet at 25,000 yards. Its performance against surface targets was similar to the surface warning sets of the 271–3 series.

The two deficiencies in the British system of fighter direction from ships were that there was no accurate way to find the height of an aircraft and that cover at low angles was bad. There was also the problem of the fading of echoes as the target passed from one lobe to another. The lobes of the Type 279 on 7 m. and the 281 on 3½ m. were different and it was found that by fitting both in one ship, detection was continuous. This was only possible in the larger ships such as the new aircraft carriers *Implacable* and *Indefatigable* (Plate VI). To meet the requirement for low cover and height finding a new 10 cm. set under development as a replacement for the 271–3 series was adapted. This was the Type 277 of 500 kw. which had an aerial which could be elevated as well as trained. With this it was possible to detect low-flying aircraft out to twenty-five miles and also to find the height out to the same distance. Both the 277 and the latest version of the Type 281 were now trained continuously by power and the echoes read off by P.P.I. display. It was therefore no longer necessary to stop and 'investigate' an echo as all-round cover was continuous. By fitting a number of P.P.I.'s and later an improved display called a 'Skiatron' the number of simultaneous interceptions was only limited by the number of 'Skiatrons' available. A new air warning radar, the Type 960, did not come into service until the end of the war (Note 7).

During 1943 the Germans introduced two kinds of guided weapon for use by aircraft against ships. The first of these, known as the FX 1400, was a heavy free-falling bomb which could be guided visually by radio signals from the parent aircraft. It weighed 1,400 kg. (about 3,000 lb.) and had a terminal velocity of 800 ft/sec. and so was armour piercing. It could only be carried by heavy bombers of the He 177 and Do 217 types and was released from between 12,000 and 19,000 feet, at which heights anti-aircraft fire was very little use. The second weapon was a winged self-propelled flying-bomb known as the Hs 293. It had a speed of 570 m.p.h. using a jet engine, had a warhead of 1,100 lb. of explosive and a range of eight miles or so. It was also guided visually by radio from the parent aircraft. Both weapons had a green flare in the tail to make them easier for the controller to see.

The FX 1400 was used without success in a raid on Malta early in 1943 and in small numbers in the Sicilian campaign. In September 1943 when the Italian fleet left Spezia to surrender it was attacked by eleven Do 217 bombers off Sardinia using the FX 1400. Both the battleships *Roma* and *Italia* were hit; a bomb penetrated to a magazine in the *Roma* so that she blew up and sank and the *Italia* was seriously damaged, but reached Malta. Two days later the same German squadron based near Marseilles attacked the ships supporting the landings off Salerno. The U.S.S. *Philadelphia* was near-missed several times but the U.S.S. *Savannah* and H.M.S. *Uganda* and *Warspite* were heavily damaged and completely disabled. All were towed to Malta but in every case the bombs penetrated right through the ship and blew the bottom out. Meanwhile He 177 aircraft using the Hs 293 had appeared in the Bay of Biscay in support of the U-boat campaign. On August 27 eighteen aircraft attacked the First Support Group off Cape Finisterre and sank the sloop *Egret* and badly damaged the Canadian destroyer *Athabaskan*.

By the time of the landings at Anzio in January 1944 a number of counter-measures had been devised. Three ships were fitted with radio sets to monitor the control frequencies of the bombs and with jammers to try to interfere with them. Tactical counter-measures included concentrated close-range anti-aircraft fire against the Hs 293 and smoke against both types. All these had some success but at Anzio H.M.S. *Spartan*, an anti-aircraft cruiser, as well as the destroyer *Inglefield*, were sunk by Hs 293 while the destroyer *Jervis* was damaged. These weapons were used on a small scale against convoys crossing the Bay of Biscay and in the Mediterranean but never proved more than a nuisance, and the counter-measures were able to compete with them. Nevertheless this was the first use of airborne guided missiles in war and was a pointer to the future.

This book would not be complete without another reference to the minelaying campaigns of the combatants. Not only did they continue in Europe but also in the Far East by the U.S. Air Force against Japan. The British air minelaying campaign against German traffic in the Baltic proved by far the most effective weapon used by aircraft against merchant ships and forced the Germans to deploy huge minesweeping forces. The Germans, well before 1944, had developed yet another type of influence mine. This was not strictly an electrical mechanism but had electrical components and is relevant because the long-term counter-measures were mainly in this field. This was the 'Oyster' or pressure mine which was actuated by the pressure or rather suction when a ship passed over it. Its merit was that it was almost impossible to sweep except with a ship. The Germans were afraid if they used this type of mine in the ordinary campaign against shipping that it would be compromised and the Allies might employ it against them in the Baltic with disastrous results. They therefore held it back in reserve to be used to oppose the invasion of Europe. Four thousand of them were manufactured, and the day after the invasion of Europe by the Allies authority was given to use them. The first pressure mines were not laid until 11 June 1944, however, and the early casualties from mines were from magnetic and acoustic types. On June 20 the British recovered one of the pressure mines and were able to discover how it worked. This mine had limitations as it was essential that the waves should not set it off. It was found that if ships went slowly enough they would not create sufficient suction to fire it. Speed restrictions in shallow water were therefore rigidly enforced, and although by the end of July all 4,000 'Oyster' mines had been laid they failed to cause sufficient damage or to delay the build-up of the armies ashore. Nevertheless no method of sweeping the mines was found and it was clear that the mine could be developed to catch ships moving slowly too. A pointer to what might have to be done in the future was shown during the clearance of Cherbourg harbour by divers who had to search every inch of the bottom.

At this point the time has come to summarize the effect of the electron on sea power during the Second World War. If one of the great innovations in the Russo-Japanese War was the use of wireless for communications and in the First World War the advent of radio interception, direction finding and cryptography, the equivalent in the Second World War was the development of the two new methods of detection, radar and asdics. Of these radar was the more important as it had many applications whereas asdics was only of use for the detection of submerged submarines. There were many other developments and effects of the electron upon sea power during the struggle but none was in the same category as these two devices.

Radar, coupled with the use of voice radio, was the key to the defence of fleets against air attack. Long-range warning of attack; fighter direction; the use of radar in fighters themselves; vastly improved anti-aircraft gunnery using radar control and proximity fuzes all played their part and when present made it possible for warships to compete with aircraft. In 1940 the British Home fleet, with few radar sets, no system of fighter direction and inaccurate anti-aircraft gunnery, was driven from the coasts of Norway by the Luftwaffe. In 1944 in the Pacific the U.S. fleet with every electronic advantage was able to defeat the first-line Metropolitan Air Force of Japan. Of course it is not asserted that the electron was the only cause of this transformation but it is claimed that it could not have taken place without it.

Radar, by virtually turning night into day, made night action by surface ships normal and something to be sought by the strongest fleet. It progressed from providing an additional excellent lookout at Matapan in 1941 to an action such as that at Surigao Strait in 1944 in which the whole battle was fought by radar without it being necessary to see the enemy at all.

Although radar in some form was present on both sides on occasion, it was for practical purposes the 'secret weapon' of the Allies. German and Japanese radar sets were never very effective and little, if anything, better than their lookouts. Their sets were to the Allied sets as a pocket torch is to a car head-lamp. Nevertheless for some time the superb Japanese night-fighting technique with their long-range torpedoes had the measure of American radar-fitted ships. Without radar, however, the Americans would not have been able to compete at all and would probably have lost Guadalcanal. It was not until radar was developed to make night fighting possible at long range that the Americans mastered the Japanese tactics and then its use became devastating. Eventually radar took the element of risk out of night action which had discouraged admirals from engaging in the dark for so long. It superseded first the searchlight and then starshell. Its use became virtually unrestricted and the early fears that it might give away a ship's position to the enemy did not materialize during the Second World War.

Asdics proved a very effective U-boat detector and it was responsible for most of the 246 German submarines sunk by ships during the war. It did not, however, prove to be the answer to the submarine as had been hoped it would before the war; this was mainly because of its comparatively short range. It did not often provide protection and seldom prevented a torpedo attack being made. The majority of its successes were achieved in counter-attacks or in following up detection by other means such as radar. The German U-boat tactics of operating on the surface at night exploited the weakness of the asdics, and if it had not been for radar the U-boats would probably have won the Battle of the Atlantic. Nevertheless, as Winston Churchill said, 'The asdics did not conquer the U-boat, but without the asdics the U-boat would not have been conquered.' It was radar fitted in ships and aircraft, especially aircraft, which provided the answer where asdics failed, and it drove the U-boats off the surface so that asdics came into their own again. When radar was fitted in aircraft it turned them from minor harassing agents into lethal U-boat killers. Most of the 290 U-boats destroyed by aircraft were initially detected by radar, which was unquestionably the most important reason for the defeat of the U-boats in the Atlantic. It defeated Admiral

Dönitz' chosen tactics of operating in packs at night on the surface which promised to be the only way in which he could sink ships fast enough to win the war.

On the other side of the world in the Pacific, the American submarine campaign, far from being vanquished like the U-boats, won a victory which virtually paralysed the Japanese Empire and was a large factor in its defeat. They achieved their results largely by pack tactics on the surface, and were able to do this as they had efficient radar whereas the Japanese escorts and aircraft had not. It can be said with some confidence that, although many other factors were involved, it was radar that was the key to why the U-boats were defeated in the Atlantic and to why the U.S. submarines in the Pacific won.

If we now turn to wireless communications we find that the most significant changes were in the volume of traffic handled and in the advent of voice radio, especially on very high frequencies, to control ships and aircraft at sea. Wireless already provided world-wide coverage in the inter-war period, and although this was strengthened and made more reliable this was no more than a refinement. The huge number of messages sent, however, gave the cryptographers plenty to work upon. Cryptography had astonishing successes and these were fairly evenly divided between the combatants. The Germans gained priceless information from the British in Norway and in the Battle of the Atlantic but it is of interest that they did this without breaking any of the really top-grade British ciphers. This is why they were therefore completely surprised by the North African landings in 1942 and in many other major operations. The Germans obtained their information from the mass of less important messages in low-grade ciphers, and this continued until the British tightened up their security in 1943. The British seem not to have learnt so much from deciphering German messages but gained a wealth of information through their high-frequency direction-finding system. With this they were able to work out, as in the First World War, the positions of most U-boats at sea. The Germans knew they must be giving something away but the wolf-pack tactics controlled from the shore necessitated much signalling and would not have been possible without it. Undoubtedly the British were on occasion able to read some German signals especially when they captured material, but it seems that they were never able to repeat the astonishing successes of Room 40 in the First World War. The Americans read the Japanese ciphers throughout the war and after a very bad start at Pearl Harbor were conspicuously successful. The victories at Midway and Coral Sea were made possible by reading the enemy's signals, as was the shooting down of Admiral Yamamoto and a substantial proportion of the sinkings by the American submarines. The Japanese, on the other hand, gained little or no information from Allied signals.

It is impossible to come to any other conclusion than that the influence of the electron on sea power in the Second World War was immense. It was so bound up in every sphere of naval warfare and so important as to be completely indispensable. There were countless other uses which there has been no space to mention in this book, radar for navigation, minesweeping and combined operations being amongst them. It is fair to say that the use of the electron in its various forms conferred advantages of the same order as the advent of the gun or steam power in naval warfare in the past.

XI

Since the Second World War

As AT THE END of all wars, demobilization was the order of the day and the expenditure on defence research was drastically cut. The exploding of the first atomic bombs brought the methods of waging war at sea, indeed the relevance of sea power itself, into question. At the same time the need for military expenditure did not appear urgent as Soviet Russia was still an ally and there did not seem to be an enemy. The post-war period was therefore one of stagnation as far as new equipment was concerned. Long-distance wireless communication, commercial as well as naval, still used the high-frequency beam system developed by Marconi in the twenties. There had been many improvements, of course, but communication was seldom possible continuously throughout the twenty-four hours. Systems of relay stations and the use of several receivers and aerials on a number of frequencies helped reception but the greatest advances made were in the amount of traffic that could be handled. Manual transmission of morse had been largely replaced by high-speed automatic systems (Note 1). Nevertheless in 1948 sixty-four per cent of the long-distance traffic was still being sent by cable. For ship-to-shore communications, the morse code was still used for both naval and commercial traffic, the signals being sent by the high-frequency network developed during the war. With the return of peace, although defence research was cut down, commercial communication research was increased with a consequent benefit to both.

After VJ-day in 1945 radar was released to commerce and ceased to be a secret military weapon. Private companies began to develop and sell navigational radar sets which were fitted in merchant ships on a large scale. The sets in use in the post-war period in most navies were those developed during the

war. The design of sets conceived during hostilities was completed and others were modified and improved. The new
metric Type 960 of increased coverage and power replaced the
Types 279 and 281 for air warning and fighter direction and the
Type 277 was retained for height finding. The centimetric
Types 274, 275 and 262 replaced the 284, 285 and 282 for
gunnery control, making completely blind fire possible. The
Type 295 replaced the 271–3 series for surface warning and also
met the need for target indication and for air warning in small
ships. H.M.S. *Vanguard*, the last British battleship, completed
in April 1946, had fourteen sets of these types: the cruiser
Superb, completed in November 1945, had seven and a 'Battle'
class destroyer had four. These sets were satisfactory for all
purposes for about five years; they gave adequate air and
surface warning and efficient fighter direction for piston-engined
aircraft. The advent of the jet aircraft, however, generated a
need for speed and quickness of reaction, and by the end of the
forties requirements for new systems had been stated.

   In the immediate post-war period the British concentrated
much of what research effort they could afford on the anti-
submarine problem. They fully realized that the Type XXI
U-boat was a menace and that it might well have renewed the
Battle of the Atlantic with success. They produced a British
sono-buoy, experimented with homing torpedoes and put much
effort into a new asdic set and anti-submarine weapon system.
The Type 170 asdic did not do very much more than its predecessors but it did it very much better. The depth finding was
integrated into the main set and a split-beam technique with a
stabilized oscillator gave the direction of the submarine without
having to sweep across the target. The new 'Limbo' weapon
system which went with the Type 170 was the 'Squid' with much
longer range (which could be varied) and with all round
training. At the same time a new high-speed dome increased
operating speeds to twenty-five knots. The result was an anti-
submarine system, coming into service in the early fifties, which
could be used to attack a fast-moving submerged U-boat such
as the Type XXI. In the U.S.A. a new sonar set was developed
which sent a single 'ping' out in all directions simultaneously
and showed the echoes on a P.P.I. type display; this was also a
great advance for tracking a fast-moving submerged submarine.
Much effort was also put into the problem of producing a new

detecting system to find submerged submarines from aircraft, but without much success. Sono-buoys had hitherto been of the passive acoustic, non-directional type. The first step was therefore to produce a directional sono-buoy and this was developed during the fifties. Sono-buoys could of course, as they were hydrophones, be countered by the submarine slowing down to silent speed. A very great deal of effort had been put into silencing submarines and the Type XXI could proceed at five knots without making any noise. It was clear, therefore, that there was also a requirement for an active sono-buoy which could 'ping' and much effort was expended upon this project.

The development of radar to detect the Schnorchel, or 'snort' as it came to be known, was obviously important too. To pick up a small echo such as a 'snort' head required a high frequency, and the small commercial 'high definition' navigational radars which worked on the 3 cm. band proved quite successful in this role. New types of ASV also had moderate success but the break-through was obtained as a by-product of a radar set developed in the U.S.A. for quite another purpose. It was for detecting low-flying aircraft approaching a task force, a problem which had never really been solved during the war. The use of picket destroyers had proved too expensive, and little better was the U.S. Navy's equipping of a number of submarines with large radar sets in the hope that they would be able to avoid attack by diving. A more promising line was to carry a radar set aloft in an aircraft where it would be able to 'see' beyond the horizon. This had been tried during the war in a small way but if it was to have much chance of success, a very much more powerful radar set was needed. The result was the AN/APS 20 radar set. This was built into a variant of the Douglas Skyraider aircraft which consequently had a huge and ungainly dome below the fuselage. A number of these aircraft were supplied to the Royal Navy at the time of the Korean War. This new radar set not only achieved the purpose for which it had been designed and provided far better warning of the approach of low-flying aircraft, but was an outstanding success in a number of other ways too. This was the radar which was found to be able to pick up submarine snorts at substantial ranges. It was also extremely useful for what was known as 'strike direction'. The aircraft with the AN/APS 20 could often take up a position from which echoes of the aircraft carrier and the enemy were obtainable at the same time; it could, therefore, direct attacking aircraft to their target. The AN/APS 20 aircraft was often able to pick up ships at distances of 200 miles or so and it proved a very effective general reconnaissance aircraft in its own right. It could search a large area that would have taken many aircraft to search visually, and the problem became not one of finding ships at sea so much as of identifying the many echoes obtained.

By the early fifties when the British aircraft carriers *Ark Royal* and *Eagle*, laid down during the war, were completed, some new radar sets had been developed and other war-time sets improved (Plate VI). These were by no means revolutionary but embodied many improvements. Long-range air warning was still given by the existing Type 960 metric radar but low-angle coverage was improved by a pair of a new Type 982. Height finding was by two of another new set, the Type 983, and an improved Type 293Q was used for surface warning and target indication. For gunnery the older types 275 and 262 were still used and the outfit was rounded off by a small commercial 3 cm. navigational radar. These sets gave better coverage than their predecessors but the information was still processed and plotted by hand. The action information organization was far better laid out with much more room, but ranges of detection remained much the same. When jet aircraft entered operational service it was clear that the speed with which they had to be operated required still more sophisticated equipment.

During the fifties there were some new developments in communications. The first of these was Ionospheric Forward Scatter followed by Tropospheric Forward Scatter. These methods of communication were not new but dated from before the war. It had been found that under certain conditions VHF and higher frequencies could be reflected or rather scattered from the ionosphere or troposphere giving much longer ranges. This was done by using very high power and a directional aerial aimed just above the horizon. Tropospheric scatter in the UHF band could obtain ranges of 650 miles using a transmitter of 50 kw. The importance of these methods was that they filled in the gap which usually existed between the longest range obtainable on medium frequency and the shortest range by high frequency at the point where the sky waves first returned to earth. Because of the very high frequency that was used it also meant that more channels were available and so it increased the amount of traffic that could be transmitted. These systems were mainly of use for fixed services at moderate distances. In 1956, for instance, the Admiralty used an ionospheric scatter transmitter from Gibraltar to send signals to the United Kingdom.

The second development was not new either. It had been used before the war with a radio-telephone circuit between London and New York. This was the single sideband technique in which only one sideband (Note 2) is transmitted. This has the effect of economizing power and frequency bandwidth which allows more channels to be used and also, when used on high frequency, it gives better protection against fading introduced by the vagaries of the ionosphere. By 1963 the Royal Navy and most other navies had gone over entirely to single sideband transmission from ships as well as shore stations. Considerable use was made of a Marconi transmitter NT204 with a power of 500 watts which used single sideband and covered the whole high- and medium-frequency maritime band and with which frequency could be changed by pressing a button. By international agreement, ships completed after 1 January 1973 had to have single sideband equipment.

During the fifties, radar development was also rapid. Various advances, notably a new Klystron amplifier, allowed a substantial increase in the power of transmitters, and those of new radar sets tended to be measured in megawatts rather than kilowatts. Considerable increases in the range of radar sets was therefore possible although it must be remembered that to double the range, sixteen times the power is required. Radars, which were normally now in the higher-frequency bands, were much more accurate. The use of transistors and other technical improvements made radar sets more reliable, smaller and easier to maintain.

In this period the British designed a new generation of radars. The largest of these was a new air defence radar for aircraft carriers called Type 984 which first went to sea in H.M.S. *Victorious* in 1959. The Type 984 replaced the Type 960 air warning, Type 982 low warning and the Type 983 height-finding radars. It was what was known as a 3D radar as it gave height as well as a P.P.I. presentation of the situation. The aerial, which looks like a huge searchlight fifteen feet in diameter, was stabilized and trained mechanically in azimuth but elevated electronically (Plate VI). A narrow pencil beam scanned very rapidly in the vertical plane and there was also a fixed beam at low elevation for long-range warning. It had a special display in which the echoes could be identified by symbols shown alongside them on the screen. The Type 984 was a great advance and met the requirement for the control of a number of high-speed jet fighters. It was, however, very heavy and could only be used in large ships such as aircraft carriers (Note 3).

For frigates and destroyers a new Type 965 in the metric waveband was selected (Plate VII). It had a mattress type aerial, megawatt power and gave a far better coverage than earlier metric radars as well as increased range. This set was also fitted in the 'County' class guided missile destroyers which relied upon it to indicate the target to the Type 901 radar which controlled the Seaslug missile. Subsequently it became the standard long-range air search set for all classes of ship of the frigate type and upwards. Some ships had a double aerial array which improved the coverage still more. Other new radar sets were the Type 993 to replace the Type 293 which came into service in the mid-sixties and the Type 992, an S-band set for air warning in frigates. Some new commercial navigation sets of better design also became available.

Development of radar in the U.S. Navy followed much the same pattern, but with rather more sets. Some, such as the SPS 39 as fitted in guided missile ships from 1960, were three dimensional. The most advanced radars were the SPS 32 and SPS 33 fitted in the nuclear-propelled aircraft carrier *Enterprise* (Plate VIII) and guided missile cruiser *Long Beach*. This set has a completely fixed aerial array in the form of four large flat surfaces which are, in fact, the sides of the bridge structure. Scanning for both azimuth and elevation is electronic from all four sides simultaneously and the beams are electronically stabilized. The beam sent out is in the 10 cm. band and is fan-shaped in the vertical plane giving three-dimensional coverage. The power that can be used in this type of aerial is considerable and long ranges, probably well over 300 miles, can be assumed. A companion SPS 33 radar fitted alongside the SPS 32 is very similar but is for tracking targets and emits a pencil beam. A similar Anglo-Dutch project, which was to have been fitted in the ill-fated CVA 01 aircraft carrier and the Type 82 guided missile ships, was cancelled in 1966. Radar is now designed and manufactured in France, Italy, Japan and the Netherlands as well as in the United States, Great Britain and the Soviet Union. Every navy in the world is equipped from one or other of these sources.

We have seen how guided missiles were used during the war by the Germans. These missiles were, however, launched only from aircraft against surface targets. Post-war research was directed principally at the problem of launching missiles at aircraft from the surface. It was clear that even with radar control and proximity fuzes, anti-aircraft gunfire had little chance of competing in the future. It already took thousands of rounds to bring down a piston-engined aircraft and jet aircraft flew at much greater speeds. Furthermore jet aircraft could fly very much higher and there was little hope that anti-aircraft guns, even of large calibre, would be able to reach them. The solution clearly lay in a new kind of guided weapon fired from the ground or from ships against aircraft. Any such missile would obviously rely heavily on radar and radio to get it to its target. Specialized radars would be required and it was the development of these sets which took much of the effort during the fifties.

The guidance of these missiles was effected by one or a combination of two out of a number of methods. The first was to hold the target with a special radar set using a narrow pencil beam and to design the missile to run up this beam until it hit the target. The British Seaslug, which came into service in 1961, used this method. The warhead was exploded either by a direct action or a proximity fuze. Seaslug therefore 'beam-rides' all the way, using Type 901 radar for the purpose. The American 'Terrier' missile, produced in 1956, and the much larger 'Talos', which came into service in 1959, also start their flights as beam-riders, using SPG 49 or SPG 56 radars. Both Terrier and Talos use semi-active homing for the final phase of their flight. In semi-active homing the target is 'illuminated' by a powerful radar set in the ship; a radar receiver in the missile then picks up and homes on the reflections from the target. This can be done at considerable ranges as was shown when the U.S.S. *Long Beach* off the coast of Vietnam shot down two MIG aircraft 105 kilometers away. The much smaller U.S. Navy 'Tartar' missile, which went to sea in 1961, and the new British 'Sea Dart', of 1972, also use semi-active homing but the initial course is found by a computer using the data from an accurate tracking radar. The Tartar uses the SPG 51 radar and the Sea Dart the Type 909, both of which track the target as well as illuminating it.

The new French medium-range 'Masurca' missile can use either radio command guidance or semi-active homing. In the first version the position of the target is accurately tracked by the DRBi-23 radar and the missile guided to it by radio. The DRBi-51 radar is used for illumination in the homing version. The radars used by all these systems necessarily have very narrow concentrated beams and therefore have to be put on to the target by information from long-range search radars on which they depend.

The medium- and long-range surface-to-air guided missiles have proved extremely effective against high-flying aircraft and have a high kill rate which has rendered anti-aircraft artillery completely obsolete. They have not, however, proved so success-ful against low-flying aircraft where their homing and guidance systems suffer from interference from the sea. To meet this problem, new small short-range guided missiles have been developed. The first of these was the British 'Seacat', weighing only sixty-eight kilogrammes with a range of 3·5 km. It uses optical-tracking and radio-command guidance. A later version incorporates a 'lock-on' tracking radar as well. The U.S. Navy adapted the air-to-air missile 'Sparrow III' for use from ships but this had semi-active radar homing and the target had therefore to be illuminated. The French 'Murene' system, just coming into service, was adapted from a land weapon already in existence and consists of rockets controlled by radio using optical or radar tracking.

The advent of jet aircraft greatly increased the speed of the fighter but at the same time increased the speed of the bomber. In fact the margin of speed was then smaller than before and attacks from astern were seldom possible. With the tremendous speeds of approach and short time available to fire in a head-on attack, it became very difficult to use guns in fighters at all. It therefore became essential to produce a better weapon and this led to the development of the air-to-air missile. At first sight this may not seem to be much to do with sea power but, of course, the need to equip fighters operating from aircraft carriers made it important in this sphere as well as in pure air warfare. The first air-to-air guided missiles were produced in America in the mid-fifties. The early 'Falcon' missile produced in 1954 had semi-active radar homing and required the aircraft to illuminate the target with its radar until it hit. The new 'Sidewinder' missile, the British 'Firestreak' and later versions of the 'Falcon' had infra-red homing on the enemy aircraft's exhaust and were in service in 1956–8. The fighter could then break away as soon as it had fired. All these early missiles could only be fired by a fighter pursuing a target and could only attack from the rear hemisphere. The British 'Red Top' missile used by Sea Vixen fighters also had infra-red homing with a range of 12 km. and could engage supersonic aircraft from any direction even from right ahead. The U.S. Navy's 'Sparrow III' could do the same and formed the armament of the supersonic Phantom fighters. It had a longer range and used semi-active radar guidance and a proximity fuze. In addition to jet propulsion and a missile armament, it was found essential to equip all fighters with radar. In the Second World War the principal fighters were single seaters with no radar for use by day. At the end of the war the two-seater night fighter fitted with air interception radar joined the air groups of aircraft carriers. Initially its purpose was to provide fighter protection by night. By the fifties, however, it was being called an 'all-weather' fighter and was increasingly being used by day. With aircraft approaching the speed of sound it became normal practice to use radar interception even in good visibility. By the sixties nearly all fighters were of the 'all-weather' variety.

The use of air-to-air missiles enormously improved the lethality of the fighter but of course the armament of the strike aircraft had not stood still. The greatest progress in this field was made in the Soviet Union. By the early sixties they had produced two of what were known as 'stand off' weapons; one called 'Kennel' (Note 4) with a range of fifty nautical miles and another called 'Kelt' of 100 nautical miles. These were what were known as 'cruise missiles', that is they were flying-bombs with some sort of guidance and terminal homing. It is not known whether they use radar-beam riding or command guidance for the first part of their trajectory and semi-active or infra-red homing for the rest. Terminal homing would scarcely be necessary if they have nuclear warheads.

The British and Americans had tactical nuclear bombs for use by carrier-borne aircraft and were not so interested in air-to-surface missiles. The U.S. Navy did, however, produce 'Bullpup' in 1959 which was little better than the German Hs 293 of the war years and which used optical tracking and radio command guidance. During the sixties more attention was paid to this kind of missile and a number of countries produced their own versions. In the U.S.A. new homing devices were designed for 'Bullpup' and a new and much longer-ranged missile called 'Condor' was produced by the early seventies; this was a supersonic cruise missile with a range of over 60 km. using a TV camera in the nose and radio guidance. In the United States they also produced a smaller anti-shipping missile called 'Harpoon' with radar terminal homing. Sweden had their R604 air-to-surface missile and France their AS30 which was supersonic, using radio command guidance with a flare in the tail. In the early seventies West Germany produced the 'Kormoran' with an inertial system for initial guidance and then terminal homing which was either active radar, passive infra-red or passive homing on to electro-magnetic emissions. Finally the Anglo-French 'Martel' of probably about 60 km. range had either a passive system to home on to electro-magnetic emissions or radio command guidance using a TV camera in the nose of the missile.

It was the Soviet Navy, too, which took the lead in surface-to-surface missiles in ships. In 1958-9 the 'Krupny' class destroyers emerged with the 'Strela' cruise missile, which had a range of about 100 nautical miles; it had radio-command guidance and terminal infra-red homing and at long range was controlled by a helicopter carried in the ship for the purpose. The 'Shaddock' missile was larger and transonic and it has a range of 300 nautical miles. It is carried in the 'Kresta' and 'Kynda' classes and is believed to have the same kind of guidance, but it is by no means clear how it is guided at the longer ranges. Finally the short-range 'Styx' missile was introduced by the Russians for use from fast patrol boats. This had guidance similar to the first two but possibly radar homing instead of infra-red. It was this weapon in the hands of the Egyptians which sank the Israeli destroyer *Eilat* in 1967. This incident had a marked effect on the development of surface-to-surface missiles. Great Britain and America had already begun to fill this gap in their armouries by modifying their surface-to-air missiles so that they could be used against ships. Israel designed its 'Gabriel' missile, a surface version of the Anglo-French 'Martel' was produced, while the French brought their 'Exocet' into service which was adopted by the Royal Navy (Note 5). All these missiles, although they vary considerably in size, are cruise missiles flying low above the surface of the sea. They use either a computed directional launch, beam-riding or radio command for most of their flight with terminal infra-red or radar homing.

All these anti-ship missiles, of course, showed a need for other guided missiles which could shoot them down in flight. It was one of the main requirements of the new British 'Sea Dart' and 'Seawolf' surface-to-air missiles and the U.S. 'Aegis' system that they should be able to do this. It also stimulated what is known as Electronic Warfare, that is the need to interfere with the control of these weapons in some way and so render them useless.

Before any electronic counter-measures (ECM) can be devised it is essential to obtain a great deal of information or Electronic Intelligence (Elint) in order to find the frequencies, pulse repetition rates, pulse lengths, power and many other facts about how enemy radars and radios work. This of course is the purpose of the many Russian 'spy trawlers' which appear at NATO exercises. Electronic counter-measures can be of several kinds. They can be completely passive and simply obtain information that certain equipment is being used, and about its direction and rough position so that something can be done about it. They can be active, such as by jamming the enemy transmissions or introducing confusion in some way so that ranges or bearings are made inaccurate. Steps can be taken to confuse the picture with false echoes or by making small ships look large with radar reflectors. Electronic counter-measures in their turn give rise to electronic counter counter-measures (ECCM) which are mostly built in to radar or radio sets to increase their resistance to ECM. For instance the thinner the beam of a radar set the harder it is to jam as it will not be able to 'hear' the jammer unless it is pointing directly at it. Radar sets can also be designed so that they can be rapidly switched from one frequency to another, or can sweep in frequency or make random variations in frequency. Equipment for detecting and analysing enemy emissions can be carried on board as well as jammers and direction finders. The equipment can be very extensive, and in the U.S. Navy there are special aircraft devoted entirely to electronic warefare.

By the time the first nuclear-propelled submarine had put to sea in 1954, anti-submarine measures had just about the measure of submarines of the kind developed from the Type XXI U-boat. In the next few years a number of new devices became available such as anti-submarine rocket launchers in France and Sweden which were equivalent to the British 'Limbo'. Active directional sono-buoys for use from aircraft and better homing torpedoes also came into service Submarines had also increased their capability, using passive sonar and homing torpedoes, to destroy their own kind. The British Mark 20 was an electrically propelled passive homing torpedo for submarines which was effective against a snorting submarine. The Mark 24 was wire guided, and an operator in the submarine could monitor the transducer in the nose of the torpedo. It was therefore less likely to be worried by decoys. The American Mark 44 was a light-weight homing torpedo for dropping from aircraft or helicopters. The most important advance, however, was the 'dunking sonar' used from helicopters. This was an asdic set lowered into the water from a hovering helicopter. As the transducer could be lowered to the best depth for results, since it was stationary and there were no propeller noises, it obtained much better ranges than sonar in a ship. Nevertheless the nuclear submarine had such advantages that it was clear that it left even these new devices far behind.

At about this time, however, the ranges of new ship's sonar sets were substantially increased by lowering their frequency and increasing their power. In 1961 the Royal Canadian Navy produced a variable depth sonar (Type 199) which was towed behind a ship. This allowed a transducer to be lowered, as with helicopter sets, to the best depth and so competed with poor asdic conditions and temperature layers. It also considerably cut down interference from the ship's noise. This set was adopted by the Royal Navy and is installed in a number of frigates.

Better weapon systems were brought into service to take advantage of these increased ranges of detection. The U.S. Navy's 'Asroc', which became the primary anti-submarine weapon for their destroyers and frigates in 1961, was a rocket-propelled ballistic missile which could carry either a nuclear depth charge or a small homing torpedo to a distance of 10 km. At the same time the British introduced their 'Match' system which consisted of a small helicopter, carrying a homing torpedo, which could be vectored out to drop it on a long-range sonar contact. In 1965 the French produced their 'Malafon' system which was a guided weapon which carried a homing torpedo out to a range of 13 km. This was followed by the Australian 'Ikara' which was a similar system, the missile using an auto-pilot and a radio command link.

While these anti-submarine improvements were being introduced, the development of armament of the submarine did not stand still. In the Soviet Navy some of their conventional submarines began to be fitted with the 'Shaddock' cruise missile carried in large containers. In 1965 the U.S. Navy produced 'Subroc' which is fired from a torpedo tube, leaps into the air and becomes a missile. The head then separates from the rocket and continues ballistically finally becoming a nuclear depth charge. New torpedoes in many navies took a number of forms including the active sonar homing variety. Finally the British began to develop a small guided missile which could be fired from a submerged submarine and which could shoot down a helicopter or a maritime aircraft.

We left mine warfare at the end of the war with a virtually unsweepable pressure mine against which the Allies had been lucky to be able to devise passive counter-measures. It was clear that this mine could be redesigned so as to make these measures ineffective. In any case, with magnetic and acoustic mines, the problem of minesweeping was already extremely difficult. It had become impossible to declare an area swept and safe from mines well before the end of the war. Not only might the field include some pressure mines but it might not have been swept enough times to work off the anti-sweeper setting; moreover the arming delays might have kept the mines inert during the whole sweeping period and make them dangerous after the sweepers had finished. It was therefore only possible to reduce the risk of mines by what was known as statistical sweeping and so some casualties were inevitable. After the war in consequence attention began to be paid to what was known as mine hunting as well as minesweeping. In mine hunting the bottom is searched by some method with the aim of destroying every individual mine. It does not matter then whether it is a

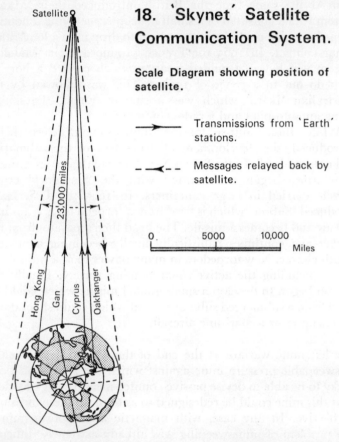

18. `Skynet´ Satellite Communication System.

Scale Diagram showing position of satellite.

$\longrightarrow$ Transmissions from `Earth´ stations.

$-\!-\!\blacktriangleleft\!-\!-$ Messages relayed back by satellite.

Satellite

23,000 miles

Hong Kong　Gan　Cyprus　Oakhanger

0　　　　5000　　　10,000　　　Miles

pressure mine or any other type and it will be disposed of even if it has an arming delay. Most of the early mine-hunting devices were cumbersome and dangerous to use; they swept very narrow paths and often missed mines altogether. The solution was found by the end of the fifties by using a very high definition asdic set with visual presentation of the echoes. The latest Type 193 sonar for this purpose is used in conjunction with a local but very accurate electronic navigation system together with a method of destroying the mines by counter-mining.

In 1957 when the U.S.S.R. put the first artificial satellite into orbit round the earth, high frequency was still the main way to achieve long-range radio communication. In spite of many modern techniques it was still subject to the vagaries of the ionosphere and there were considerable periods in every twenty-four hours when no communication was possible, as well as occasions in which inexplicable fading occurred. In 1962 the famous Telstar demonstrated the possibilities of satellite communication by relaying television programmes between the United States and Europe. Satellite communication can be achieved either by just using the satellite as a reflector or by installing in it a receiver which picks up the signal, amplifies it and retransmits it. The early communication satellites were in low orbits and so constantly moving round the earth, consequently a considerable number of them had to be in orbit if communication was to be always available. Later it became possible to place satellites in high equatorial orbit where they could be made to appear stationary relative to the earth, and so be constantly available for communication between places which could see the satellite. Various systems were used in the U.S.A., and in 1969 the United Kingdom Defence Satellite Communications System known as 'Skynet' came into operation. The satellite, built in the U.S.A. but embodying a number of British features, was put into orbit by the United States and is stationary relative to the surface of the earth some 23,000 miles above the Indian Ocean (Diagram 18). In this position it can be 'seen' from nearly all the eastern hemisphere from the Western Atlantic to east of Hong Kong (Diagram 19). It is of the type which relays messages and has to be replaced every two to three years. A second stand-by satellite is kept ready on the ground to be launched if the first one fails. Eight 'earth' stations are included in the system, four being fixed, two in H.M.S. *Ark Royal* and *Hermes* and two more are air transportable ready to be set up where required. The terminal in the United Kingdom is at Oakhanger in Hampshire, and it is from here that the satellite is controlled and monitored with a very complicated system of telemetry.

The main advantage of satellite communication such as 'Skynet' is that it is available all the time. There is no fading and it can be used day and night with complete reliability. As it works in the millimetric band, a very large number of channels are available and its message capacity is very large. As it is necessary to use a highly directional aerial to transmit to the satellite, the position of a ship passing on a message at sea is not revealed. On the other hand it is likely that in war a satellite could be destroyed by an enemy although this would require large and expensive rockets to do the job. With the emphasis on deterring war rather than fighting it, however, it is well worth while using satellite communication in peacetime.

19. 'Skynet' Satellite Communication System. Showing area covered by messages relayed from satellite.

Also showing:-

σᴺ Permanent 'Earth' Stations

σᴺ Possible positions of Ship Stations

σᴺ Possible positions of air portable stations.

+ Geographical position immediately below position of satellite.

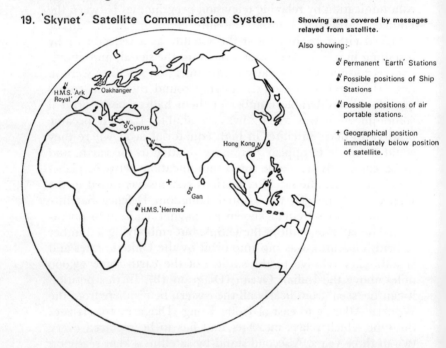

Modern communication systems are, of course, largely secret and it is only possible to comment in a very general way. Practically all messages are now sent by radio teletype at roughly five times the speed of morse, which today is seldom used. With multi-channel working the capacity of communications systems is enormous. The three British defence services send something of the order of forty million messages a year.

The U.S. Communications System transmits over a quarter of a million messages every day and is manned by 30,000 men. Computers have to be used to sort and route this vast traffic. What is known as 'on line' ciphering is now standard and is virtually instantaneous, and so all messages can be ciphered in a high-grade system as a matter of routine. At the same time secure speech equipment is available so that nothing need be given away by voice circuits. Obviously there is no information available on modern methods of cryptography or their effectiveness. It seems certain, however, that computers have made the task easier. It is known that in the U.S.A. a huge organization, employing 10,000 people and known as the National Security Agency, was set up in 1958. It is believed to handle interception, deciphering and traffic analysis for all American Government Departments and to check the security of U.S. ciphers too. It seems unlikely that such an organization would continue in being if it was not achieving anything. The effect of rapid, reliable and secure communications which can be used without restriction is clearly to centralize the control of ships and operations much more than in the past. It is only a matter of time before the Ministry of Defence will be able to talk to every ship wherever it may be on a secure voice net day and night (Note 6).

The electronic computer began to be used in navies for anti-aircraft fire control at the end of the Second World War. It replaced the complicated electro-mechanical systems which consisted of differentials, cams and graduated scales and was able to deal with a greater range of situations. Computers were also extensively used in many of the control systems of the various missiles which have been described. The British MRS3 fire-control system for guns which came into service in 1958 uses an analogue computer. Computers also form an essential part of the Polaris ballistic missile system in submarines of the U.S. and British Navies. A computer in the submarine stores the target information for each missile and receives information all the time on the submarine's position. The submarine's position is obtained from the Ship's Inertial Navigation System which is a conglomeration of gyroscopes, accelerometers and computers. Before a missile is fired the ship's computer works out the trajectory and passes it to another computer in the nose of each missile where it is stored. When the missile is fired it severs all connection with the submarine and the computer it carries guides the missile until the second stage rocket is released when the head becomes ballistic, and if it is not by then on exactly the right trajectory it will miss.

The action information organizations developed during the Second World War were worked by a large number of men using the information from radar, asdics and direction-finding systems with an automatic plot. Communication was entirely by telephone circuits which were either internal in the ship or by very high-frequency voice radio from other ships and aircraft. It required a large number of trained men to work the system, and the command made up its mind what to do from the information it presented. With jet aircraft and then guided missiles it was often not possible to compile the picture quickly enough and automation was clearly needed.

In 1964 the Action Data Automation System (ADA) emerged in H.M.S. *Eagle* after an extensive refit in Devonport Dockyard. This system was based on computers and co-ordinated air defence information from the ship's own radars, from other ships and aircraft by data link (Note 7), and from visual sightings. This information was either stored in the computer's memory or displayed. The computer was capable of evaluating threats, calculating interceptions and passing out information required by fighters, guns and missiles. It was able to perform tasks which formerly took some sixty men. In 1965 the Action Data Automation Weapons System (ADAWS) entered service in the second batch of the 'County' class guided missile destroyers. Based on digital computers this system gives automatic assistance in the compilation of the tactical situation not only in the air, but on the surface and below the surface as well. It produces threat evaluation and recommendations for action not only by fighters but by guns and missiles.

With such a wealth of new equipment it is very difficult to predict what would happen if it came to be used in war. All that can be done is to describe the equipment of one of the latest ships and one of the latest maritime aircraft, and to speculate to a certain extent.

The new British guided missile ship *Bristol*, which has just been completed, is a suitable example. She was originally designed as an escort for a new generation of aircraft carriers but is typical of a ship of the guided missile era. She is of 7,000 tons and is armed with one 4·5 in. Mark 8 completely automatic gun, a twin Sea Dart surface-to-air missile launcher, an 'Ikara' anti-submarine launcher, a single 'Limbo' (Mortar Mark 10) and two Seacat short-range surface-to-air missile launchers. Air warning is provided by Type 965 and combined warning by Type 992 radar. Two Type 909 radars are provided for target tracking and for 'illuminating' for Sea Dart. The ship has the latest sonar and electronic counter-measures equipment as well as nearly double the number of radio channels and data links formerly available. The whole is co-ordinated and controlled by a new combined action data information and weapons control system called ADAWS Mark 2. This system stores the information obtained from all the usual inputs and keeps it available for display according to what the operator asks to see. Its computers not only evaluate the threats from in the air, on the surface and below the surface, but recommend action according to the tactical situation. They do this by storing a large number of programmes on tape which can be selected as required. ADAWS 2 therefore upon request produces practically an automatic response to a situation including the allocation of weapons to meet the threat. The system is also able to pass information to other ships and aircraft including a simplified picture for ships with less sophisticated systems. H.M.S. *Bristol* is therefore, in spite of a dearth of gun barrels, probably the most versatile ship the Navy has ever had. She could not compete in an age of missiles, jet aircraft and nuclear submarines without the vast quantity of electronics she has on board (Note 8). They are essential not only to give warning of the enemy's approach, above, on or below the surface of the sea but to direct the missiles on to their targets. Without computers and automation of the action information system the tactical situation could not be appreciated quickly enough or the missiles fired in time.

R.A.F. Coastal Command aircraft are now of equal sophistication. The new 'Nimrod' is equipped for the detection and destruction of submarines and for general reconnaissance with a limited strike potential against ships. It has first, a powerful ASV radar set capable of picking up ships at long range and submarine snort masts at shorter ranges. It carries three types of sono-buoy; a long-range passive omni-directional buoy; a shorter-range passive buoy, which is directional, and a short-range active buoy. It also carries a powerful searchlight, a device known as 'Autolocus' for 'sniffing' for the exhaust fumes of snorting submarines and a Magnetic Anomaly Detector for pin-pointing a submarine when right overhead. In addition to advanced communication systems the 'Nimrod' also carries electronic counter-measures equipment which is able to detect radar emissions, analyse them and pinpoint the user. The 'Nimrod' can carry anti-submarine homing torpedoes and the 'Martel' air-to-surface missile as well as more conventional bombs, depth charges and rockets. The whole of this very complicated system is co-ordinated by computer which provides a picture of the situation. Computers are also used to keep the position of the aircraft up to date and accurate.

In the period since the Second World War, the most notable change in navies has been the gradual replacement of the gun by the missile. The gun is now secondary and obsolescent. In this final stage it is only really kept to give warships some authority over unarmed vessels. A shot across the bow is more effective and very much cheaper when used to enforce an order to stop than to launch a missile. For practically every other purpose, the missile is vastly superior. Although expensive it represents an entirely new order of offensive power in which hitting is normal and a miss the exception. This is achieved by guiding the missile to the target rather than by projecting it in its direction as with a gun. The guidance systems are entirely dependent upon and would never be possible without electronics. The Royal Navy has now nearly completed the transition from a gun to a missile armed navy. Most of the guns remaining are of small calibre (Note 9) and there are already eleven types of missile in service with others under development (Note 10).

Although H.M.S. *Bristol*, which has been described, is not to be repeated, the new 'Through deck cruiser' and three rather smaller types of ship will carry similar equipment and armament (Note 11). There is no doubt that these ships are the very least that can compete in modern naval warfare. Ships of these types will fight using electronic means almost entirely and will probably never see their enemy. They will fight in exactly the same way and just as effectively by night as by day. They are, however, entirely dependent on their electronics which must

work with 100 per cent efficiency all the time. This is a formidable challenge to the maintenance organization on which
everything depends. A beam-riding missile will not beam-ride
if there is no beam and a semi-active homing missile will not
home unless the target is illuminated. Furthermore it would be
virtually impossible to engage aircraft if there was no warning
radar to put the guidance radar on to the target. It seems also
true that in this kind of warfare it will be essential to get in the
first shot because these modern ships are of light construction,
are unprotected and very unlikely to work at all when damaged.
This will be so even when attacked with high-explosive missiles
and more so if tactical nuclear weapons are used (Note 12).

In spite of all this the temptation to go for simpler ships and
more of them is strong especially as they would be able to
compete with most routine peacetime tasks, but there is no doubt
that such a policy would surrender the command of the sea to
those with sophisticated electronics and missiles, and do so
without a fight. Ships and aircraft become obsolete quickly
enough without building them that way in the first place. It
follows from this that nothing but the best will be any good
in the future. This fact has serious implications: a war expansion
programme such as the corvette-building programme of the
Second World War will be of no value in the future and it will
be useless to put asdic sets and a gun in such ships as trawlers.
Nothing but a highly sophisticated warship will be able to
compete; and this will be very expensive and depend entirely
on a highly developed industrial base and maintenance
organization.

The story of the electron and sea power now draws to a close.
It will suffice to say that in this period its influence has been of
increasing importance and that it has fallen in the three main
spheres of communications, detection and the control of missiles.
In communications it grew from the linking of ships through
their bases by the telegraph cable to the reliable two-way
world-wide high-speed transmission of messages between ships
at sea by satellite. The communication between ships by voice
and data links is at such a speed and in such quantity that it
almost amounts to a system of thought transference. In detection it grew from the invention of the searchlight, the first factor
in making night fighting possible, to a system able to sense the

presence of aircraft, ships and submarines which would otherwise be far outside the limits of the human eye and ear. Finally electronics have made the age of the missile possible. The electron has risen from its humble beginnings into something which has penetrated every aspect of naval warfare.

Electronics are now essential to fight on the surface, in the air or under the sea. One cannot escape the feeling that the push-button warfare of science fiction is not far off. Inevitably with so much depending on electronics, counter-measures are bound to increase and become more effective. In the future the lethality of modern weapons is so obvious that it may well be the unseen electronic struggle which precedes their launching which will really matter. The shooting down of satellites may replace the cutting of cables, and it is possible that the frustration of the cryptographers may lead to wholesale jamming. Whatever may transpire there is no doubt that Sir Henry Tizard was right when he said in the late forties (Note 13) that the electron was the third great influence, after the submarine and the aircraft, on sea power in the twentieth century.

Bibliography

Baker, W. J. *A History of the Marconi Company.* London:
    Methuen and Co. Ltd, 1970.
Bangay, R. D. *The Elementary Principles of Wireless Telegraphy
    and Telephony.* Third Ed. revised by O. F. Brown. London:
    Iliffe and Sons Ltd, circa 1930.
Churchill, Winston S. *The Second World War, Vol. 1, The
    Gathering Storm.* London: Cassell and Co. Ltd, 1948.
Cole, Major D. H. *Imperial Military Geography.* London: Sifton
    Praed and Co. Ltd, 1937.
Corbett, Sir Julian S. *Naval Operations,* Vols 1–3. London:
    Longmans Green, 1920–3.
Dönitz, Admiral. *Memoirs.* Trans. by R. H. Stevens. London:
    Weidenfeld and Nicolson, 1959.
Douglas, Archibald C. *Life of Admiral Sir Archibald Douglas.*
    Totnes: Mortimer Bros, 1938.
Encyclopaedia Britannica. London: William Benton, 1963. Esp.
    parts on Radar, Radio and Electricity.
Ewing, A. W. *The Life of Sir Alfred Ewing, the Man of Room 40.*
    London: Hutchinson and Co., 1939.
Fremantle, Admiral Hon. Sir E. R. *The Navy As I Have Known It.*
    London: Cassell and Co. Ltd, 1904.
Gibson, R. H. and Maurice Prendergast. *The German Submarine
    War 1914–18.* London: Constable and Co. Ltd, 1931.
Grant, Robert M. *U-boats Destroyed.* London: Putnam, 1964.
—. *U-boat Intelligence 1914–1918.* London: Putnam, 1969.
Hale, John Richard. *Famous Sea Fights.* London: Methuen and
    Co. Ltd, 1911.
Harris, Admiral Sir Robert Hastings. *From Naval Cadet to
    Admiral.* London: Cassell and Co. Ltd, 1913.
Howeth, Captain L. S. *History of Communications – Electronics in*

the United States Navy. Washington: U.S. Government Printing Office, 1963.

Hoy, Hugh Cleland. *40 O.B. or How the War was Won.* London: Hutchinson and Co. Ltd, 1932.

James, Admiral Sir William. *The Eyes of the Navy.* London: Methuen and Co. Ltd, 1955.

Jane's Fighting Ships, 1900–73. London: Sampson Low, Marston.

Jellicoe, Admiral Viscount. *The Grand Fleet 1914–16.* London: Cassell and Co. Ltd, 1919.

Kahn, David. *The Codebreakers.* London: Weidenfeld and Nicolson, 1968.

McLachlan, Donald. *Room 39.* London: Weidenfeld and Nicolson, 1968.

Morison, Samuel E. *History of the United States Naval Operations in World War II.* 15 vols. London: Oxford University Press, 1948–62.

The Naval Annual, 1886–1900. Ed. by T. A. Brassey. Portsmouth: J. Griffen and Co.

The Naval Annual, 1914. Ed. by Viscount Hythe. London: William Clowes and Sons Ltd, 1914.

Navy Records Society, Publications of
Vol. LXXXIII   Russian War, 1854.
Vol. LXXXIV   Russian War, 1855.
Vol. LXXXV   Russian War, 1855.
Vol. XCV   Second China War, 1856–60.
Vol. CVIII   The Jellicoe Papers, Vol. I.
Vol. CXI   The Jellicoe Papers, Vol. II.

Newbolt, Henry. *Naval Operations, Vols. 4 and 5.* London: Longmans Green, 1928–31.

Parkes, Oscar. *British Battleships.* London: Seeley Service and Co. Ltd, 1957.

Pears, Commander Randolph. *British Battleships 1892–1957.* London: Putnam, 1957.

Politovski, Eugene S. *From Libau to Tsushima.* Trans. by Major F. R. Godfrey. London: John Murray, 1906.

Price, Alfred. *Instruments of Darkness.* London: William Kimber, 1967.

Raeder, Grand Admiral. *Struggle for the Sea.* Trans. by Edward Fitzgerald. London: William Kimber, 1959.

Roskill, Captain S. W. *The War at Sea 1939–45,* 3 vols. London: H.M. Stationery Office, 1954–61.

Scheer, Admiral. *Germany's High Seas Fleet in the World War.* London: Cassell and Co. Ltd, 1920.

Semenov, Vladimir. *Rasplata.* Trans. by L.A.B. London: John Murray, 1909.

—. *The Battle of Tsushima.* Trans. by A. B. Lindsay. London: John Murray, 1906.

Sueter, Commander Murray F. *The Evolution of the Submarine Boat, Mine and Torpedo.* Portsmouth: J. Griffin and Co., 1907.

Tirpitz, Grand Admiral von. *My Memoirs, Vols. 1 and 2.* London: Hurst and Blackett, 1919.

Usborne, Vice-Admiral C. V. *Blast and Counterblast.* London: John Murray, 1935.

Waldemeyer-Hartz, Hugo von. *Admiral von Hipper.* Trans. by F. Appleby Holt. London: Rich and Cowan, 1933.

Watson-Watt, Sir Robert. *Three Steps to Victory.* London: Odhams Press Ltd, 1957.

Notes

Chapter 1

1. Paddington to West Drayton in 1837 and Washington to Baltimore in 1844.

2. From 1837 this service was carried out by contract with the P. and O. Company.

3. There were no regular overland routes across the North American continent. California did not belong to the United States at the time.

4. They also agreed with the company to open the electric telegraph for an hour on Sundays.

5. In fact they used Rogers' and Black's *Semaphore Dictionary*.

6. Not the same Admiral Dundas as in the Baltic.

7. A particularly fast paddle despatch vessel of sixteen knots, the fastest ship in the Royal Navy.

8. Captain Freemantle had unwisely decided to 'hasten' their Lordships and this was probably the reason for his admonishment.

9. H.M.S. *Iris* and *Mercury* of eighteen-and-half knots which were, in their turn, the fastest ships of their day in the Royal Navy. They were of 3,730 tons and the first British warships with steel hulls. They were later converted into second-class cruisers.

10. Notably the attack with fireships by the English on the Spanish Armada at anchor off Calais in 1588; the pursuit of du Casse by Benbow in the West Indies in 1702 and the action between Saumarez and Linois in the Straits of Gibraltar in 1801.

11. It is of interest that in the Saumarez–Linois action, a Spanish ship engaged one of its own side.

12. Ten times as bright as an arc light using current supplied by primary batteries and able to stay alight four times as long.

13. The Russians and other nations subsequently used electricity to fire independent mines which then carried batteries within the mine case. These mines simply had an alternative firing mechanism (which was probably more efficient) to the older mechanical or chemical devices.

14. The *Capitan Prat*.

15. The searchlight was not really put to the test during this period since all the major actions namely, the Battle of the Yalu 1894, Santiago de Cuba and Manila Bay 1898, and the bombardment of Alexandria in 1882, were fought, as in the past, by day.

Chapter II

1. A spark gap when no current is flowing has a very high resistance which can only be broken down by a very high voltage. Once the spark is established however its resistance falls drastically and the spark can be maintained with a small current. It is used in a radio transmitter as a switch which is broken while the condenser is charged and then made so that the condenser discharges itself into the oscillating circuit after which it is broken and the cycle begins again.

2. The principle of the 'coherer' was discovered by Professor Branly in 1890. The conductivity of iron filings increases when electro-magnetic waves are encountered. It can therefore be used to detect such waves.

3. Instead of the coherer being actually in the aerial circuit, it was coupled to it by a transformer.

4. The actual messages were '*Alexandra* from *Juno*. Communicated with *Europa* about sixty miles off convoy rendezvous. She was there with convoy and has now returned to squadron. Convoy following at about nine knots. No enemy sighted by her or us', and forty minutes later '*Europa* alone. *Vindictive* follows two hours later. Afterwards remainder of division with convoy'.

5. Originally the intention was to employ them at the ports to help with the organization of the many troopships arriving and unloading.

6. The distance from Kosi Bay to Lourenço Marques was only eighty miles but direct communication was not possible because of intervening hills. The *Magicienne* was therefore stationed off Delagoa Bay to relay the messages.

7. The comparative trials are of interest and the best ranges obtained at sea were:

Slaby-Arco	62 miles	Braun S. Halske	25 miles
de Forest	54 miles	Ducretet	24 miles
Lodge Muirhead	33 miles	Rochefort	13 miles

8. Her only operator had become involved in some disciplinary trouble and was languishing 'in the brig' at the critical moment!

9. The Telefunken Company had been formed in 1903 by the amalgamation of the Slaby-Arco and Braun-Siemens-Halske concerns.

10. By 1905 already 110 ships of various nationalities were equipped with wireless, and interference at sea was becoming a serious problem.

11. The Russian cruisers under Admiral Enquist also kept their searchlights off and escaped to the southwards.

Chapter III

1. P and Q Tunes were the commercial waves established by the International Conference, that is 300 m. (1,000 kc/s) and 600 m. (500 kc/s). The part of the radio spectrum between 600 m. (500 kc/s) and 1,600 m. (187·5 kc/s) reserved by the Conference for ships was then divided into four tunes which were at the time the most that could be used without unacceptable interference. These were:

R Tune   788 m.   (380 kc/s)
S Tune   1,000 m. (300 kc/s)
T Tune   1,273 m. (235 kc/s)
U Tune   1,515 m. (198 kc/s)

It may seem odd that such precise wavelengths were stipulated when tuning was so inaccurate. The reason was that the British laid down the wavelengths in feet, e.g., 1,515 m. is 5,000 feet.

2. V Tune   1,727 m. (174 kc/s)
   W Tune   1,970 m. (152 kc/s).

3. Transmitting wavelength of destroyer set was Tune D 212 m. (1,415 kc/s). It could receive messages on all tunes from D to W. The wireless office was a small box-like compartment between the bridge and the fore funnel. It remained in this position in British destroyers until just before the Second World War.

4. If a signal was to be sent to the shore, Tune T would be used for a naval station or Tune Q for a commercial station. Within the fleet itself, Tune S was used to keep in touch with detached ships. Destroyers used Tune D but as they only carried one operator, watch would only be set when ordered. Destroyer flotilla cruisers would normally keep watch for them and Tune U was set aside for these ships to communicate with the flagship. Tune R was kept in reserve for use in case of enemy jamming. The range at which a message could be sent from a ship at sea depended on the size of the transmitter in the ship and, as the signal had to be answered, of the shore station as well. It also depended on whether it was night or day. Most of the shore stations had low-power sets and so communication might only be possible at 100 miles by day but as much as 300 miles by night.

5. The American companies were Shoemaker, Massie, Stone, Fessenden, de Forest and two smaller firms.

6. There were thirty-five of the original 1·25 kw. Slaby-Arco sets which had, however, been modified and improved. The new sets varied from the 1 kw. Fessenden set fitted in the battleship *Illinois* to the 5 kw. set made by the Stone Telegraph and Telephone Company in the new battleship *Kansas*.

7. Which was supposed to be 400 m. (750 kc/s).

8. An attempt had been made to remove the ionized air by an air jet. This 'blown spark' was used in the British Service Installation Mark II.

9. The spark transmitter can be compared with a man hitting an iron plate with a rapid succession of blows with a hammer. A continuous wave transmitter could be compared with a factory hooter.

10. The rotary and quenched spark transmitters could be compared to the rapid striking of a gong.

11. In more scientific language, the electric arc was capable of setting up continuous oscillations in a circuit containing inductance and capacity.

12. Rinella was not actually commissioned until 1913 when it was given a 150 kw. spark transmitter. Until then communication with the Mediterranean was by cable. Ships at sea in the Mediterranean could receive messages from Gibraltar in the western basin and from the

low power transmitter at Malta when in its vicinity, but there was nothing for the eastern end.

13. The actual wavelengths used were as follows:

Tune U	1,527 m.	196 kc/s	Communication with low-power stations.
Tune V	1,729 m.	173 kc/s	Communication between Admiralty, Whitehall and Cleethorpes, Ipswich, Aberdeen and Pembroke Dock.
Tune W	1,987 m.	150 kc/s	Communication between ships and medium-power stations.
Tune X	2,998 m.	100 kc/s	Broadcasts by Cleethorpes and North Front, Gibraltar.
Tune Y	3,660 m.	82 kc/s	Communication Horsea Island to North Front, Gibraltar and Rinella in Malta.
Tune Z	4,260 m.	70 kc/s	Broadcasts by Rinella.

It may be of interest to anyone who wishes greater detail to follow the routes of one or two messages:

(*a*) An Admiralty general message to all ships of the Royal Navy: Enciphered in Admiralty thence by Tune X to Cleethorpes then broadcast on Tune X at next routine time. This should be received by all ships in Home waters north of 47 degrees N. and east of 25 degrees W. It would also be sent from the Admiralty to Horsea and would be sent at the next routine time to Gibraltar and Malta on Tune Y, Malta and Gibraltar would broadcast at the next routine time to all ships in the Mediterranean and in the Atlantic between latitudes 47 degrees N. and 24 degrees N. and east of 30 degrees W. The Admiralty would also send the message by commercial cable to all other foreign stations where it would only be received by ships at sea within 100 miles of the low-power wireless stations at the naval bases. Other ships at sea would not receive it until they next reached a port with a cable office.

(*b*) A message from the C.-in-C. Atlantic Fleet at sea off Madeira to the Admiralty: His flagship would call the medium-power station at Gibraltar on Tune W and pass his message. Gibraltar high-power station at North Front would then send it on to Horsea Island at the next routine time. Horsea would send to Admiralty.

(*c*) A message from H.M.S. *Superb* at sea off Cromarty to H.M.S. *Bulwark* at sea in the eastern Mediterranean: *Superb* would call Aberdeen on Tune W and pass the message. Aberdeen would send it to Horsea through the Admiralty. Horsea would send it to Malta on Tune Y at the next routine time. Malta (Rinella) would broadcast at the next routine time on Tune Z and it would be received by *Bulwark*. If *Bulwark* was with the fleet and was not the Tune Z guardship then it would be received by the guardship and passed to *Bulwark* by visual signal or if fitted by auxiliary wireless.

(*d*) H.M.S. *Good Hope* exercising off Portsmouth wishes to report her expected time of arrival: She would call Culver W/T station on Tune U and pass the message. Culver would send to C.-in-C. Portsmouth by land-line.

14. *See table overleaf.*

15. The early heterodyne receivers themselves used a small arc to generate the heterodyne frequency.

16. The first of these was to be that used by the International Conference of 1906, that is 600 m. (500 kc/s) to call ships and shore stations and 1,000 m. (300 kc/s) for one shore station to call another. Six ships which had low-frequency transmitters were also permitted to use 1,000 m. (300 kc/s) to call shore stations.

17. In the 'Marconi scandal' allegations were made that the Postmaster-General and other Cabinet ministers had dealt in Marconi shares and that the contract had been awarded because the managing director of the company was the brother of the Attorney-General.

Chapter IV

1. These cables went from Emden to Vigo, Tenerife and the Azores where they connected with other cable routes. These cables were subsequently diverted to the use of the Allies to improve communications across the Channel, and one was re-laid from Brest to Casablanca and Dakar.

2. The same Captain Jackson of the early days of wireless.

3. In 1918, however, the large cruiser submarines *U155* and *U151* succeeded in cutting cables off Lisbon and New York.

4. Two of these ships were lost by enemy action.

5. Two messages sent by Admiral Cradock on October 8 did not reach the Admiralty until October 11 and 12, and their Lordships did not reply until October 14.

6. Her escape cannot be entirely attributed to the interception of British signals; it was mainly good luck.

7. In fact the *Minotaur* was ordered by the Admiralty to leave the convoy and proceed to the Cape as the convoy approached Cocos Island. She had to acknowledge this signal which was sent by Cocos Island wireless station, having been received by cable. The acknowledgment was, in fact, intercepted by the *Emden* but she does not seem to have heeded the warning.

8. The first actual use of an enemy signal was on 4 October 1914 when the captured wireless station at Samoa intercepted a signal from the *Scharnhorst* in the secret German mercantile code, which had already been captured, giving away the information that Admiral von Spee was on his way from the Marquesas to Easter Island.

9. When the submarines were submerged and he wanted to get in touch with them Keyes steamed about with a black ball hoisted which meant 'surface'; he then passed the new orders to them by visual signal.

10. The diode had in fact been developed as early as 1906 and the triode well before the war.

Table of Royal Navy's Wireless Sets 1914 (*See Chapter III, Note 14*) All are spark transmitters with crystal receivers

Type no.	Power kw.	Purpose	Fitted in	Range N. miles	Frequency range Transmitter (m)	Receiver (m)	Notes
1	14	High-power ship set	Dreadnought battleships battle cruisers, armoured cruisers, medium-power shore stations	500	300–1,987	109–4,260	Late service installation Mark II
2	1½	Standard ship set	All other surface ships larger than destroyers. Low-power shore stations	100	300–1,987	109–4,260	Late service installation Mark I
3	1	Auxiliary set	Second set in battleships	5	126	126	
4	1	Destroyer set	Destroyer flotilla cruisers, destroyer and torpedo boats	50	213	213–1,987	
5	½	Portable set	Boats and landing parties	5	300	300	
6	½	Harbour defence set	Defended ports	5	157	157	
7	100	High-power shore stations	Cleethorpes, Horsea I, North Front	1,000	1,729–3,660	1,729–3,660	
8	150	High-power shore stations	Rinella	1,800	3,660–4,260	3,660–4,260	
9	1¼	Cruiser auxiliary set	Second set in battle cruisers, armoured and light cruisers	30 m.	126–157	126–157	
10	1	Submarine set	Submarines of 'B', 'C', 'D', 'E' classes	30 m.	157–231	157–231	

Chapter V

1. The raider *Möwe*, which left Germany at the end of 1915, got to sea without any warning from radio intelligence.
2. These were ciphered cables sent by the German Ambassador in Washington through neutral countries.
3. Originally it was *U20* but she developed a defect.
4. Another nine U-boats sailed between May 20 and 24.
5. The accuracy of the D/F stations is illustrated by the fact that this was, at 300 miles, only a change of bearing of 1½ degrees.
6. After the battle the British feared that the Germans knew about Room 40. The First Sea Lord called Admiral Jellicoe's attention to these changes being made just before sailing and said great care must be exercised in using intercepts in future.
7. The signal was not finally deciphered until the next afternoon when it was too late. It read: 'Head of 3rd squadron will pass Jade war lightship A at 0430. 2nd squadron will take part in the operation from the beginning and will join up astern of 1st squadron, Wilhelmshaven 3rd entrance will control W/T in German Bight.'
8. This was made at 0916 by the Rear-Admiral Scapa addressed to the R.A. Invergordon but intended for interception by the Commander-in-Chief, the words 'For C.-in-C.' being enciphered in the text.
9. The Tenth Cruiser Squadron enforced the blockade of Germany.
10. Admiral Scheer again made his position at 1631 just before he sighted Admiral Hipper. This message was received and decrypted by Room 40 but only reached Admiral Jellicoe a quarter of an hour before he had to deploy and was too stale to be of much use.
11. Oddly enough this was the first knowledge the Admiralty gained of Admiral Jellicoe's night intentions.
12. The Admiralty were always afraid of compromising this priceless source of information. Arrangements had already been made to use a special cipher with a very limited distribution to pass on radio intelligence.
13. The main value of the larger German searchlights was that they could illuminate a target at longer range. At Jutland the night was very dark and all contacts were at very close range at which even 24 in. searchlights were fully effective. The larger German searchlights, however, had a greater dazzling effect which was useful.
14. This mistake also meant that Admiral Jellicoe continued towards his rendezvous at cruising speed when he might have pressed on and brought the enemy to action earlier in the day with a better chance of victory.
15. The *Ostfriesland* struck a mine after the High Seas fleet had entered the Horns Reef Channel and was with difficulty got into harbour. *Breslau* struck five mines and sank, *Goeben* struck three and was so seriously damaged that she had to be beached. The Dreadnought *Audacious* was also sunk by a mine early in the war and this was not a danger to be dismissed lightly.

16. In fact there was a difference in reckoning of twelve miles between the *Lion* and the *Iron Duke* and twenty miles between the *Southampton* and the *Iron Duke*. A system of 'Admiral's reference positions' was, in fact, in force at Jutland but this only ensured that all ships in company with Admiral Jellicoe were using the same position relative to each other. It could not apply to the battle cruiser fleet as it had not been in visual touch with the battle fleet since leaving harbour.

17. The Grand fleet battle orders certainly told subordinate commanders to use their initiative and watch the Commander-in-Chief's movements as signals might take too long or be indistinguishable. 'It is hoped that difficulties in signalling will be largely overcome by the use of wireless telegraphy.'

18. The Fleet Wireless Officer.

19. The Harrison system was vapour cooled and gave a greatly increased light.

20. In fact the old book but with a new cipher key was used at Jutland.

Chapter VI

1. At the end of the war, German battleships had three wireless offices: main, auxiliary and after-action. They had both quenched spark and Lorenz arc main transmitters and a quenched spark auxiliary set. The after-action set was simple and portable.

2. The interception and sinking of the raider *Leopard* in March 1917 was due to the vigilance of the northern patrol and radio intelligence was not responsible for this success either.

3. In March 1917 *U64* sank the French battleship *Danton* off Sardinia and that night was able to report the fact by wireless to the German cruiser *Arkona* in the Ems.

4. A 'diagraphic substitution' system in which a codeword is used to jumble an alphabet in a 5 × 5 square, pairs of letters can then be read off in various alternative positions.

5. Some of the very early hydrophones were of the stethoscope variety and so strictly not within the scope of this book, but electric microphones with valve amplifiers similar to those used in radio sets were soon found to give better results.

6. At night when the U-boats were likely to be on the surface using their diesel engines, hydrophone patrols normally remained stopped and listening all the time.

7. There is little evidence, in fact, that the Germans used starshells to any great extent at Jutland. Large Very lights were probably mistaken for them.

8. A minor though important improvement at this time was the introduction of metal filament instead of carbon filament light bulbs which proved more shock resistant.

Chapter VII

1. The Lafayette station near Bordeaux, completed in 1920.

2. They were keyed by changing frequency. When the key was pressed they transmitted the transmitting frequency and when it was not they emitted a compensating frequency.

3. The power that could be obtained by an alternator was, however, limited and the largest at Annapolis was 50 kw. With its greater efficiency, however, this was equivalent to a 100 kw. arc or a 350 kw. timed spark.

4. In 1922, however, water-cooled valves of from 10–15 kw. were developed in both the U.S.A. and Great Britain.

5. In 1921 the U.S. Navy developed a radio-controlled target ship, U.S.S. *Iowa*, which was used in tests of bombs against ships.

6. They had already had to surrender the band from 500 to 1,500 kc/s to civil broadcasting.

7. The Fourth International Radio Conference held in Washington in 1927 prohibited the use of spark transmitters after 1 January 1935 or their installation after 1 January 1930.

8. No doubt this was to some extent because of the extraordinary power held during the war by Admiral Hall, the Director of Naval Intelligence, who decided virtually what was good for the Foreign Office to know and what was not! The 'Zimmermann telegram' affair is an example.

9. This was set up in July 1919. In 1924 economy cut down its activities and in 1929, with the arrival of Mr Stimson as Secretary of State, it was closed down on ethical grounds. Its records and some of its staff were then transferred to the War Department.

10. A transposition cipher is one in which the letters of the message are jumbled up in some systematic manner, e.g., writing the message backwards. A substitution cipher is one in which a jumbled alphabet is used, e.g., a = e, q = w, etc.

11. The doppler effect is that which causes the echo from a moving object to return with a higher or lower note than the transmission according to whether it is moving towards or going away.

12. Contact was generally lost at close range.

13. Radar in Great Britain was originally known as RDF.

14. This was, of course, not the seventy-ninth radar set produced. It was numbered in the wireless transmitter series.

15. Two lobes were transmitted pointing in slightly different directions. The transmitter was switched rapidly from one to the other and when the size of echoes in the receivers was the same, it was pointing straight at the target.

16. The 'ten years rule' was a Government directive made in the twenties to the Service chiefs to base their forward planning on the assumption that there would be no major war for the next ten years. This policy was adhered to well into the thirties.

17. This was also found to be essential during the 1937 Home fleet exercises.

18. There were intercept stations in Great Britain at Flowerdown and Scarborough and abroad at Bermuda, Malta, Trincomalee, Aden and Hong Kong.

19. This was the very maximum speed and equivalent to twenty knots in the British asdics when there was a considerable falling off in performance. Asdics could operate at full efficiency at fifteen knots and the U.S. Navy's sonar at about six knots.

20. The actual stations were Esquimault, Ottawa, Halifax, Bermuda, Gibraltar, Malta, Simonstown, Aden, Falklands, Durban, Ceylon, Bombay, Singapore, Hong Kong, Darwin, Belconnen (Australia), Wairouru (New Zealand).

21. The high-frequency network in the U.S. Navy was much more successful, partly because of better equipment and partly because they had a greater choice of frequencies and were able to use the best one.

Chapter VIII

1. *Renown, Suffolk* and *Norfolk* had been refitted well before September 1939 and were too soon to have radar fitted. Other ships completing large refits were the battleships *Valiant* and *Queen Elizabeth,* the cruiser *London* and the anti-aircraft cruisers *Curacoa* and *Carlisle.*

2. Ships due to complete within a year were the battleship *King George V,* the aircraft carrier *Illustrious* and a number of cruisers of the 'Fiji' and 'Dido' classes.

3. *Exeter* and *Ajax* after the River Plate, *Nelson* after being mined and later *Suffolk* after serious damage in the Norwegian campaign.

4. Dönitz *Memoirs,* page 63.

5. In much the same way as a piece of iron can be magnetized or demagnetized by stroking it with a permanent magnet.

6. In the 'LL' sweep two trawlers in line abreast towed the floating cables directly astern. The first length of cable was double and so its magnetic field was nil but the last part was single, the current returning through the sea. By the two trawlers pulsing together but with the current in opposite directions a powerful vertical field was set up between the second lengths of the cables which would fire the German mines. The double portion of the cable prevented the mines being fired too close to the minesweepers.

7. Also possibly due to the 'degaussing' of British ships.

8. Influence mines are mines fired by any influence other than by contact. This term therefore includes acoustic as well as magnetic mines.

9. In fact before the days of radar the fighters often failed to sight the attackers altogether.

10. Nevertheless it still needed a large expenditure of ammunition to bring down an aircraft.

11. The corvettes ordered just before and on the outbreak of war were coming into service; there were the fifty old American destroyers acquired during the autumn and destroyers were being released from the narrow seas where the invasion threat had declined.

12. David Kahn's book *The Codebreakers* says that a Mata Hari type

spy called Cynthia in Washington inveigled the Italian Naval Attaché into parting with his ciphers.

Chapter IX

1. This was what they had done earlier in 1941 during the Japanese invasion of French Indo-China.
2. She was also torpedoed by a Japanese submarine.
3. *Patterson*'s enemy report on sighting the Japanese was 'Warning, Warning, Strange ships entering harbour', which except as a general alarm told the ships very little.
4. The U.S. Navy thought this was the maximum range of Japanese torpedoes at the time.
5. U.S. Intelligence did not realize the outstanding performance of these torpedoes and assumed they were no better than those in service in their own navy.
6. *Washington* at the Battle of Guadalcanal got nine hits out of seventy-five rounds fired from her 16 in. guns on *Kirishim* at 8,400 yards.
7. It was often not the nearest one by any means. The author well remembers calling Ceylon from the Malacca Straits and being answered by Halifax, Nova Scotia.
8. In fact a new magnetic pistol type Pi2 was successfully introduced in December 1942. This was much more effective than the contact pistols in use in 1941–2 and a single torpedo was enough to sink most ships. It was estimated that it virtually doubled the torpedo capacity of a U-boat.
9. They read sixteen signals giving advance information about both convoys including their route and the stragglers route and later they read the signals ordering the diversion of both convoys.
10. Known by the British as the 'Gnat'.
11. This was the 'Foxer', described by Professor Morrison as 'a contraption of parallel rods which clacked together when towed, making an unholy racket designed to attract and detonate the new German acoustic torpedo.'
12. Four motor torpedo boats, eight motor gunboats and four motor launches. All of them were fitted with radar.
13. This was probably the Mark II Model 2. A 10 cm. set but at first of only $\frac{1}{2}$ kw. power. It does not seem to have been able to pick up ships as far away as Japanese lookouts with their excellent binoculars could see them.
14. This could obviously pick up the SG radar.
15. *See page 306.*
16. By this time joined by four fleet destroyers from the convoy escort.
17. These destroyers had, in addition to Type 286 and Type 285, two Type 271 among them.

Chapter X

1. Before the advent of VH/F 'doubtful' enemy reports were generally sent on low frequency at low power in the hope that the enemy would

not pick them up. It was also possible to take bearings of ships making enemy reports on M/F or L/F and so establish relative position.

2. The comparison is with the conventional Type IX D2 of similar tonnage to the Type XXI.

3. A new ship replacing the one sunk at the Battle of the Coral Sea.

4. Unmanned wireless-controlled aircraft target in common use in the U.S.

5. It also had a large part in the defeat of the German V-1 flying-bomb attack on London in 1944.

6. The enemy were in fact sighted by some ships before firing.

7. Typical radars fitted in ships at the end of the war were as follows: the battleship *Duke of York* had the Type 281 BQ air-warning radar, a Type 293 P for surface warning and target indication, two Type 274 for the main armament control and four Type 285 P for the anti-aircraft batteries. Close-range guns still had the Type 282. The aircraft carrier *Implacable* had Types 279 B and 281 B both with single transmitting and receiving aerials and continuous rotation for air warning, Type 277 for height finding and low cover, Type 293 P for surface warning and target indication and Types 285 and 282 for anti-aircraft gunnery control. The cruiser *Swiftsure* had the same as the *Duke of York*, but only one Type 274 and three Type 285.

Chapter XI

1. With direct printing this was at about seventy words per minute. With recording but no printing it could be as high as 1,200 words per minute but this did not pay commercially as there were so many mistakes.

2. Both sidebands could in fact still be transmitted and each could carry a different message.

3. In fact it was only installed in the aircraft carriers *Victorious*, *Hermes* and *Eagle*.

4. These are the NATO nicknames for Russian equipment.

5. Others include the Swedish Rbo8a of 1967, the Italian 'Nettuno' and 'Vulcano', the Norwegian 'Penguin' and the Franco-Italian 'Otomat'.

6. This would no doubt be considered a great advance by politicians and staff officers of the Ministry of Defence. This author is more inclined to agree with the Generals in the Crimea in 1855 and regard it with horror!

7. A data link is simply a communication channel which passes encoded information direct in the form of digits. It is normally associated with the transfer of information to or from a computer. An early data link was from the AN/APS 20 radar in an aircraft and it displayed what the radar set detected on a P.P.I. in a ship.

8. The increase can be illustrated to a certain extent by the generating power provided. The *Bristol* has 7,000 kw. which is substantially more than the 'County' class of ten years before which had only 3,750 kw. and not far short of the aircraft carrier *Eagle* when she was modernized in the early sixties with 8,250 kw. Even the 'Leander' class frigates of the first batch completed in the early sixties had 1,900 kw. which was 300 kw. more than the battle cruiser *Hood* had when she was completed in 1919,

and roughly the same as the battleship *Rodney* when she was commissioned in 1928.

9. Nearly all of 4·5 in. calibre. The largest is 6 in. and there are only four of them.

10. The eleven missiles in the Royal Navy are:

'Polaris'	Submarine-launched strategic ballistic missile.
'Sea Dart' 'Seaslug' }	Medium-range ship to air missile.
'Seacat' 'Sea Wolf' }	Close-range ship to air missile.
'Exocet'	Surface-to-surface missile.
'Ikara'	Surface-to-submarine missile.
'Bullpup'	Air-to-surface missile.
'SS.11'	Helicopter to surface missile.
'Firestreak' 'Red Top' }	Air-to-air missile

11. The Type 42 destroyers of the *Sheffield* class have 'Sea Dart' and 'Exocet' but not 'Ikara' and are therefore not quite so versatile.

12. In the atom bomb trials at Bikini in 1946 it was found that radar and radio antennae were particularly vulnerable and were liable to be destroyed even when a ship was undamaged structurally. With large nuclear weapons, radar and radio aerials could be damaged by an explosion as much as ten miles away.

13. If my memory is right, he actually said 'electro-magnetic waves, Marconi and all that . . .' I have broadened this to include electrics as well as electronics of all kinds.

Typical Equipment of British Ships with Radar 1943 (*See Chapter IX, Note 15*)

Type of Ship	Long-range air warning and fighter direction	Surface warning	Short-range air warning	Surface fire control	Anti-aircraft fire control	Close-range AA control	AA barrage for main armament	Total number of sets
Battleship	279 ⎫	273	–	284 M	285 M	282	283	14
Aircraft carrier	or ⎬	–	–	–	285 M	282	–	9
Cruiser	281	273	–	284 M	285 M	282	283	8
Destroyer	–	272	286 P	*	285 M	–	–	3
Atlantic escort	–	271	–	†	–	–	–	1
East Coast escort	–	–	286 P	‡	285 M	–	–	2

* 272 and 285 M could assist; † 271 could assist; ‡ 285 M could assist.

Index

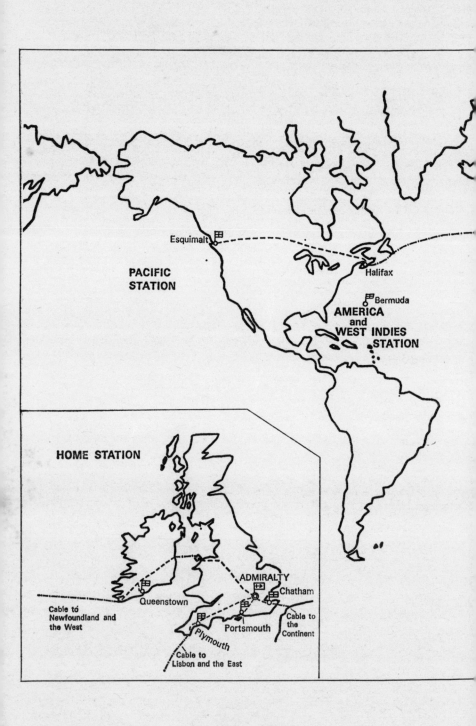

Esquimalt

PACIFIC
STATION

Halifax

Bermuda

AMERICA
and
WEST INDIES
STATION

HOME STATION

ADMIRALTY

Chatham

Queenstown

Cable to
Newfoundland and
the West

Portsmouth

Cable to
the
Continent

Plymouth

Cable to
Lisbon and the East